BOATBUILDING ONE-OFF IN FIBERGLASS

BOATBUILDING ONE-OFF IN FIBERGLASS

Allan H. Vaitses

INTERNATIONAL MARINE PUBLISHING COMPANY
CAMDEN, MAINE

©1984 by International Marine Publishing Company

Typeset by The Key Word, Inc., Belchertown, Massachusetts
Printed and bound by McNaughton & Gunn, Inc., Ann Arbor, Michigan

All rights reserved. Except for use in a review, no part of this book may be reproduced or utilized in any form or by any means, electronic or mechanical, including photocopying, recording, or by any information storage and retrieval system, without written permission from the publisher.

Published by International Marine Publishing Company
21 Elm Street, Camden, Maine 04843
(207) 236-4342

Library of Congress Cataloging in Publication Data

Vaitses, Allan H.
   Boatbuilding one-off in fiberglass.

   Includes index.
   1. Fiberglass boats. 2. Boat-building. I. Title
VM321.V348 1984   623.8'207   82-48431
ISBN 0-87742-156-0

To those libertarian owners who dream of different boats, and those creative builders who keep finding better ways to build such boats one-off.

Contents

        Preface   ix

PART I   **Choosing a Method**   1

Chapter 1   **The Boat You Want to Build**   3
One-off systems • Boat design and construction • Sorting out the methods

Chapter 2   **Molded One-Offs**   10
Building in a mold or over a form • Assembling a hatch mold • Material to laminate a hatch • Building a one-off deck mold • A molded hull

Chapter 3   **PVC Foam**   63
A PVC-foam one-off hull • A PVC-foam one-off deck • Other PVC-foam one-off structures

Chapter 4   **C-Flex**   79

Chapter 5   **CVC**   88

Chapter 6   **Str-r-etch Mesh and Fer-a-lite**   98

Chapter 7   **WLP (Wood Left in Place)**   106
WLP-lined, single-skin fiberglass construction • WLP-fiberglass sandwich construction • Other WLP one-off constructions

Chapter 8   **A Boat From an Existing Boat**   127
The male-mold method • The female-mold method • Laminating and releasing the one-off or one-off mold

PART II Techniques and Finishing 143

Chapter 9 Hand Layup Procedure 145
Resins • Fiberglass materials • Layup technique • The second layer • Local strengthening layers • Laminating in a mold

Chapter 10 Finishing Raw Fiberglass 166
Fairing • Smoothing • Painting

Chapter 11 Keels, Sumps, Rudders, Centerboards, and Tanks 176
Keels • Sumps and oil pans • External ballast keels • Pouring your own keel • Direct keel molds • Sand-cast keels • Bolting keels on • Internal ballast keels • Rudders • A shoal-draft rudder • Rudder stops and steerers • Centerboards • Other boards • Centerboard cases • Centerboard hardware • One-off tanks • All-fiberglass tanks • The metal-lined fiberglass tank • Integral tanks

Chapter 12 Installing Bulkheads, Engine Beds, and Other Parts 228
Bulkheads • Engine beds • Shaft logs, stuffing boxes, stern bearings, and struts • Mast steps, chainplates, and their reinforcements • The cabin sole • Deckhouse and full-width-cockpit soles

Chapter 13 Finishing Details 256
Joinerwork • Hatches and coamings • Companionway doors and fisherman slides • Deadlights and fixed windows • Opening portlights • Opening windows • Ventilation • Exterior trim • Deck hardware

Glossary 282

Index 285

Preface

Several years ago, Roger Taylor, President of International Marine Publishing Company, sent me a book about one-off fiberglass boatbuilding and repair. Along with the book came a question to ponder: Is the book still up to date, having been published 10 years ago, or has enough changed with regard to building one-off in fiberglass to make it out of date? It was fascinating to read, and undoubtedly a good book in its time, but that time was a memory, even to those of us old enough to have watched the beginnings of one-off fiberglass boatbuilding. No way, I assured Roger, should a current would-be one-off builder in fiberglass look to any book published a decade ago for guidance in how to go about it. After a little while, he answered my report with another question: "I don't know which of us was setting up the other here, but would you be interested in writing a new book on building one-off in fiberglass?"

I was—and this is that book. But I am glad that I read the older book before putting this one together, for it has been a constant reminder that growth and change are natural parts of one-off fiberglass building. Regardless of past successes, no building system long remains the best, and even at the peak of its popularity, no system is best for all types of boats, or under all conditions. I was also reminded that it should not be so much the intention of this book to tell anyone precisely how to build his boat one-off in fiberglass as it should be to acquaint him with a number of the many methods open to him, and, as a result, to inspire him to develop some methods of his own.

Warm thanks to the dozens of co-workers, customers, designers, boatbuilder friends, and suppliers of one-off materials and know-how who are each in his own way responsible for the subject matter of this book.

A good boat is a thousand jobs done right.

Part I

Choosing a Method

1

The Boat You Want to Build

Unless you want to do some boatbuilding more for its own sake than for the product—and I have known such people—we can begin with the assumption that you intend to build a particular boat. The kind of boat you want makes a difference, because some of the many one-off building methods are more adaptable to a given type than others. Also, in a book addressed specifically to one-off in fiberglass, it is only fair to point out early that your projected boat might possibly be better built one-off with another material.

If, for instance, yours is to be an extremely high-performance craft, where saving weight is crucial, you should at least consider one of the two lightest materials in use at this writing: cold-molded wood and wood-foam-wood sandwich. However, if you envision frequent trips through logging streams, polar ice, canal locks, or areas where frequent groundings on stony bottom are unavoidable, then a steel boat would probably suit you better than fiberglass. Again, if you are short of cash for materials, you will find that you can get a lot more boat for your dollar with wood or plywood than with fiberglass, as long as you don't offset the savings with expensive fastenings and/or ultraexpensive adhesives and coatings. Also, it would be a foolish mistake to build a cheap hull and then load her with expensive gear. A cheap boat should be kept cheap (since it will never be worth more than its hull), and the best way to do that is to keep it very plain and simple.

I mention these considerations and encourage you to weigh them carefully because, from my experience with most of the known boatbuilding materials, I have found that no one material is best for all boats. At the same time, 90 percent of all current boats or yachts are built of fiberglass because of its dependability and low maintenance cost. Thus, it should be obvious that the material is suitable if not preferable for most designs and that this book stands to lose very few clients to other materials. Certainly, when I next build a boat for our family, I will build it of fiberglass, simply because the maintenance of any of the several wooden boats we usually have on our property either preempts too many precious hours or is shamefully neglected.

One other factor might possibly turn you away from building one-off in fiberglass: physical problems with the materials. Glass fibers or particles can irritate the skin of some people so seriously that they cannot even handle the fabrics, especially chopped-strand mat (CSM), without itching or breaking out in a rash. When grinding fiberglass, anyone who allows the fine particles to lodge in the skin of arms and face can itch temporarily; but covering up as much as possible, dusting off or changing outer clothes, and showering after exposure are usually all the precautions the average person needs to take to avoid discomfort. Yet I know one man who has constant sores on his legs up to the knees just from walking around in a fiberglass shop where he is a master boat carpenter. People who have had respiratory problems cannot and should not breathe the fumes of either curing polyester resin or the acetone that we use to wash the resin from our brushes, rollers, and hands.

Although I know many people who have worked in fiberglass every working day for 20 to 35 years with no apparent ill effects—and I myself have bathed pretty freely in the stuff from time to time—I advise you to undertake a small project or two to make sure you are not allergic to the materials before you tackle a whole boat. I further advise you that it is not hypochondria to wear goggles and mask or even a throwaway paper suit and gloves when grinding and to keep the area well ventilated when mixing and applying materials. Nor are you an alarmist if you forbid smoking near the job. These precautions are the only sensible ones to take.

ONE-OFF SYSTEMS

Now that we have considered seriously the negative aspects of the subject, let's switch to the pleasant business of contemplating how you can build the boat you want one-off in fiberglass. In the following chapters you will find that you have many options. Actually, I have omitted several one-off systems that I know about because they have been generally abandoned as inferior in some way. Also, such is the ingenuity of boatbuilders that I'm sure there are or have been many other systems that I don't know about. At first, the wide choice of one-off systems might confuse you. Conversely, you may already have a strong prejudice in favor of a particular system and be tempted to skim over the chapters discussing others. Whatever your feeling, I hope you will be patient while I attempt to sort them all out in the light of my experiences with each over about 25 years of custom boatbuilding. As we go through them you should begin to see the advantages and disadvantages of working in each system. More important, you should get a feel for the variations in the physical strength, durability, weight, cost, and last, but quite significant, appearance and livability of the finished products. As you consider the possible effects of each system on the boat you want and balance them against the work you would have to perform, it is likely that you will decide to build her with a combination of systems. If she is to be a fast power cruiser, you might feel that a polyvinyl-chloride (PVC)-foam-cored hull is best. But if you desire low maintenance on the outside and the pleasant warmth of varnished wood on the inside, you might opt for fiberglass over left-in-place wood for the decks and pilothouse. However, if your boat is to be a shoal-draft sharpie with a stout, stiff, heavy bottom, you might build it of wood or plywood thickly fiberglassed. But on this same boat you might also be determined to have an absolutely watertight, well-insulated deck with all of its details molded in, including a nonskid pattern. In that case, you would lay up the deck in a throwaway deck mold with PVC-cored fiberglass.

BOAT DESIGN AND CONSTRUCTION

For all of the one-off systems except taking a boat off an existing boat, you need a plan of the boat you want. If no plan exists of what you have in mind, it would be well worth the cost to have a designer draw you one. A good plan makes your building job infinitely easier. More important, it ensures good looks, good performance, and someday a good resale value. But you might not need a custom design. Designers have innumerable "stock plans" of boats they have already designed, usually to customer specifications, but sometimes to their own specifications of what somebody should want to build. Literally hundreds of stock plans are regularly advertised in yachting magazines.

If the plans you have are not designed for a fiberglass boat, you can ask the designer to draw you a construction section for fiberglass—a plan of a typical section near midships showing the details of the construction. A laminate schedule is noted either on this plan or on a separate specification sheet, stating the material and weight of each layer in the sequence of its application. It is also noted on the plan how far each layer should extend, since on almost all boats there are more layers in the bottom than in the topsides and many more in the keel. The core material may stop short of the keel and of the rail, too, for reasons we explore later.

If for any reason you cannot get such a plan, the next best aid would be a recommendation of the thicknesses of laminate and/or core to use. If that, too, is unavailable, you can figure it out for yourself by comparing well-built boats similar to the boat you want. To aid you in this, I include some typical laminate schedules on the several systems. But there's no magic to it. You don't need a

Fred Ford–designed one-off ocean-racing sloop Bright Star, *one of two boats built in a wooden temporary mold. Her hull was single-skin fiberglass; her decks were laminated plywood, wood left in place; her tanks were one-off fiberglass over metal liners. Built in the late 1960s, these boats were early specimens and exemplars of many methods described in this book. (Robert E. Mann photo)*

degree in engineering to make a sound judgment based on what has been proven to work well already—just good old common sense.

In order to build the form on or mold in which to build your boat from plans, you have to do some lofting; that is, you have to draw at least some parts of the lines plan full-size. A complete job of lofting—the reproduction of the entire lines plan full-size, fairing the lines as you go—is not mandatory in one-off fiberglass systems that are based on stringers over section moulds. (Note the distinction between a boat or part mold and a station or section mould.) It is just as easy—indeed for the most part easier—to find and correct any unfairness after you fit the stringers on the moulds and can study the boat's shape in three dimensions rather than to fair the many two-dimensional lines on the floor. Because the one-off structure is not a part of the boat, you can shim up the stringers or let them down into the moulds as much as needed with nothing but good results on the boat itself.

To keep this book from being overly long (and expensive), I assume that you can loft the necessary parts to set up your one-off system or that you can get someone to help you. If you are willing to study lofting for its own sake, there are good sections on the subject in several standard boatbuilding books and a whole book about it that I wrote myself.

For the same reason, I assume that you have familiarity with basic carpentry and/or how to fashion wooden parts and install them in boats. A neat job of measuring and cutting wood; of fastening it with screws, nails, bolts, or glue; and of sanding and painting it is about all that is needed to build one-off in fiberglass. So, while I tell you what to do with wood, I hope you forgive me if I avoid making this a woodworking primer.

However, since the boat you want is going to be fiberglass, I feel compelled to discuss the handling and application of fiberglass materials in all the detail I can muster. After 25 or more years of laying out work for an average of 20 employees, I may tend to belabor details; but so might you after you'd lost enough money from misunderstandings. Anyway, I'd rather have you suffer a bit of pedantry than needless worry about your fiberglass work. Worse, if you are inexperienced, I'd just as soon you didn't fall under the spell of somebody who "did some fiberglassing" once. So there is a whole chapter on, and a running mention of, the techniques of hand layup. Should you happen to be experienced, I can only ask your indulgence and hope you don't disagree with my version in any crucial way.

That fiberglass is an excellent boatbuilding material needs no confirmation here. I think if you give it a chance you will enjoy working with it. Only an insensitive person feels no trace of wonderment at what can be fabricated with glass-fiber-reinforced resin. Once you become familiar with it, the urge to put it to work for your imagination, for the satisfaction of your creative instincts, can be as compelling as with any other material. No, it will never smell as good as cedar to you, but many other materials are not as pleasant to work either. That didn't stop the Chinese from using mud and flames to form their pottery, the Greeks from

COMPLEXITY OF ONE-OFF TECHNIQUES

Code
- 0 None
- 1 Minimum
- 2 Moderate
- 3 High
- 4 Maximum

	Mold		PVC	C-Flex		CVC		Str-r-etch Mesh Wire out		Str-r-etch Mesh Wire in		WLP Lining		WLP Wood boat		Off Existing Hull Direct		Off Existing Hull Mold		Cores			
	Single Skin	Sandwich	Sandwich	Single Skin	Sandwich	Single Skin	Sandwich	Single Skin	Sandwich	Single Skin	Sandwich	Single Skin	Sandwich	Glued Construction	Traditional	Single Skin	Sandwich	Single Skin	Sandwich	Wood	Balsa	PVC	Polyvinyl Ribs
Extra Cost of Materials	2 to 4	3 to 4	3	3	3 to 4	0	2 to 3	1	2 to 3	1	2 to 3	var.*	2 to 4	var.*	var.*	0	2 to 3	3	4	1	2	3	1
Extra Cost of Labor	2 to 4	3 to 4	2	0	2 to 4	2	2 to 3	0	2 to 3	0	2 to 3	2 to 3	2 to 3	2 to 3	2 to 3	0	2	3	4	1	2	2	4
Amount of Skill Needed	2 to 4	2 to 4	1	1	1	1	1	1	1	1	1	2	2	2	3 to 4	0 to 1	1 to 2	2	2	1	1	1	1
Need for Tools and Equipment	2 to 4	2 to 4	1	1	1	1	1	1	1	1	1	2	2	2	3 to 4	1	2	2	2	1	1	1	1
Shelter from Wet Weather	4	4	1	1 to 2	1 to 2	1	1	1	1	1	1	2 to 3	2 to 3	3	3	2	2 to 3	2 to 3	2 to 3	2	4	1	3
External Fairing and Finishing Work	0	0	2 to 3	1	1† or 3	2 to 3	2 or 3	1	1 or 3	1	1 or 3	1 to 2	2 to 3	2	2	2 to 3	2 to 3	2 to 3	2 to 3	1	0 to 4	2	0 to 4
Weight for a Given Strength	2 to 3	0 to 2	0 to 1	2 to 3	1 to 2	2 to 3	1 to 2	2 to 3	0 to 2	2 to 3	1 to 2	1 to 2	1 to 2	var.*	var.*	2 to 3	0 to 3	2 to 3	0 to 1	2	1	0	0
Bending for a Given Weight	2 to 3	1 to 2	0 to 1	2	1 to 2	2 to 3	1 to 2	2 to 3	1 to 2	1 to 2	1	2	0 to 1	0	1	2 to 3	1 to 2	2 to 3	1 to 2	1	0	2	1
Interior Sweating and Noise	2	1 to 2	0	3	1 to 2	3	1	3	1 to 2	3	1 to 2	2	1	1	1 to 2	3	1 to 2	3	1 to 2	2	1	2	0
Difficulty of Attaching Joinerwork	2	0 to 1	0	2	0 to 1	3	1	2	0 to 1	2	0 to 1	2 to 4	1	2	0	2	0 to 2	0	0 to 1	0	1	0	0
Difficulty of Installing Deck Hardware and Through-Hulls	0	0‡ to 4	4	0	0 to 4	0	0 to 4	0	0 to 4	0	0 to 4	0	0 to 4	0	0	0	0 to 4	0	0 to 4	0	3	4	4

* Variable: Full range is possible.
† Depends on whether her core is applied on inside or outside of starting skin.
‡ Depends on core.

chipping stone, or the industrial West from working in the iron, steel, and concrete on which it burgeoned. I once asked L. Francis Herreshoff what he would do about fiberglass. "If I were your age," he said, "I'd be up to my elbows in it."

A lot of people misquote this most artistic designer because of his famous outburst of disgust at the prospect of a flood of cheap, plastic production boats. Indeed, he was a bit of a prophet, but also a pragmatist who refused to ignore any material that might make it possible to build a better boat.

I mention these things so that you don't build the boat you want with an inferiority complex because it happens to be one-off in fiberglass. Sure, bad boats are being built with this material. They have been with all materials—and more with wood than with all the others combined simply because there have been so many wooden boats. The boat you want can be as fine as any. The material is up to it; the rest is up to you.

SORTING OUT THE METHODS

Because the wide variety of building methods available to the one-off builder can cause confusion, I have attempted to compare them in the condensed form of a chart. You can acquire an excellent boat, from one point of view or another, with each system; thus, the chart does not rate the methodology, the materials, or the product of the systems. Rather, it only quantifies the disadvantages or limitations of each, relative to the others. In the column under each system, the numbers 0 to 4 indicate the degree of complexity of each of the most common disadvantages of one-off fiberglass constructions. The number 0 means that a method or its product has the least of the particular disadvantages. The number 4 means that the method or its product has the most of that disadvantage. In other words, like the soundings and bottom characteristics on a nautical chart, these ratings don't tell you which way to go, only what sort of water you are getting into.

I see little point in working out "scores" or playing mathematical games with the chart. There are too many heavily weighted subjective unknowns (your preferences) that it does not represent. I say, go the way you want the most to go, and use the chart only to avoid unnecessary hardship. As the building of your one-off proceeds, you may feel at times as though you are aground, or that your anchor is dragging, but if you have worked out your itinerary before you start, you shouldn't get into anything disastrous. About the worst that can befall you is enough disenchantment to cause you to mutter, "There has to be an easier way! Next time I'll try that other route."

2

Molded One-Offs

BUILDING IN A MOLD OR OVER A FORM

One of the first decisions the builder of any one-off fiberglass part has to make is whether to build it in a mold or over a form. Because glass-fiber materials are relatively limp and polyester resins are sticky, a part is easily built up, or laminated, with them in a simple, open mold. Neither pressure nor heat is necessary to form or cure the part, although both can be used. When the part cures, it is an exact mirror image of the mold; and if the mold has a surface like a mirror, so will the part.

Such simplicity of fabrication is one good reason for the tremendous growth of the fiberglass industry. It is also the reason why you should never overlook an opportunity to mold any of your one-off parts. It takes approximately the same amount of time and materials to lay up a part in a mold as on a form. However, when lamination is complete, the molded part, unlike the formed part, is finished.

One test, then, of whether to use a mold or a form is to balance the extra cost of finishing a formed part against the cost difference between building a mold and building a form. For example, suppose the boat you want to build is a V-bottomed, straight-sided boat. There's an awful lot of surface to sand, fill, and paint on such a hull when you build it over a form. This procedure is bound to be more work, and to most people more unpleasant work, than lining essentially the same size structure you would build as a form with a smooth sheet material to make a mold.

However, if the boat you want to build is a very curvaceous round-bottomed boat, you would probably rather do the finishing on a formed hull than diagonally plank the interior of a mold for it. Only if you had a couple of friends who wanted the same hull might the labor invested in such a mold be worth considering. In my boatshop years ago, we built many diagonally planked, "short-run," round-bottomed hull molds, which, although not strictly one-off boatbuilding, I describe later just in case you want the capability of building two- or three-off. After all, the boat you want could be a catamaran or trimaran, which calls for two or three identical, symmetrical hulls. In fact the three hulls of *Gulf Streamer*, a 60-foot trimaran, were all taken from a single diagonally planked mold by an ingenious method her designer, Dick Newick, worked out with us.

In my enthusiasm for molds, however, I have wandered ahead into that complex area of mold construction from which most builders, amateur or professional, begin to back away, unless very wooden-boat building oriented. To allay any anxiety you might have that I'm pushing you toward something you'd rather not tackle, let's drop back to some molds so simple and easy to build that you'd be foolish to try to get a fiberglass part without them.

ASSEMBLING A HATCH MOLD

A hatch—whether a companionway, trunk-top, seat-locker, or cockpit-sole hatch; whether high sided or flush; whether flat or curved—is just a box. Yet a hatch is a good thing to make of fiberglass, for it must remain watertight while subjected to as much wear and tear as is anything on a boat. With fiberglass, you can build an almost indestructible hatch that will stay tight for its life; you can build it in a fraction of the time it takes to build a wooden hatch; and you can build it best in a mold.

To construct the mold, you need only to build a box, the inside of which will be the outside of the hatch. For just one hatch, the simplest, cheapest mold is a pine frame with a sheet of good-one-side material on it. The frame can also be light mahogany, poplar, rift-grain fir, or any other soft, fine-grained, easily sanded and filled wood. The sheet material can be pressed fiberboard, which is marketed under such trade names as Pressboard and Masonite. You want the "tempered" variety with one hard, smooth face, which can be plain or melamine coated, the latter having the advantage that resin won't stick to it. But there are innumerable other sheet materials you can use for mold surfaces. Formica or Micarta with a polished surface, sheet metal, and even sheet fiberglass with an appropriate surface are all good. Any material that resin won't attack will do, as long as it is also stiff enough to withstand a little brushing and rolling.

If the hatch is to be flat, the easiest way to make its mold is to lay out its perimeter on a piece of the sheet material on a table; then make up four sticks of pine as wide as the hatch is deep and longer than its sides, with one end of each cut off square; and arrange them on the outside of the perimeter lines in pinwheel

The E.S. Brewer–designed Centennial. *Working radius wax into a hatch mold's corners. (Loy photo)*

fashion. You can nail the side sticks down with box nails or finish nails if you want, but I like to glue them down with hot-melt glue, which comes in sticks that you push through a cheap, little electric gun with your thumb. These sticks are readily available in hardware or building supply stores. Hot-melt glue is very handy in mold making because you can tack or spot-glue things in place quickly and just as quickly break them away when you remove the part.

When the mold is assembled, you might want to glue in a patch of textured material to make the top of the hatch nonskid. Alternatively, you can use a textured sheet material to *make* the top. In the first case, you might leave a border of smooth surface around the nonskid for looks. To make a border in the second case, mark off the center of the textured surface with masking tape and paint the sides smooth with resin.

To get round edges and corners on your hatch, you can thumb into the seams and corners of the mold a fillet of ordinary modeling clay, of fiberglass body putty, or pattern-maker's beeswax. The wax comes in small, preformed strips like cove molding, in a wide range of radii, from pattern-makers' supply houses. These establishments also sell a metal ball on a rod to wipe the wax into place. But for a very small radius, you can wipe in a little bowling alley wax with your finger or a round-ended dowel.

Now it's time to wax the interior of the mold with mold-release wax, sold in both paste and liquid form. You wipe it all over the surface with a sponge or saturated rag. When it has dried a little, go back over it with a soft cloth to smooth it. Then go away and let it really dry. If it is dry, you can put on another coat; but if it isn't, you'll only dissolve the first coat and move it around. For a small mold like this, two or three coats might be enough; but the thicker the layering the better to ensure release. More important, to keep the part from sticking in the mold, you should let the first two layers of fiberglass harden for some hours, preferably overnight until you are experienced, before you put on more. Too many layers at once generate too much heat, melt the wax, and allow the laminate to stick to the mold.

If you have several flat hatches of different sizes to make, you can lay them out simultaneously on one large sheet of the mold top surface material and save considerable time by performing each operation on one after the other.

To build a small curved-top hatch, you want to assemble the four side pieces, two of which are curved and two straight, with the top of the mold (what will be the bottom of the hatch) down on a flat table and then bend and fasten the sheet material over it. However, should the hatch be so big, or long, that the sheet material doesn't have a straight centerline and dishes in at the middle, you had best preform a truly cylindrical curve in the sheet material. To do this, fasten the material into the hollow curve of several outside ribs or formers and then fasten the side pieces of the mold to the inside.

So far we have been assuming that the top of the mold is the bottom of the part. Thus, when the hatch is laminated, the fiberglass extending above the top of the mold should be trimmed flush with it, either with a knife as you go along, when the fiberglass has gelled just enough, or with a grinder at the end. This leaves the bottom edge of the part fairly straight and true. It is cut or "raw," however. Should you want the edge to come out of the mold in a more highly finished state, you can provide a stop, an extra strip of wood around the top of the mold that extends inward, against which you can terminate the laminate. If the stop overhangs just the thickness of the laminate, it can be a guide to getting the bottom edge of the hatch an even thickness, too. Of course, you have to remove this piece before you can remove the hatch from the mold; but because the mold is a one-off, you'll probably knock it apart anyway. If you wish to make more than one hatch out of the same mold, you have to have a less tack-it-together, anything-goes attitude in building the mold. You might use ring nails or screws so that the mold can stand your prying out the part. You might attach a stop with screws so that you can reinstall it. And above all, you must see that the mold either has "draft"—a slightly larger size at the top than at the bottom—or at least has no undercuts— larger areas in which the part becomes locked because it cannot pass through the smaller areas to come out of the mold. Obviously, if there are any undercuts, the mold has to be taken apart to release the hatch. But that's one of the joys of truly one-off, onetime molds: you can plan on knocking the mold apart, destroying it if need be, and forget about draft.

You may want to work some special details into your hatch. You can make recesses for hinges or other hardware by gluing strips of wood into the mold and glassing over them. Or you may want to form the slide notches in the corners of the ends of a companionway hatch, which calls for gluing in and glassing around some small blocks. You can also make a rabbeted hole to receive a deadlight by gluing in first a block that is slightly bigger and thicker than the glass of the light, then on top of it another block that is the size of the opening and the thickness of the laminate. It is good to apply such blocks or pieces of wood with a bit of hot-melt glue after waxing the mold. The fiberglass, as it dries, usually shrinks around them, seizing them tightly. As a result, the part tends to stick fast to the mold even when the mold is knocked apart. The wax, however, lets the glue break away, the blocks come out with the part, and you can then knock or pry them loose.

Now suppose you would like a raised boss or base for some piece of hardware, or a coaming across the aft end of the companionway hatch. Such features call for holes or slots in the mold with shaped blocks underneath. This takes a little more woodworking ingenuity than that required to insert blocks into the mold; but you will find that with a moment of thought you can build some neat and useful details into the part. For practicality and freedom from breakage, you can't beat a detail that's an extension of the part.

MATERIAL TO LAMINATE A HATCH

After you have constructed a mold for a particular hatch, the next problems are how much material to use, what kinds of material to use, and in what sequence to lay it up. During ordinary use, it is a most unusual hatch that doesn't get stepped on once in a while; so even a hatch that is not supposed to be walked on should be made strong enough to take it. This can be done easily and without excessive weight. Therefore, the only excuse for a weak hatch is to cheapen the boat, which it certainly does. A practical test for any hatch is to jump up and down in the middle of it. If you don't weigh much, carry on a cement block or two to get yourself over 200 pounds, or do as a production superintendent friend of mine used to do: jump from a height of several feet to add a little impact. It is nice to read tables and "standards" of construction; but it's better to develop your own instincts and make your own simple tests so that you gain a sense of proportion about scantlings. If you go only by what you read (including what I write) and not by what you see, you may misinterpret the facts or adopt the mistakes and prejudices of others. You'll certainly never build a better boat.

Because fiberglass is somewhat flexible, stiffness is a primary concern. The stiffness of a material does not always indicate its strength, however. In a fishing pole or archer's bow, the same material can be bent deeply for thousands of cycles, even millions, without breaking. Nevertheless, where boat parts are attached to other parts, too much bend results in dislocation or breakage. For this reason, the seats of fiberglass dinghies are best hung from the rail. Sailors have a strong aversion to flexibility underfoot. And why not when stiffness in this circumstance is a tangible gauge of the capacity to take punishment?

In a single-skin hatch of the larger sizes, you'll find that you can't get proper stiffness without the hatch being rather heavy and wasteful of materials. At 1 foot square, you need at least four layers of 1½-ounce mat, and at 16 inches square, no fewer than five. Adding in or substituting some layers of woven roving yields more stiffness with less total weight. But roving is difficult to push into sharp corners, so the easiest way to use it in a small hatch is to cut a square patch that fits the top panel and then to overlap it with a piece of mat on the sides. Roving, I have found, is best alternated with layers of mat, a subject discussed later on. Thus the number of layers of roving you can use overall is limited. Not only the span but also the shape of the hatch has a bearing on the number of layers, or total thickness, of laminate needed. The more crown it has, the more it resists bending.

The best way to obtain sufficient stiffness for your hatch is to use a core material with fiberglass on each side of it. This "sandwich" construction has a lightweight or filler material that holds the fiberglass apart and together—as trusses do the main members of a bridge—throwing the glass into tension and compression, in which it is many times stronger than in bending strength. Please forgive the pedantry, but I have had so many people say to me, "I only trust solid fiberglass—I don't like sandwich construction," that I like to trot out its perfectly sound principles in hope of squelching the prejudice.

Like all good things, sandwich construction has been abused, mostly by builders who have used it to mold a part (or a whole boat) that is stiff enough to "get by" with a minimum of fiberglass. Also, there is a vast difference in the strength of the various core materials, and in their capacity to adhere to fiberglass, both of which determine the strength and durability of a sandwich. Cores that are too weak tend to collapse as the fiberglass tries to buckle. Bending also creates a lateral stress that shears a poor bond between the fiberglass and the core. Alternatively, the top of a weak core itself shears off just below the bond. To be right for your hatch, probably right for your entire deck, and possibly for your hull, a core should be light in weight, adequately resistant to compression and shear, and above all, capable of an unshakable bond with fiberglass. It is also best if the core won't absorb or permit the migration of water, although this is more important in the hull than on deck. As of this writing, the cores that meet these requirements, in ascending order from good to best, are natural softwoods, plywood, end-grain balsa, and PVC foam.

Thousands upon thousands of decks, including their hatches, have had balsa cores. Balsa is the lightest of woods, and, in end-grain blocks, sufficiently strong and easily glued for many core applications. It is also relatively inexpensive. But, in my opinion, if you want the best hatch, you should use PVC foam (making sure it is not a low-heat-deforming type). The bond of PVC to fiberglass is just about perfect, for the resin bites right into the foam chemically. It absorbs no water, it is tough and resilient, and the impact resistance of a PVC sandwich is fantastic. As if these qualities were not enough, PVC foam also has good insulating qualities, so PVC-foam-cored parts are warmer or cooler as the season requires, free of "sweat" or condensation, and quieter, too.

Core materials are readily available in sheets from ¼ to ¾ inch thick. Your selection of what thickness to use depends on the room you have for it, the span, or unsupported length and width, of the part, the desired stiffness, and in some cases the cost.

A fairly rugged laminate for a medium-sized cored hatch 24 by 30 inches with ½-inch crown and 3-inch-high sides would be:

1. Gelcoat
2. Two layers 1½-ounce mat all over
3. Two layers 1½-ounce mat: one all over and one to fit the top surface only
4. The core weighted down in the number 3 layers while wet
5. Body putty or strand roving to fill and radius the corners between core and sides
6. Three layers of 1½-ounce mat all over

Six layers of mat in the sides and seven layers plus the core in the top should yield sides that are a scant ¼-inch-thick solid fiberglass and a top that is a fat ¼-inch-thick solid fiberglass, divided into two skins by the core. Given a core thickness of ½ inch, the total thickness of the top will be ¾ inch, capable of withstanding several hundred pounds of pressure or impact without noticeable deflection.

The completed hatch will weigh roughly 16 to 18 pounds, depending on the core's density and on whether your workmanship is resin rich or resin starved. You can drop the weight by about 4 pounds if you leave off a layer of mat on each side of the core, but you will reduce it only about 1 pound if you cut the thickness of the core in half. You can increase the stiffness some by substituting a layer of woven roving for one layer of mat on each side of the core. If, in addition to all of these measures, you also cut the weight of each glass layer by one-third and squeezed all the resin you dared out of the laminate, you could get a barely strong-enough hatch that would weigh under 10 pounds. That's what some production builders do (more or less) to cut costs and what some custom builders of high-performance boats do to save weight (while perhaps adding a layer of carbon fibers or some other material to increase stiffness). A wooden hatch approximately ½-inch-thick of cold-molded cedar and mahogany would weigh about the same. A more traditional mahogany hatch of ¾-inch to 1-inch splined and glued stock would weigh about the same as our 16- to 18-pound fiberglass hatch.

BUILDING A ONE-OFF DECK MOLD

Leaving the actual procedure of laying up your hatch to Chapter 9, let's consider the possibility of building your one-off deck in a mold. Just as with a hatch, there is no better way to combine good looks, integrated detail, ruggedness, and watertight integrity in a deck than by molding it. However, let me quickly interject that while molding is the best way to make a one-off deck, it is by no means the easiest or the cheapest. The honors for the easiest should go to lamination on a form with either C-Flex or PVC foam, depending on the deck's configuration; whereas covering wood or plywood with fiberglass is the cheapest, the choice again hinges on configuration. So here we are back to the reason for my writing a book, not a monograph, on building one-offs in fiberglass. There is no "correct" one-off system for all boatbuilders or boats. Each method has disadvantages, not the least of which being that it might take more time and materials to achieve some of the advantages than you are willing to invest.

Anyway, a one-off or "throwaway" deck mold is not a mind-boggling project, nor does it demand the utmost boatbuilding skill or know-how. To avoid frustration, expense, and complicated construction, you should bear in mind at all times the temporary, throwaway nature of the mold. Its only purpose is to present a single face for a few hours or days on which to lay up the fiberglass. How and with what materials that face is fabricated and supported are irrelevant. Anything goes as long as it serves well to make the one part you want. When that purpose is uppermost in your mind, the perfectionist in you can relax and your instincts for shortcuts and innovative details can have free play.

Essentially, a deck mold is a big tray. Its surface represents the top of the deck, which is built in the mold upside down. To visualize this, turn your boat's profile plan upside down. Now the sheerline of the boat corresponds to the outboard edge of the tray or mold. A horizontal line drawn below the upside-down deck parallel to the waterline will represent the line of the floor on which the mold will stand. If you intend the main deck mold to include the cabin trunk, which would be a large cavity in the middle of the mold, you should draw the floor line a few inches below the deepest part of the upside-down trunk, so the bottom of the trunk clears the floor. However, if you want to include a cockpit as one piece with the main deck, it should appear as a rectangular mound above the level of the mold; at the same time, a coaming around the cockpit should appear to be a moat or deep gutter around that mound. Whatever projects upward on a deck, then, is a depression in its mold, and any depression in a deck is a bump on its mold. Also, the starboard side of the mold is the port side of the deck, although fortunately for those of us who are absentminded there are very few asymmetric features on most decks.

Your boat might have a deckhouse that is so high or complicated that you would be better off to leave it out of the mold. In that case, you can just leave a hole in the main deck over which it will fit. It is best, however, to turn up a flange on the deck (which amounts to turning fiberglass down around the edges of the hole in the mold) both to provide a good overlap for fastening on the house and to turn away deck water. It is difficult to envision a tub-type sailboat cockpit that would not be built most efficiently into the main deck mold. A big cockpit that goes right out to the sides of a motorboat, however, is often done more sensibly in its own mold and fitted to the boat later, even though the arrangement shows a connecting surface between coaming and sole.

Deck Mold Design and Materials

The traditional way to build a direct deck mold is to make up a set of section moulds of plywood or cheap softwood boards, which are either lined with a sheet material directly or fitted with wood stringers first and then lined with sheet material. Although it may seem more work to put in stringers, their stiffness reduces the number of moulds and/or the thickness of the lining material necessary to get a fair structure fore and aft. Most building-supply houses or lumberyards sell ¾-by-2½-inch stock called strapping, which house carpenters use across joists to provide nailing for ceiling materials. It is usually spruce or some fairly tough wood, often rather coarse stuff with knots and warpage, which create considerable waste; but it is cheap and handy to use as ready-made stringers in one-off work. To make your own stringers, you can rip up fir, hemlock, or most any inexpensive softwood.

On a small deck, or one with closely spaced moulds, you can usually either eliminate stringers or use them only around the edges of the mold and in back of any seams in the lining material. What few stringers you use to back up seams have to be notched into the moulds, but this doesn't call for precision fitting widthwise. Without stringers to back up joints, you might have to use some cleats or butt straps under seams in the sheet material between the moulds; you should not forget hot glue as a method of fastening these. However, what works very well on the back of both flush joints and corner joints is fiberglass "tabbing." You can back up most or all of a seam with a couple of layers of 2-inch-wide, 1½-ounce mat, or you can spot-tab it with spaced patches about 2 by 4 inches. Working on the underside of a deck mold, spot-tabbing is easier than trying to put up tape. If you presaturate the patches, you can almost pop them in place on the end of your brush. Yet another way to steady butted edges of the lining material, which might wobble past each other and leave a line in the part, is to simply run a bead of hot glue along the joint on the outside. The choice of one method or another should depend primarily upon whether you are going to have to walk on the mold, as you must with big decks, or whether the light pressure of brush and roller is all it will ever suffer.

Along with the need for stringers, you must decide what type and thickness of liner material to use considering the mold's size and the amount of human traffic, if any, it will have to endure during its building. Fortunately, tempered hardboard or Masonite is commonly available in both ⅛-inch and ¼-inch thicknesses. The ⅛ inch is fine for little deck molds, the ¼ inch is stiff enough for the biggest molds with fairly frequent stringers to back it up. I have built some huge molds with ⅛-inch Masonite on stringers spaced not over 6 to 8 inches apart (so that nobody would put his foot through the stuff).

Plywood is stronger than Masonite, but it is more expensive. Also, its surface is more porous, which means you have to seal it with one or more coats of resin to keep its grain from showing up in the part. But if most of the deck is going to have a nonskid pattern glued to it, and it certainly should, not much of the lining material will show on the walking surfaces. The cabin trunk and cockpit sides and the coamings are another matter. These should be lined in the mold with smooth materials, such as melamine-coated Masonite, polished Formica, or sheet fiberglass, so the part comes out with a minimum of blemishes. Such materials are more expensive than plain tempered hardboard, but you can often get damaged sheets or discontinued patterns at a reduced price, and the resulting good finish on the part saves you a lot of "rework." Since these materials are usually too thin to stand alone—and the thinner the sheets the cheaper they are—you probably will have to line the area with plywood or Masonite first and glue the sheets to it.

Once you have decided what thickness of lining materials to use and whether to fit stringers between the lining and the moulds, you can adjust the section, or station, lines in your lofting to allow for those thicknesses before you pick up the moulds from the lines. If you had rushed ahead and made moulds to fit the section lines, and had then lined the moulds with a certain thickness of materials, the part you took out of the mold would be smaller than the lines by that thickness.

You also need to consider the relation between the spacing of the moulds you pick up from the lofting and the construction details of the mold as you plan to build it. Normally, you would pick up a mould at each station line in the lines plan, because for each line there is a section already lofted in your body plan on which you can easily draw the deck crown, house, or other features. But the distance between stations, and therefore between moulds, can affect your decision on what lining to use, whether you need stringers, how stiff they need to be, and/or how closely spaced.

It should become apparent now why we are backing into lofting, picking up section moulds, and setting up to build the deck mold from a discussion of the lining and stringers. You need answers to the following questions before you do anything.

1. What lining material and stringer combination will make a usable mold built on section moulds spaced according to the station spacing of your lines plan? Or,
2. Should you put in more section stations to support a lighter lining construction that you have in mind?
3. What dimension do you have to add on to the lines to allow for the thickness of the lining and any stringers before you pick up your moulds?

An additional question to which you must have the answer before you start building your deck mold is how to attach the deck to the hull. Obviously, the type of deck joint determines how you should prepare the edge of the deck. Now, if you build the deck in a mold but intend to build the hull on a form, you can set up your hull's form on top of the deck while it is still in its mold and overlap the hull and deck laminates to form one piece. If your boat has bulwarks included in the deck mold, the deck and hull laminates can be joined there when the hull is built atop the deck. If the deck does not have bulwarks, you can turn a flange down into the topsides, which would be a flange turned up on the deck mold, and the hull-on-deck's laminate can overlap it just as it would a bulwark.

Building a one-piece hull and deck is quite feasible with any of the usual one-off, form-built systems; and if you know about the trouble deck joints have given over the years, you will agree that the elimination of that joint is an extremely desirable advantage. The hull-on-deck method also eliminates the need for legs on the hull moulds and for setting up these moulds on a level base. The builder who builds his one-off out of doors has another advantage: when the boat is turned over, it is essentially weatherproof.

However, before the prospect becomes too euphoric, one large disadvantage of the method is that all of the interior work must be accomplished within the confines of the closed-in boat. This work starts with ripping out the hull form; and if you are using a sandwich construction, it might include laying up the inner skin as well as the usual tabbing of joinerwork to the hull. For that much fiberglass work, you need a hefty exhaust fan. Then there is the problem of getting large pieces of joinerwork, tanks, and the engine down the hatch and into place. For this you need a generous companionway, ingenuity, and a strong back. Right from the start, with the deck in place, there is also more than the usual amount of working in dark corners and crawling in and out of tight places. For this you need to be part raccoon and part rodent.

Nevertheless, I prefer to build any boat that is adaptable to it this hull-on-deck way. To me, the perfection of the joint alone is too appealing to give up without more compelling deterrents than those already listed. In addition, cruising sailboats that have cabin trunks, cockpits, and numerous deck details but hulls too shapely for a one-off mold are without question better boats at a lower cost when built hull-on-deck than by any other combination of one-off methods.

If, however, the boat you want to build is mostly flush decked, you will find other deck-building methods quicker and less expensive. In addition, if she is to have tall deckhouses and/or a large sunken cockpit, you will want to choose a more convenient method of building the hull than hull-on-deck, even though you might still be leaning toward molding some part or parts of the deck or deck structures.

If you are not going to build your hull on the deck, you still need to decide how to prepare the molded deck and the hull to fit together. There are several deck joints you might use. The simplest close-fitting joint is a plain-edged deck lying flat atop a flange turned inboard on the hull. The most difficult move in making this joint is laying up the flange, which tucks under the upside-down hull. Another difficulty is cosmetic: the joint itself and/or the edge of the deck does not come out exactly flush with the topsides. The usual ways of improving the appearance are:

1. Apply fiberglass putty and gelcoat or paint
2. Cover the deck edge with a guardrail
3. Hold back the edge of the deck from the topsides an inch or more, and cover the seam with a rabbeted toe rail
4. Drop the deck into a rabbet in the hull flange (which makes the flange even more difficult to lay up), and then cover the seam with a toe rail

If your boat has a hollow bulwark, you can turn a flange in on the hull at the top of the bulwark and one out on the deck that will overlap it. If the space inside the bulwark is too narrow for screwing nuts on bolts, you have to use tapping screws or pop rivets, as well as the filled resin or mastic-type bond and sealant that should be used in all deck joints. With a hollow bulwark, it is stronger and wiser also to plug the lower part of the space with foam and to laminate a knee in place from the underside of the deck to the hull. This joint also shows the same deck edge, which can be covered by a wooden railcap, a guardrail, or a combination of these.

Probably the most watertight deck joints are the "shoe box" and the "coffee can." In both of these joints, the deck fits down over the hull. In the shoe box, the deck just hangs down along the outside of the topsides; but in the coffee can, the hull has a rabbet that accepts the deck's down-turned edge, so it is flush with the topsides. The coffee can joint is best because it can be made tight the easiest. After the two parts are set together in whatever mush and bolted, you can cover both the bolt heads and the seam with a couple of layers of mat, which seals out all possible leaks, and then the whole area with a guardrail. With the shoe box, however, the tabbing of fiberglass must cover the lap at the deck's lower edge, which calls for a rabbeted guardrail. Such rails are made for production builders in aluminum, with a vinyl insert that both covers the rail's fastenings and serves as a rubbing strip. No doubt you can obtain such if you don't care to build a guardrail of wood.

Note that both of these joints require that the matching surfaces of deck and hull don't flare outward. If they did, it would be physically impossible to get the deck down over the hull. To simpify the lofting and construction of the parts, it is customary to build a vertical flange around the top of the hull 1 to 2 inches wide (proportional to the size of the boat) and a similar vertical flange on the deck that is bigger than the hull all around by the thickness of the deck's own skin, plus a mite for clearance.

While on the subject of deck joints, I should mention the "pout," which is made, as the name implies, by turning out flanges or lips on both hull and deck. It is the most common joint seen on early fiberglass production boats. This is not surprising. The joint has a wide tolerance of mismatch and the flanges are easily fastened on the outside of the boat. The flanges are also easily laid up in the molds, requiring no removable mold parts. However, this protrusion around the sheer mandates a guardrail, which is a nasty thing to build in wood decently. Production builders in the past usually took the easy solution to the problem by snapping a U-shaped extrusion of vinyl over the assembled flange; and this sort of guard is still produced in many sizes for those who use the pout. If you intend to build this type of deck joint and wish to use a vinyl guard, you should purchase a suitable extrusion, or know when it will be available for purchase, before settling the details of the flange. Extruders tend to backorder an item for months or even years until they can run a large volume of it; thus, a boatbuilder can have trouble getting a particular extrusion in a reasonable amount of time. I hope, however, you will think twice before you use the pout-type joint. It's not very desirable to have your deck joint hanging out where it can get beaten up by pilings or worse. More important, the joint has a poor record in watertightness. This could be due partly to its vulnerable location, but also to its configuration. For some reason the joint doesn't handle the strains that the wringing and bending of the hull place on it as well as some others.

Lofting the Deck Mold

Once you have all of the details of how to build the deck mold in mind (if you want to do good work, it should always be completed in your mind before you start it), you can now go back to the first step, which is the lofting—the full-size laydown of the lines. Assuming that the hull is lofted, the first move in lofting for a deck mold is to draw the main deck crown on each station, or mould section, in the body plan. Most designers give you a single deck crown measurement for the entire deck. Others might draw a line on the profile plan that is the "top of deck at centerline," expecting you to loft a different crown at each station that fits between the high point at the centerline and the low points of the "deck at side," or sheer. The easiest way to draw these crowns is to nail two long boards together like roof rafters with their inside apex on the center point and their lower edges on the deck-at-side points. By putting a pencil in the apex and sliding the boards from side to side against nails or picks in the sheer points, you can draw the crown of each station. If that method is not practicable, you will have to "construct" a crown for each station in one of the several ways indicated in boatbuilding or lofting instructions, or sometimes shown on designers' plans. Still another method is to find by trial at each station the radius the arc of which fits the three points.

Now, when you have drawn the main deck, with which the sides of the cabin trunk, cockpit tub, seats, and coamings intersect, you can draw these on the body plan. To find their dimensions at every station, you will probably have to loft their outlines in the profile and half-breadth views. A few designers include a drawing among the plans with heights and widths at each station, but most give only a few overall measurements, and some expect you to scale it all off the plans. Anyway, these parts have only a few lines, which should not take you long to lay out on the floor. There is also a crown pattern for the trunk top, which is usually steeper than the main deck crown.

When the section at each station is complete, you should add on the thickness of the stringers and lining material and draw a line parallel to the section line to represent the edge of the section mould. It is very likely that your body plan will soon become a confusing mass of closely drawn and overlapping lines. One way to avoid mistakes is to use different colored pencils to draw the various lines. Another is to build each mould as soon as the line of that section is completed. If you do it the first way, it is prudent to use the nailhead method to pick up the lines; the grooves the nails leave will indicate the lines already picked up.

Picking Up the Section Moulds

The nailhead method is much the best for picking up lines that generally have many angles, like those of a deck mould. You should use plasterboard nails or nails with fairly wide, thin heads. Lay each nail with its head on the line, its shank at right angles to the line, and tap the edge of the head into the floor until the shank is flat to the surface. When you have put in as many nails as needed to record the shape, lay a piece of the mould board or plywood gently in place, put your weight on it so that it won't shift, and either stamp it (with one foot at a time) or hammer it down. This makes a nice set of imprints, easily drawn through with battens and straightedges. If the piece you have marked is for one side of the deck, nail another to it and saw out the two at once, so they will be identical. If you have drawn only half of the section, but intend to mark a piece the full width of the deck by printing one side and then its reverse side, you can accurately reposition the piece for the second impression provided it has one straight edge. You can fit this edge against blocks or picks set parallel to a waterline, pick up the centerline on the first impression, and then square it over the edge to index the reversed side to the centerline.

If your cabin trunk's ends are vertical, you can pick these up off the floor as easily as any moulds of the station sections. You might be lucky and find that one or even both of them are either on a station or close enough to be used for the mould in that area, saving some nearly duplicate construction. When a trunk end is raked and/or curved, and you feel that lofting and picking it up as a mould are too complicated, you can pick up a vertical mould just forward of the forward end or aft of the aft end, run the stringers and lining to this mould, and construct the true trunk end in place in the deck mold. In general, you will find that cobbling strange shapes up in place in the mold is quicker and gentler on the mind than lofting and building them on the floor.

Setting Up the Moulds

Although you certainly can use softwood boards to build your moulds, plywood is better adapted to the deep cutouts and notches on many deck mold sections. It saves the awkward and time-consuming business of cleating small pieces together. Whatever cleats or butt blocks you do use on moulds are best fastened with either ring nails or screws, lest they work loose in the handling and setting up. The use of screws, particularly if you have a reversing electric screwdriver, allows quick and less destructive salvaging of mould parts, too. Fastening stringers and lining materials to the edges of the moulds is the worst aspect of using plywood; but using steel screws and boring a hole of the right size improve holding power, slanting the screw so it crosses the plywood layers helps, and you can resort to softwood cleats alongside the edge of the plywood for stringers that refuse to stay sprung into place.

As long as the results are accurate and fair, the beauty of one-off-mold building is that the quickest and least expensive way you can get it all together for that one shot is the best way. You're not building the boat, just a very temporary inside-out facsimile from which the boat will take its shape. If you find that a couple of layers of ⅛-inch plywood makes a sharp curve, use it; but if you can make the curve more easily with fiberglass putty coped into shape with a ping-pong paddle and scrubbed smooth with sandpaper on a curved block of wood or foam, go that way.

Because you will be tearing the mold apart after your one deck is built, you need not be overly concerned with draft, the slight angle given all mold surfaces that would otherwise be parallel to facilitate drawing out the finished part. In fact, as long as you plan how to get the mold apart without a prodigious and possibly damaging struggle, there is no harm in building it so that the deck could not possibly be pulled from it. However, there are some other more or less related factors to bear in mind:

1. You have to be able to reach inside deep, narrow places, or at least to get a resin brush into every corner of them. The strong taper (and great thickness) of coamings seen on production boats is so designed that you can easily fit your hand and brush inside as well as easily pull the part. It's also handy to reach into with backing plates, nuts, and washers when bolting on hardware.

2. You should be careful not to build the cockpit sole on the mold with a single piece that extends out to all four sides. Otherwise, the laminate, once it shrinks tight around it, may make the part impossible to remove without chopping it up in place, as I mentioned earlier in regard to molding hatches.

3. You should be alert to the laminate's tendency to come out slightly concave when laid up on a dead flat surface and to pull away from the top edge of the mold as it cures. You can head off concavity by building the mold's flat surfaces with a touch of convexity, about as much as you would get using the round side of warped sheet material for the molding surface. You can also bulge these surfaces faintly with braces against the backsides, or with curved boards clamped across them.

Setting up the moulds level and squarely on their stations is crucial to a fair deck. If you are setting up on a straight and level wooden floor, the process is relatively easy. It requires but a centerline with station lines properly spaced along it and normal (squared) to it. If the floor is not level, and perhaps not straight either, you can create a true floor line most effectively by setting up a centerline batten. This should be a fair, stiff batten fastened to the floor with one edge along the drawn centerline. It should be shimmed or cut so that its top face is straight and level. Now you have a true floor line at the centerline, and a long level (or level and straightedge) can widen it into a true floor plane. To prepare for setting up each mould, set your long level across the centerline batten over the station line and build up blocking (or slide two matched wedges together) at the spots where the mould's legs will rest until the two blockings and the centerline batten are in a straight, level line. Set your mould up with its legs on the blocking and its face on the station line, and center it with the level by shifting the mould athwartships until its centerline is plumb over the centerline edge of the batten.

This is a time-honored way of setting up any boat moulds with legs on an uneven floor. It can be used on a cement floor, too, in conjunction with a spider of boards laid flat on each station line and either tacked to nailing strips or braced off to each other so that they can't shift. However, for setting up on a dirt floor or bare ground, the best arrangement is a bed consisting of a pair of nominal 2-inch-thick-by-6-to-12-inch-wide planks on edge "boxed off" parallel to each other with crosspieces of the same, braced diagonally (or staked) to prevent shifting, and blocked up with the plane of their tops level. It is also a perfectly good method to use when you set up on polished floors into which you can't nail, or when you want to be able to move the mold about bodily.

In setting up all section moulds, whether of a boat mold or of a boat, you should start with the midship mould and work toward the ends. It is easiest to measure and tie off the progressively smaller moulds from this biggest one. Also, starting in the middle of the boat reduces potential "progressive error" by half. To make the midship mould an accurate base from which to work in setting up the others, double-check that its station line is square to the centerline and that the mould itself is accurately leveled, well braced, provided with a stiffener to hold it straight if at all bowed, and horned at its outboard top corners. Horning is measuring with a tape (or two tapes) from a fairly distant point on the centerline to matching points (like the sheer) on each side of the mould to check its squareness with the centerline.

Once all the moulds are set up, as well as a false stem piece on which the stringers and lining can converge and terminate, you can install your stringers and lining. Almost enough has been said about these for the purposes of the relatively simple shape of a deck mold. But I would like to mention that a stringer that must be butted along a curve should neither be butted on the edge of a mould nor butt blocked with a full piece of its own stock. These practices result in an unfair joint. You will find that the quickest way to make a really fair joint is to use a longish butt block or "splint" of the stringer stock that is tapered from full thickness at the center to not more than half its thickness at each end. Also, in fastening the lining material to the stringers, you should use a very shallow countersink so the fastener heads lie just below the surface. If you countersink the fasteners too deep, you will have an unnecessary amount of putting to do. But if you do not countersink them deep enough, the fastenings will leave craters in the gelcoat or, worse, the gelcoat will get hooked under their heads, which will tear a chunk out of the deck as it is separated from the mold.

Building in the Details

When the basic structure of the deck mold has been lined, you can go to work on the details. These might include provisions for the companionway, deck hatches, seat lockers, trunk portlights or deadlights, bulwark scuppers, mast collars, and bases for winches, cleats, ventilators, smoke-pipe deck iron, and other hardware items. Some of the most cost-effective time you can put into a one-off boat is spent building these details into your deck mold. You can create many of them more quickly in the mold than the best of boatbuilders could hope to on the raw deck. More important, any details that you lay up as part of the deck laminate will remain clean-cut, sound, and waterproof for the life of the boat.

Portlights and Deadlights

Let me begin with a real work saver. Why lay up a blank cabin trunk, on the sides of which you will have to lay out and cut out holes for the portlights, when blocks of wood cut to the shape of the holes and screwed to the mold will automatically incorporate them into the part? If you are going to have deadlights, a block a bit bigger and thicker than the glass placed next to the mold liner and another block ¼ inch to ½ inch smaller in outline on top of the first block will form the rabbet into which the glass will fit. You can set the glass in bedding compound and retain it with a bolted-on frame, or you can make the rabbet deeper and "glaze" (putty) in each deadlight. If the trunk side has much curve, to which you don't want to bend Lexan, you can shape the outboard side of your first block to fit the curve, leave its inboard face flat, and come up with a straight rabbet to take a glass light.

The Companionway

It also wastes time, and materials, to lay up fiberglass across the companionway area that is going to be cut out later. At the very least, you should install stops, strips of wood fastened to the mold just inside the perimeter of the opening, which will form a true, finished edge in the laminate. You can then readily fit wooden hatch runners and a frame for doors or "fisherman slides" to this edge. The stops should be the same height as the anticipated total laminate thickness so that you can use them as a guide to keep the thickness of the edge consistent, which you will appreciate when you come to fit wood to it, especially rabbeted wood.

However, you need not settle for wooden hatch runners, or even a wooden door frame, if you prefer that they be fiberglass. Fiberglass runners are created by cutting slots in the trunk top of the mold and fitting open-top wooden boxes beneath the slots. When the fiberglass is turned down into one side of one of these channels and back up the other, a runner forms that will never get loose, leak, or rot. Of course, runners laid up as such are hollow, but you can fill them up flush with "applesauce" (resin thickened with glass fibers, sawdust, or some other filler). Please heed a word of caution here: use a strong enough laminate to depend on before you fill it; that is, don't skimp on the laminate and then depend on the filler to give the runners the strength they need. Filler adds to the stiffness, but not much to the strength.

A third piece goes with every set of runners—the little athwartship coaming between them that keeps water on the trunk top from washing under the forward end of the hatch and into the cabin. This coaming can be formed the same way the runners are—by a channel under the trunk top in the mold. This channel should be curved to match the crowns of the deck and hatch. Although not easy to fashion in one piece of wood without a shaper, a curved channel is a breeze if you build it up with three sawn pieces and radius its inner corners with wax or putty.

The channels for the coaming and the after half of the runners that border what will be the deck opening of the companionway do not have to be fitted under slots in the trunk top of the mold, however. You can cut out the opening in the mold, and fit these parts of the channels up to the edge of the cutaway top. While on the subject, you can also cut out the opening of the doorway part of the companionway in the bulkhead; or, with foresight, you can build the companionway opening into the mold. Whichever way you make it, an opening here provides a convenient place to stand while doing this detail work, as well as good access to hard-to-get-at areas when you lay up the deck.

To form in fiberglass the jambs of the frame for doors or slides, you can make a stop along the sides of the opening as deep and wide as you want the rabbet to be, then turn the glass of the bulkhead up the side of the stop and across its forward face. To retain fisherman slides in such a rabbet, usually a piece of wood is fastened on the outside of the bulkhead so that it overhangs the opening and makes a channel of the rabbet.

It is not, of course, impossible to build the entire channel for slides in fiberglass; but it means fussy work in some tight corners with an increased likelihood of bubbles in the laminate and future "breakouts." Usually in fiberglass work, complicated configurations like this are considered more trouble than they're worth. Still, if your time is your own and you want to try it, why not?

A useful configuration that is not quite so difficult to lay up is formed by making the notch or rabbet first mentioned, then turning the laminate forward, and then outboard again. This forms a hollow fiberglass post in back of the rabbet that stiffens up the edge of the companionway more than a plain flange. It also creates a pocket to accept the edge of interior finishing materials and is easier to take hold of or lean against. The same configuration can be carried across the bottom of the opening, where its flat surface is useful as a threshold or as a base for one of wood.

Whatever shape door jamb or slide channel you use, it must end at the top at a height that permits the companionway hatch to slide over it, covering the tops of the doors or slides from the weather.

Deck Hatches and Skylights

You should also make some sort of provision in the mold for whatever deck hatches and skylights you plan to use. Whether you use an aluminum-frame stock hatch or a custom-built hatch of wood or fiberglass, it is best in the long run to mold a fiberglass coaming as part of the deck. Even a low base a fraction of an inch above the deck provides some runoff, raising the joint of a bolted-on coaming or frame out of the surface wetness that attacks it and its bedding constantly. But if you want, you can just as easily mold a full-height fiberglass coaming with a rabbet or other arrangement to receive the hatch. Forming a hatch coaming is similar to making the companionway runners: you have to cut out the part of the mold where the coaming will be and install suitable formers for the coaming beneath it.

The Mast Collar and Other On-Deck Features

Because it is an on-deck part, a mast collar is also formed below the surface of the mold. Here again you have a worthwhile project, for there's no better way to get a collar that is bound to be watertight for life. Because you are building one-off, you can include two important undercuts in your collar mold: one to form a lip projecting outward around the top of the collar to keep the lashing of the mast boot from working up and another to form an outward flare from the top of the collar to its base at deck level, so the collar is larger than the mast partner and its wedges.

To form the mast collar mold, you saw a hole the size of the outside of the collar and the shape—round, elliptic, or rectangular—the mast requires in a block of softwood the thickness of which is equal to the height of the collar without the lip at the top. The collar will be laid up on the inside of this hole. To form the lip, you simply add a thin piece of wood with a slightly bigger cutout to the "top" of the block (this will be the bottom when it is put in under the deck mold), then another thin piece of wood or Masonite as a stop for what will be the top edge of the collar. To fit the collar mold to the deck mold, you should trace a line around the block on the surface of the mold liner, cut out a hole to this line, fit the block up through the liner flush with the mold surface, and hot-glue it in place.

It is important to fit the whole block up through the mold liner. Then after you have split the block off the laid-up collar, there will be a generous hole in the liner for the collar and its lip to pass up through as the deck is removed from the mold. Also, you can tilt the block to the exact angle or rake at which the mast enters the deck, scribe around it, and cut it flush with the mold surface or grind it down flush after it is installed.

The description I give may make molding in a mast collar sound much more involved than it really is. However, once you are accustomed to building on-deck parts in the mold, you'll find it the quickest and easiest way to get most of them to the finished, installed state. Some other on-deck features that you might consider molding into the deck are winch bases, ventilator cowls, smoke-pipe deck-iron bosses, dodger coamings, and, of course, toe rails. You can even build in solid handrails of the C-section type, although I must confess I never cared for these except along the edges of house roofs where they serve both as grab rails and as gutters to control water runoff.

When molding above-deck details, which require recesses in the mold, you should remember the following:

1. Build the formers for these parts in such a way that they are easily broken up or pried off the laid-up part, and fasten them lightly to the mold. I once explained to an experienced wooden-boat builder how he should make up segmented softwood details so that they would break up easily. He followed my suggestions, but from lifelong habit he poured so many sizable screws into the mold details through the liner and stringers that they were unwilling to let the part go until we literally reduced them to splinters. So don't forget, it's only a temporary mold, not a boat.

2. Make mold details the easiest way you can think of. Anything that gives you a smooth mold surface long enough to lay up the part is acceptable.

3. Think in terms of the finished deck. What you do now will affect its viability over many decades. Don't be in a hurry and slap out a raw laminate, thinking, "I'll trim that off when it's done, cut this out later, build something there after the deck and hull are assembled." Your best chance to plan it and do it in one neat, enduring whole is right now. Moreover, hours spent on molded-in details can save you days later on.

4. Again, in a one-off mold you can do even more than a production builder can. There is a limit to the complication that is practicable in a production mold, which crews of people will use to produce hundreds of parts; but it is relatively easy for you to cobble up a one-time, disposable detail. You are not fighting labor costs, nor are you trying to make your mold as foolproof as possible to minimize labor errors.

5. At the same time, I realize that some one-off builders are reluctant to cut into a deck mold or to build the recessed formers of above-deck details. So much upside-down, inside-out work may turn them off. If that's the way you feel about it, OK; just provide for holes with stops and build some nice details out of wood or metal to fit the holes.

Cockpit Tubs, Seats, and Seat Hatches

Fortunately, details below a deck's surface like cockpit tubs and flush-hatch drains don't seem to bother builders much. A cockpit tub mold is essentially a box; and if you don't want to include its section in the station moulds, you can wait and construct it right on top of the stringers and liner of the main deck.

If the cockpit seats are at the main-deck level, the box to form the tub is as simple as can be; and here you have a good case against building the cockpit coaming integral with the deck. It is much easier to fit a wood coaming/seat back on the finished deck than to build a recessed mold detail, and the wood's thinner section steals less space from the side decks and seats. However, if the seats, and perhaps a bridge deck, are below the main-deck level, you have to build a stepped box that forms the seats and then the tub. No doubt the seat back will be a continuation of the inboard face of the coaming down to the seat level—a secure and sheltered place to sit, that's for sure. Here, it's a toss-up whether to fit wooden coamings that project above the main-deck level, or to make the whole seat, coaming, and deck integral in fiberglass. If a wooden coaming/seat back is the choice, it certainly should be applied to a laminate that is a single piece from the main deck down into the seat and on down into the tub.

When you make these boxlike cockpit tubs and seats, you should be aware that the fiberglass laid up around them will shrink tight and squeeze them as it hardens. As a result, it is very difficult to remove any solid piece of the mold that the laminate surrounds on three or four sides or edges. It is not the best idea, for instance, to use solid rectangular plywood side pieces that run from corner to corner in building a cockpit tub mold. It is better to fit the side pieces pinwheel fashion, so one edge of each piece laps over the edge of the piece on one side and one edge butts against the piece on the other side. That way you can pry the butted edge inward if you can get to it, or pound on it with a rubber hammer if you can't, and the box will tend to collapse. Also, it is best to give the bottom corner a generous radius past the bottom piece onto the side pieces, so the bottom will not get jammed in the laminate. But you can also get good release by fitting the bottom inside the side pieces and opening the back of the joint so that the bottom can be rotated out if necessary. But, needless to say, light fastening, as with plain steel finish nails and/or hot-melt glue, is as important as how you fit the pieces.

Obviously, release is easier if you give the whole tub and all of its details a little draft. But if you have other ideas for the configuration that preclude draft, such as seats that overhang their fronts, or fronts that rake inboard for more foot room, you'll have to plan the mold construction so that you can disassemble it without violence. It is desirable to screw or bolt the cockpit mold to the deck mold in such a way that it can be easily cast off when the part is pulled from the mold. Then, after the deck is turned over, the cockpit mold is easier to take apart.

The one-off builder should consider his method of mold removal not as a limitation but as a means to get what he wants. In other words, the one-off builder shouldn't feel that he has to imitate production builders, who are confined by cost considerations to the simplest mold release and repreparation for the next part. The one-off builder, who is going to throw out the mold anyway, should have no compunction about destroying it in the removal if that is what is needed to acquire the shape he would most like to have. His only concern should be that the mold be so put together that it is not an exasperating struggle to get it off the part, or vice versa.

If there are to be seat lockers, you need to construct flush hatches so that the crew doesn't have to sit on bumps. The gutters into which the hatches will fit are formed by pieces installed above the surface of the seats in the mold. Such gutters on a sailboat should be very deep on the inboard end or they will not drain when the boat is heeling. Some builders run hoses from the outboard gutters to the cockpit sole, or to through-hulls; but if the athwartship gutters slope down to the seat fronts at about 30 or more degrees, they provide simple, maintenance-free drainage. They also serve to brace the structure as hanging knees fitted in the angle of the seat and seat front.

To build cockpit seat hatches, you make molds similar to the hatch mold discussed in the beginning of this chapter. But since cockpit seat hatches must be flush, their critical dimensions differ from those of deck hatches. A seat hatch has to fit into a recess in the seat with a proper clearance around its perimeter; its laminate thickness has to be coordinated with the height of the lands, on which it rests when down, so that it sits flush with the fixed part of the seat top; and it needs down-turned edges that guide drips into the gutter. In one popular configuration, the hatch's inboard edge falls into a rabbet or pocket in the face of the seat front. With the seat front extending up under it, this edge does not need a gutter. In another, the hatch drops into a four-sided gutter that is well within the margins of the seat top.

It seems to work out best if the down-turned edges of the hatch hang in midair over the gutters when the hatch is closed and if the underside of its top surface rests on the inboard edges of the gutters for support. The gutters should be built with a flanged top that both stiffens them and provides a flat bearing surface. For all except the smallest and cheapest hatch, a cored or sandwich construction seems to resist the impacts of trampling best, which can be up to several hundred pounds in a few square inches when heavyweights hurry to reach the helm or tend a line. You can install a rectangle of core in the center of the hatch so that it falls within the supporting gutter flanges; or you can fit the whole top of the hatch with core, right up against its down-turned edges. Hatches with an island of core in the middle are light, tough, and durable, but a bit busy or stamped-out looking on the inside, no matter how neatly done. The fully cored hatch is, by definition, fully insulated against heat and sound, quite a bit stiffer, and better looking. However, its down-turned edges must be sufficiently deeper than the core to allow a decent lap of the inner skin (covering the core) onto them. This is most important with cores prone to delaminate, less so with PVC foam. To eliminate worry about a short inner and outer skin overlap, you can use the system I worked out for the tops of open boat transom cores. When setting the core in wet mat on the inside of the hatch, let an inch or two of the wet mat project above the edges of the hatch all around. After the core is pressed in place, fold the flap of wet mat down flat on the core and smooth it out. Then radius the corner with putty. When the inner skin is applied over the flap and turned up against the hatch edge, the core's perimeter is doubly sealed and bonded.

It is poor planning not to work out how a seat hatch is to be hinged and locked before you build it. One concern is that the outboard down-turned edge have ample room to rotate up out of the gutter without jamming, which is affected by the location of the pin or the axis of the hinge. Equally important are the types of hinges and locks you intend to use and the provisions for fitting and fastening them in place. Naturally, the easiest hinge installation is a piano hinge or two or three T-hinges just bolted down on top. This is simple and effective, but crude; and in the long run it can become a great way to tear up posterior clothing, at the least. Butt hinges, or a piano hinge installed as one long butt hinge, are neater looking and, except for the round edges of the hinges, are buried below the surface. An aggravating disadvantage is that you have to fasten half of each hinge to the hatch first, then the other half to the seat with the hatch propped open. Thus between the gutter and the edge of the hatch you have only a narrow slot at a poor angle through which to work with drill and screwdriver. This installation also requires careful planning if bolts are to come through on the underside of the hatch and the backside of the gutter where they can be nutted. With standard-width hinges, your chances of bolting are best if the hatch is not cored out to its edges (at least not in the way of the hinges) and the deck not cored up against the gutter. One way you can ease the installation of butt hinges is to slope the outboard face of the gutter and rake the down-turned edge of the hatch under so that you get a better angle for your drill and driver.

The best hinges I have seen for seat hatches were on an older, high-grade fiberglass boat. If memory serves, they were solid bronze (they could be welded up in stainless steel), flush with the deck, easy to install (if some small blocks were hot-glued to both hatch and seat molds to form pockets for them), and just about indestructible. Rugged hinges like these would serve flawlessly for the life of your boat and still be a joyous find in a secondhand chandlery to a future one-off builder.

Latching and locking seat hatches are companion problems to hinging them. Locking has become as important as latching to most owners today. Although there has always been the occasional threat that boarding seas might flood a boat through unlatched hatches, now, every unguarded yacht is under the constant threat of boarding by burglars and vandals. In this sad state of affairs, you are well advised to make provisions for sturdy locks in your seat hatches. You would want to form some sort of recess in the hatch or seat front for any of the usual external trunk latches and/or padlock hasps, because, when surface mounted, these can be downright dangerous to clothing and flesh. However, you should avoid such hardware altogether if possible.

Any hatch that can be reached from the interior, say, through the engine space or from a quarter berth, is best locked with sliding or rotating dogs from below and left unblemished on deck. For hatches over lockers that are sealed off or inaccessible without strenuous contortions, there are a number of remotely actuated below-deck locks that have been devised over the years. I have installed both spring catches with pull wires and long rods or tubing with rotating or sliding dogs attached along them. Because different boats need different arrangements, and because I was never fully satisfied with any we worked out, I won't bore you with their details. No doubt you can devise your own system, if you want, and configure your hatches to accommodate it.

I cannot remember ever having seen a simple, rugged piece of hardware for clamping a flush hatch tight and locking it from the outside. However, I'm sure such either exists or could be invented by a mechanically inclined individual with common sense.

Perhaps you think I am making too much of cockpit seat hatches; yet they are integral to fiberglass-boat design. Since the first fiberglass boats were built, a drastic change has taken place under the cockpit of both sail- and powerboats. Whereas a wooden boat, with its horn timber, frames, floor timbers, stringers, beams, carlings, and stanchions, has little useful space under the cockpit, every fiberglass boat has a relatively enormous, smooth-surfaced cavern in this area. Even a pair of quarter berths in a sailboat or tanks in a powerboat leave a good portion of this space unutilized. Therefore, flush hatches, the handiest means of putting it to use, have become a standard fixture on fiberglass boats. Right in the middle of the action, they are subject to constant traffic and considerable torture. If anything goes wrong with one, it becomes a sorry nuisance. That's why you can't build and install them and their hardware too well.

Preparing the Deck Mold for Layup

When the deck mold is detailed to your satisfaction, it's time to slick up its surface to make it ready for laying up the part. But first, you should mark off the nonskid areas. This practice helps you avoid fussing too much with any of the surface that your nonskid forming material will cover. All that is needed under this material is fairness and relative smoothness. How smooth is inversely proportional to the stiffness of the material. Obviously, the stiffer the material, the more imperfection it will bridge.

What material you should use to print a nonskid pattern into your deck's gelcoat is a matter of preference. Historically, boatbuilders have used all kinds of embossed, woven, or pitted materials, including steel, aluminum, rubber, vinyl-covered fabric, and plain old canvas. But you must remember that, because you are applying this material to your mold, the pattern or texture on the deck will be reversed. To get bumps, you must use a material with pits or grooves in it. To get recesses, you should use one with a raised pattern. However, since recesses collect dirt and tend to fill in if painted in the future, you are better off with a finished part that is, in effect, many small bumps or ridges on a flat background.

On the following pages:
Centennial is a Ted Brewer–designed, shoal-draft, radius-bottom sharpie with leeboards, a ketch rig, and an outboard well. I built her for Nick and Trudy Loy in 1980. It seemed to me that the boat would be best built with a molded, Airex-core sandwich deck and a plywood-core sandwich hull, the latter to be built atop the deck while still in the deck mold. The extremely complicated cockpit arrangement, including two cockpit tubs separated by the outboard well and bordered by lockers, would have been expensive to build properly and durably except by molding it as one piece. (Incidentally, the deep cockpit carried out to the rail is the type Sam Crocker made famous.) In order to make the cockpit a one-piece molding from rail to rail, the deck mold had to change from female forward of the main bulkhead to male abaft it. In laying up the deck, the fiberglass passed through a "changeover slot" in the mold at the main bulkhead. As the following sequence of photographs begins, the deck has been lofted, the moulds have been set up and stringered, the hardboard mold lining has been installed, and blocks denoting positions of portlights, mast collars, hatch coamings, and other deck fittings have been mounted. Many of the details covered in this chapter are illustrated. (Loy photos)

Above: *The underside of the deck mold, looking aft toward the male mold for that portion of the transom above the cockpit seats.* **Right:** *The deck mold is ready for the vinyl material (roll in foreground), which has an embossed pattern to create the nonskid areas.*

Left: *Deck mold looking aft. Note nonskid, mast collar, hatch, portlights, companionway, doghouse, and cockpit tub details.* **Below:** *The deck mold looking forward, with all details in place, before laying up the part.*

Above: *Looking at the mold, the owner sees his deck inside out and upside down.* **Below:** *The bridge deck area. Note mizzenmast collar mold, companionway opening, and doghouse deadlight form. Aft of the changeover slot at the main bulkhead, the mold turns from female to male.*

Above: *Mizzenmast collar mold projecting below bridge deck.* **Below:** *Deck mold, aft end, showing cockpit tubs with hatchway of motor well between (handy place to stand while polishing), seat-locker hatch drains, bulwarks, and nonskid pattern. Five coats of wax, minimum, go on the finished mold, with over an hour between coats. Then the fiberglass won't stick, if it doesn't get too hot.*

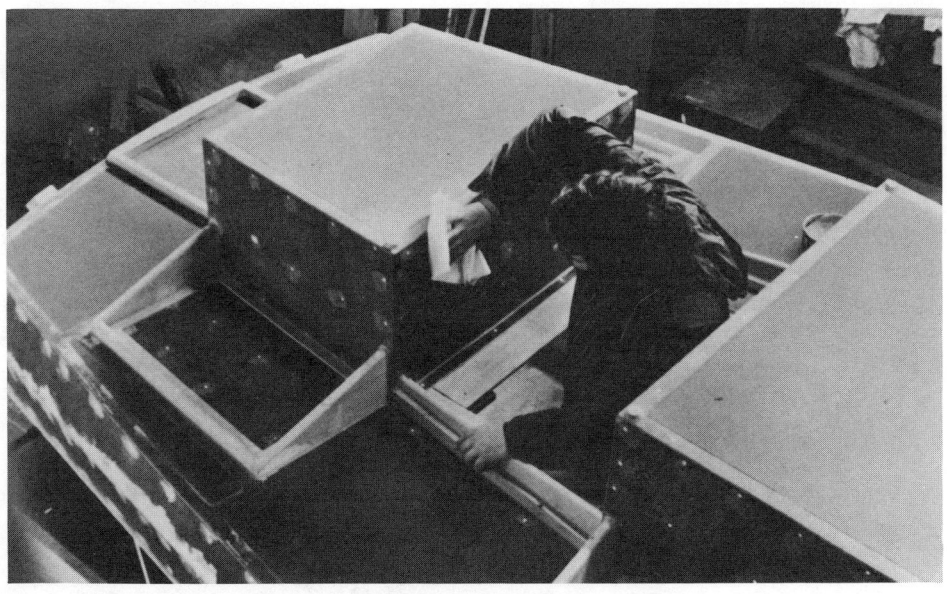

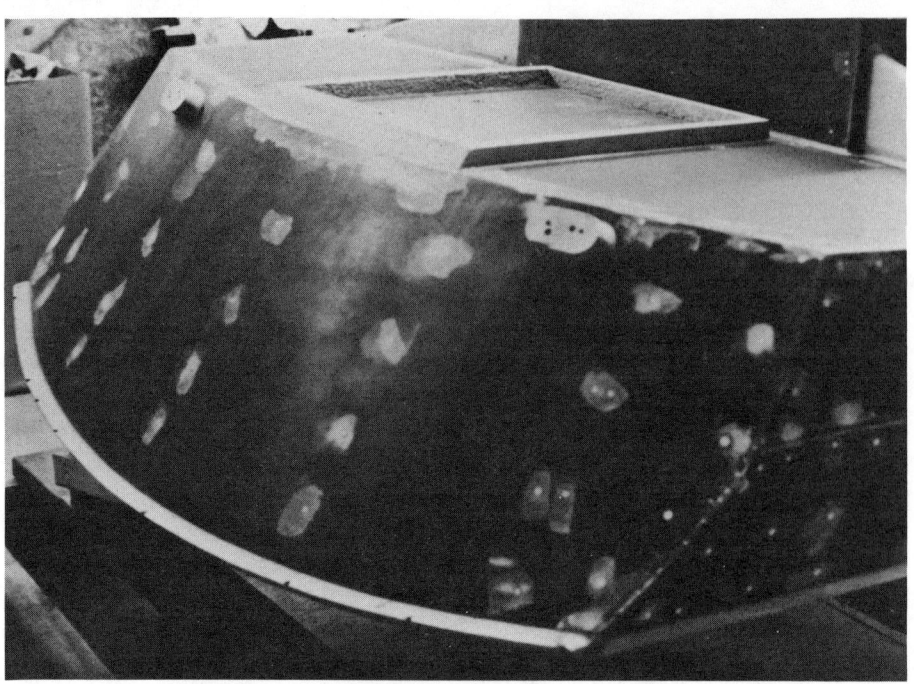

Above: *The transom, from the seat level up, in the cockpit. Note the two stern chocks (hawseholes?) just above seat level, coaming for a hatch to reach the steering, and the shine the waxed hardboard has taken.* **Below:** *Setting a second layer of plywood core replacement in place, in wet mat, atop the first layer. The first layer was set in wet mat atop the outer (upper) skin of the deck. When weighted down, the second layer will be just flush with the Airex foam already in place, which has been notched for it. Deck hardware will be fastened through the plywood core replacement.*

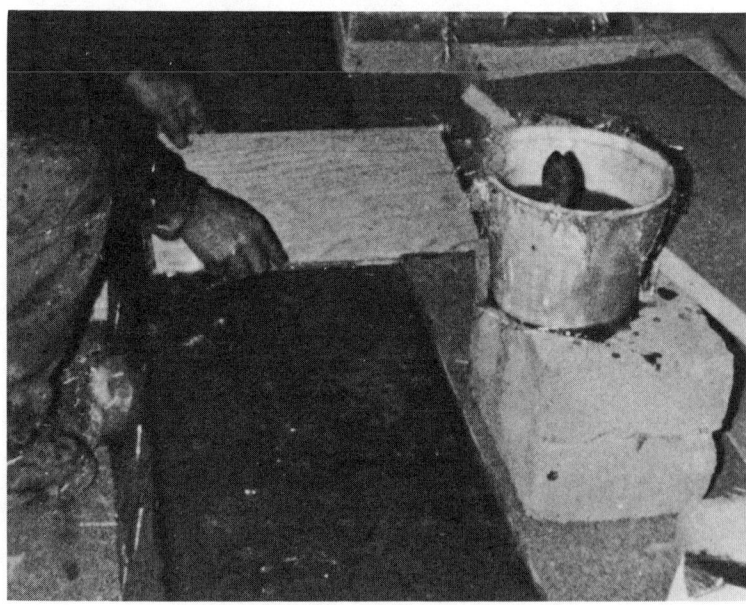

Molded One-Offs 39

Plywood core replacement (see Chapter 3) weighted down on the afterdeck (seat level), where there is bound to be some hardware bolted through. A laid-up seat-locker hatch drain is prominent in the right foreground.

The first few feet at the bow and 6 inches along the edge of the raised deck are fitted with plywood replacements of Airex foam core. The plywood is in two or three layers that add up to the thickness of the core; they bend better to fit the curve of the deck and "remember" the curve when the wet mat under and between them cures.

Right: *The bridge deck with its mizzenmast collar and the trunk or doghouse with its portlight, nonskid pattern, and companionway, as they came from the mold. The hull was built atop the deck while it was still in the mold (see Chapter 7 photographs).* **Below:** *Some of the complicated details included in* Centennial's *deck mold, all one piece: sole, seats, hatch openings, and bulwarks. They'll never leak or rot.*

The raised deck and doghouse as they came from the mold. Note mast collar. That's a fan over the forward hatch to ventilate the interior while the inner skin of the hull is being completed.

To achieve this texture on your deck, you must apply its opposite to the mold: a flat surface with many little depressions or grooves. To be sure your deck has a texture you can live with—one with enough traction but not so rough as to wear out trousers or abrade skin, it is a good idea to wax up some pieces of various materials and lay up samples on them. In the process you will discover whether there is a release problem due to undercuts or possibly a chemical reaction between the material and resin, either of which can be disastrous to your deck surface, or even to the whole deck!

If you are anxious to use a certain nonskid pattern that is available to you only in the form you want on your finished deck, you can lay up fiberglass pieces on it and glue these in your deck mold. Alternatively, you can make a mold on it and glue pieces made in that mold on the finished deck. To make pieces to be glued on mold or deck, you lay up gelcoat backed up with one layer of 1½-ounce mat, or two layers of ¾-ounce mat if the part is wider than the mat used. The idea here is to butt, not to overlap, the mat so as to keep the laminate smooth on the back side. But to make a mold for laying up a number of pieces, you should use gelcoat and three or four layers of mat backed up by a piece of ¼-inch plywood or hardboard. If the original material with the nonskid pattern is any sort of fabric, it should be glued down on a table or sheet of plywood with contact cement. Otherwise, the shrinkage of the resin will surely pull it up into a roll.

Contact cement is also good for gluing most nonskid materials to your deck mold. But resin is best for gluing fiberglass nonskid pieces to the actual deck (after sanding both surfaces). When you glue material down with contact cement, coat both surfaces as evenly as possible and let them dry until they are no longer sticky to the touch; then align one side of the material carefully over its marks, lower it carefully into place, and roll it down with one of the heavy rubber rollers made for this purpose. Contact cement is aptly named because it assumes a death grip on contact, and you're more than likely to destroy the material if you try to get it up again to adjust its position.

But I'm passing several stages of the work. After you have marked off the nonskid areas, the next move is to fill, smooth, and polish the remaining liner surfaces. This is not a long process on Formica, sheet fiberglass, or melamine-coated Masonite. As soon as you have sanded the outside corners smooth, flushed cracks where the liner is butted, and applied radius wax or a putty fillet to the inside corners, the surface is ready for waxing and polishing.

A hardboard liner is an either/or situation. If you are willing to accept a less than perfectly mirrorlike finish, you can wax and polish the liner directly; if not, you can give it a coat or two of resin to seal it, then sand and polish it before waxing. The same is true of wood. If wooden parts have been carefully sanded with finer and finer paper, they can be built up with wax to a surface smooth enough for a reasonably clean-looking, if not superglossy, part. Further, given a fairly thick gelcoat, you can polish out any wood grain or minor imperfections in the finished deck. However, the kind of wood makes all the difference in the finish you get with fine sanding and waxing. Coarse-grained woods simply cannot be depended upon. Their grain is imprinted in the gelcoat from just the heat and pressure of the shrinking fiberglass. Slash-grain fir, like the surface of most fir plywood, is a terrible offender in this regard; but clear pine, poplar, and most of the other woods with grains you can hardly detect by eye usually yield a decent surface.

If you want to save yourself rework on the part, use the finest-grained wood possible, and seal its surface with a coat or two of resin if you can spare the time. If forced to use coarse-grained wood, fill it with two or three coats of resin *before* you sand it, and sand only after the grain is filled; then use your finer and finer paper. If you must use plywood, try to get mahogany-faced plywood. The "rotary" veneer is more easily polished than the "ribbon stripe" or other fancy grains, and much less expensive. But hardboard is actually better and cheaper to use in mold work than plywood, as long as you are building a temporary mold strictly for one part.

In summary, the proper sequence of moves to prepare a one-off deck mold for layup is:

1. Lay out the nonskid areas.
2. Round off all sharp corners. (Sharp corners on the mold make nasty dirt catchers in the part.)

3. Seal all materials too porous to wax and polish with resin, and bring them up to the finish you want with finer and finer sanding. (You can always wax and polish a patch and lay up a small sample if you are in doubt about how a given surface will affect the part.)

4. Glue down the nonskid material in patches with rounded corners, leaving smooth margins around all waterways, structures, and hardware against which dirt might collect. Make the patches no bigger than the available widths and lengths of the material, for it is impossible to match two pieces of most patterns without leaving an unsightly line. Separate the patches with smooth margins or "paths" not wider than 2 inches, arranging them in a logical, balanced pattern.

5. Now, radius the inner corners of the mold with radius wax. You can also use modeling clay, but it won't give you as smooth a corner. Note: If you intend to use auto-body putty for this, you should do it as part of step number 2 of this list.

6. Wax the whole mold, polish, and let dry no less than 1 hour; wax again, repeating the process for three to five coats. Be very careful not to flip up the edges of the nonskid patches as you rub the wax on or polish the mold.

7. Lay up the outer skin of the deck. For a detailed discussion of this procedure, see Chapter 9 on fiberglass lamination.

8. Cut and fit the core material, substituting pieces of plywood, or in extreme cases pieces of solid fiberglass, under areas subject to heavy stress, such as around the mast or under an on-deck mast step, or under bolted-down hardware, such as mooring cleats, bitts, winches, genoa tracks, travelers, bow and stern sprits, boom gallows, davits, deck blocks, and lifeline stanchions. If it seems to you as though the deck will be peppered with reinforced areas, you are right, especially the deck of a cruising/racing sailboat. Most of this list pertains to such boats. The list of reinforced areas in the usual powerboat is by contrast quite short. However, if you are using balsa core, you can reduce the number of areas considerably, because end-grain balsa has enough compression strength to take the through-bolting of many items that sustain only a light pull.

Whether or not you should replace the core under a given piece of hardware depends on the size of the boat, on the size and stiffness of the backing plate used, on the size of the base of the hardware itself, and finally on the thickness of the inner and outer skins of fiberglass. There are too many variables to permit a useful rule. It's up to your best judgment whether a given piece of hardware might be torn out of a given deck laminate under the hardest use or abuse it is likely to suffer.

9. Weight down each piece of core material in wet mat, using enough bricks, cement blocks, or sandbags to ensure complete contact of its lower surface with the outer skin.

10. Once the core is fast to the outer skin, fill all voids or cracks between the pieces with fiberglass putty and grind down all lumps or ridges.

11. Lay up the inner skin.

12. Put a finish on those inner skin surfaces that will show in the overhead. Here, you have a number of options. You can glue in thin wood or plywood with

thickened resin or epoxy, or vinyl or some other appropriate material with contact cement. Or you can apply a gelcoat or paint finish directly to the inner skin. Although it isn't necessary, it is certainly easiest and most practical to finish off the overhead surfaces at this time, while they are spread out as "down" surfaces in the mold. However, if you are going to set up the hull on top of the deck in the mold, then you want to cover the finished surfaces with cardboard or polyethylene sheets, taping them down around the edges well to keep drips, runs, and foot traffic from ruining them. You also want to tab to the deck any bulkheads you are setting up on it before you finish off the overhead.

13. That's it. You should now have a good-looking, trouble-free, durable deck.

A MOLDED HULL

If it happens that the boat you want to build is a V-bottomed or flat-bottomed model, you fortunately can mold a hull almost as slick as any production boat with relative ease and with a minimum of fairing and polishing. Building a hull mold for such a boat is similar to building a deck mold. It is a matter of building a set of moulds to the outside of the lines after adding on the thickness of stringers and/or the lining material. A simple mold would have legs fitted to a floor line that is under the hull lines plan, parallel to the waterline. With these legs, it is possible to set up the moulds in one of the ways prescribed for the moulds of a deck mold. I have built molds from 12 to 45 feet this way, and it's the quickest and cheapest arrangement. Of course, once set up, the mold has to stay in this position, and all of the work has to be done either by reaching into or climbing around in it. Oddly enough, the bigger the mold you set up this way, the more time and money you save in its construction and, because you can walk around inside it, the easier it is to line the interior and lay up the hull.

In the mid-1960s, a 25-year-old boatbuilder working for me fully lofted the plans and picked up and set up the moulds for the hull mold of a 35-by-11-foot Hickman Sea Sled (the ancestor of the Boston Whaler) with one helper in approximately 200 man hours. Not everyone is as fast and accurate as that fellow was. Nevertheless, in the mid-1970s, men under my direction lofted and built the complete mold for a 45-by-15-foot V-bottomed trawler yacht at a total cost for labor and materials of about $10,000. Further, this mold was built well enough to yield several boats with only minor repairs to its melamine-coated hardboard liner. Laying up these relatively big boats, neither of which had much deadrise, was easy going for the crew. They simply trooped inside and went to work. We left the stern out of the trawler yacht mold until the hull was nearly finished to cut down on climbing. We also built the keel and "garboards" (a bit of hull near the keel) on the floor in a separate mold, dropping this central portion into the mold before we laid up the hull.

The Hickman Sea Sled was molded in a temporary mold, shown here, made of 1-inch pine board moulds and sheet plywood.

The remains of a temporary female mold in which a 45-foot hard-chine trawler yacht was built. The light framework was lined with melamine-coated Masonite, which was rubber cemented in place. It was then secured further with tapes of fiberglass laid up vertically down over the stringers on the back side, which is not melamine coated. The keel was made in a separate mold off the boat with a flange that went out onto the deadrise. It was dropped into a slot in the hull mold before the lamination was started there. The mold's transom was left off and the crew trooped in through it every day. Near the end of the laminating, the transom was put in place and blended with the hull.

Rocker Moulds

Although you can move around in the bigger molds and reach into small molds, unfortunately the medium-sized molds—from about 15 to 30 feet depending on the shape—don't allow you to do either very well. Therefore, it is often quite worthwhile to build a mold in this size range so that it can be rocked over onto its sides. To do this you can build two or three of the section moulds out wider than the rest and provide them with flats on which they can rest in one or two tipped-up positions. On a small mold, two such moulds are enough, placed between one-fourth and one-third of the boat's length from each end; but on longer molds, three give better support.

Many production molds are built with curved rockers, which allow turning the boat to any angle; but I wouldn't advise this for a one-off mold, which is lightly built and easily twisted out of shape. If you draw the rocker flats in the loft and pick them up on each rocker mould at the same time you pick up its hull section, the mold will remain true when resting on them on a true floor. If the floor is not a perfectly flat plane, you can check the flats with a level, or even sight them by eye, and shim them until parallel.

It should go without saying that, because of their great depth, the simplest and strongest way to build rocker moulds is to pick them up in plywood. But the ordinary moulds of most flat- and V-bottomed hull shapes can be built with common boards, which are a lot cheaper. In rural localities your least-expensive choice would probably be a native softwood; but in urban areas some sort of spruce, fir, hemlock, or pine boards of less-than-finish grade is usually available. You'd be surprised how big a mold you can build with lumberyard "nominal" 1-inch boards, which are really only about ¾ inch thick. When it is 6 to 10 inches wide, a board has considerable strength on edge, which is where it suffers strain in a mold. However, some very useful stock to use in building big molds is the type of board lumberyards sell as ledger boards. These boards are left rough sawn a full inch thick; they are relatively clear and straight; and, because they are used as horizontal supports and braces in wooden scaffolding, they are selected for soundness.

If you are going to use rocker moulds, you still have to set up your ordinary moulds with temporary legs, which can be removed after you make the mold rigid with stringers and install as much of the lining as convenient. The more stringers you use, with some of them laminated to improve their shape memory, and the more securely they are fastened to the moulds and at their ends, the better your mold will hold its shape when rocked back and forth. It therefore requires a little more work and material to build a mold that can be rocked. However, if you want to walk in it, the stringers have to be strong enough and closely spaced enough to bear your weight. Thus for a medium-sized boat, it costs nearly the same to build a mold to work inside as a mold to rock back and forth and reach inside, without the convenience of the latter.

But as the size of the mold grows, the same section moulds, stringers, and lining do not give it enough rigidity to withstand rocking; and you have to strengthen the more cumbersome structure with perhaps a sawn plywood flange around the sheer, a number of heavier, laminated stringers, and some plywood knees fastened to these stringers to brace the rocker moulds. Further, the rocker moulds themselves have to be made stiffer as the mold gets heavier. Such strengthening features in a mold for a big boat create quite a cost spread between the upright version and the version that can be rocked from side to side.

Nevertheless, if you are going to use sandwich construction, and if extensive areas in the topsides of your boat are vertical or tumbled home, you should seriously consider building the mold so that it can be tipped down; in this position, you can press the core to the outer skin with weights. Good contact at this stage is crucial to a strong sandwich. Yet, as long as your mold is for one boat only, an alternative that might work for you is to rock your fixed mold down at least onto its chines, after you have built enough of the boat to preclude distortion. You can install the core in the bottom—and up past the chine if some flare allows it—and lay up the inner skin over the core, dropping each successive layer back about 6 inches from the last at the unfinished edge to make a tapered scarf with the adjoining upper layers. With the entire outer skin and a good portion of the core and inner skin completed, you can safely take the legs off the section moulds and lower the mold down to rest on its chine or bilge for completing the laminate in the topside areas. If, in doing this, the outer skin wants to pull away from the mold at the rail, you can pull it back with clamps and hold it there with either tapping screws applied from the outside or some little tabs of fiberglass, which can be ground away later.

Rocker moulds on this female mold are used to tip the boat to about 45° and about 90°.

Top: *This temporary round-bottom wooden mold was started to build a single Cartwright 40 sloop, but more were sold before it was finished. Fiberglass (¼ inch) was applied to the inside of the mold, its exterior was beefed up, and it turned out about a dozen boats. It could have produced many more if the builders had not gone out of business.* Above: *The Cartwright 40 mold, showing the split centerline, reinforced stringers, and massive rocker mould for two positions: upright or approximately 75°.*

Close-up of Cartwright 40 mold. Note reinforcing stringers made by fastening plywood webs to a normal stringer and to one opposite it on the outside of the moulds. This mold was tipped so much that the rocker moulds were fitted with runners.

Even the simplest flat- and V-bottomed shapes, with the exception of scows, curve in to a stem at the bow. In the area where the bow gets narrow and "pointy," as most are in the forefoot at least, the job of fastening in the lining gets a bit ticklish. You can't swing a hammer or fit a drill or screwdriver across the narrowing chasm, and you can't screw the thin lining from the back without the screws coming through and spoiling the surface. This is when you get out your hot-melt-glue gun to fasten the lining to the stringers and stem piece.

A Split Mold

I once built a set of 20-foot akas for a trimaran that were so narrow I could hardly get my hand into the last foot or so at each end. When you're building something that inaccessible on the inside, it might be time to use a male mold as I did. You are better able to build the part, and better able to lay up a proper laminate, working on the outside, although you have finishing work to do all over the exterior.

However, as usual in the one-off game, there is another way. You can build a split female mold, a female mold with two halves bolted together down the centerline. This is not as difficult to do as it may seem. You merely pick up two pieces, one on each side of the centerline, for each centerline or backbone member and build each section mould in two pieces that meet down the centerline. To set up the mold, the two pieces of each section mould are temporarily cleated together and set up as one piece. When the moulds are all set up, the centerline pieces, which have been bolted together into one member, are dropped into slots left in the moulds; and each centerline side piece is cleated to its side of the mold. The section moulds are then stringered. At this point, you must take measures to provide shape memory when the mold is split. If you were simply to bend and fasten on a set of single-piece stringers, each half of the mold would surely bend out of shape when the bolts were released and the section moulds uncleated along the center plane. To prevent this, you laminate the stringers in place, using two pieces nailed or screwed together, preferably with glue between them. For added stiffness you can use three layers around the sheer and on one or two other stringers somewhere between sheer and keel, depending on the girth and shape of the boat. Another way to get this added stiffness is to make a girder of the sheer stringer and of one or two others. To make a girder of a stringer, you place a parallel stringer around the outside of the section moulds, fastening a sawn web of plywood between both.

As you can see, making a split mold requires considerable extra work, even if it isn't difficult. I wouldn't recommend doing it unless you need access to the fine (deep and narrow) portions of the hull and the convenience of working on each side of the hull laid down flat like the half shell of a giant mollusk. If, for instance, your boat has a very shapely bow that requires a great deal of diagonally laid planking in lieu of sheet lining material, working in the "half shell" is ever so much easier than scrambling around in the bow of the whole mold. Also, if you lay up the gelcoat and a few layers of inaccessible parts, such as deep, narrow keels and

A temporary double-diagonal hull mold for a small double-ended powerboat.

bows, out in the open, you will probably achieve better workmanship and a better finish on the outside of the boat. Needless to say, you shouldn't do too many of the layers before the mold is reassembled, and once it is reassembled, you should lay up many stout joining layers over them.

I must interject at this point that whether or not you actually make a split mold, it is very helpful to make the backbone members in two pieces, one on each side of the centerline, wherever the centerline is an acute angle. It is quite difficult to cut out a V-shaped landing for the lining material in a solid piece, but very simple to bevel each of two pieces inward, fair with the line of the section. On a flat-bottomed boat this would apply only to the stem, but in some V-bottomed boats it applies to the entire length of the keel. In a V-bottomed boat, however, you might want to go to three pieces: one for a flat place where the boat will sit on blocking or on its own keel, and one on either side to fair with the V or deadrise of the bottom. You have to work out the configuration that suits your boat's shape. Nevertheless, it is worth remembering to use two or more pieces so that you don't have to do any plowing or "hogging" out of a single piece.

When there is more than one hull to take out of a mold, it may be important to use a split mold so that you can separate the mold from each hull sideways, rather than hoist the hulls out of it. But, naturally, the best way to release a one-off hull is to tear the mold apart where it stands. In this event, it is helpful if you have had the foresight to splice in a couple of patches of short centerline pieces, stringers, and mold lining that you can remove first to expose enough keel for keel blocking under a heavy boat. This will hold her up while you tear away the mold. To keep her from falling sideways, you can brace her from the overhead to the rail indoors, or from the ground to the rail or to the ends after you have stripped some of the mold.

There is no question about the advantages of a split mold when it is a round-bottomed mold that requires diagonal planking and fiberglass sheathing so that more than one gelcoat-finished hull can be built in it. About the only way this sort of work can be done efficiently is on the two halves of the mold laid open. As I mentioned earlier in the book, we built innumerable split molds at my boatshop for "short-run" or limited-production boats. Although some of these were for V- and radius-bottomed hulls, many were for round-bottomed hulls. Some were entirely double-diagonally planked with two layers of ¼-inch wood or plywood, then fiberglass covered and polished; others were planked with one layer of a sheet fiberglass sold for large light fixtures, the seams of which were covered with household Scotch tape. Some of the most perfect and expensive of these molds were used for but two hulls; others that were relatively crude, for as many as a dozen hulls. Those were the breaks of the yacht design and building game in the years of transition from mostly wooden to mostly fiberglass boats, and therein lay the reason for building short-run molds. The first round-bottomed hull from a mold was not prohibitively more expensive than a hull built by any other method—not when you had a good crew of wooden boatbuilders to build the mold. At some point between the first and fourth boat, hulls from the short-run mold cost less than those built by any other method; and after that we were home free for as

Top: *Planking the two halves of the temporary mold for the Fred Ford–designed 38-foot sloop* Bright Star. *(See photo in Chapter 1.) The mold had two layers of ¼-inch fir plywood and a thin skin of fiberglass.* **Above:** *The gang puts a finish on one of the half-shells for the* Bright Star *mold.*

Top: *The mold for* Bright Star, *assembled and polished, being tilted onto one side for spraying with gelcoat. The gelcoat was black, the same color as the mold.* **Above:** Bright Star's hull with lead keel bolted on.

long as the mold lasted. This capability to mold a number of hulls at a small fraction of the cost of building a plug and a fiberglass production mold provided a prudent way to test the market with a new design. If the boat sold well enough to warrant a production mold, a hull from the short-run mold was used as the plug. If not, little if any capital investment was lost. This approach was a corollary of the shop rule never to speculate. We never built any boat before it was sold.

The Transom

The next item in mold building is the transom. With a female mold, even a curved, raked transom becomes relatively simple. The tedious part of lofting and building a curved, raked transom is finding the points where transom and hull intersect. Neither the shape of the transom, which is a constant cylindrical surface, nor its rake, which is a constant angle, will cause you to scratch your head, but rather where that shape at that angle meets the hull, the shape of which is changing a little every fraction of an inch that you move fore and aft along its lines. However, if in the loft you fair the hull's long lines out to a station at the aftermost point on the transom, aft of the intersection, and then extend the sides and bottom of your hull mold to a mould at that station, you can easily build the transom shape within them. This way, the points of intersection take care of themselves mechanically, and most of the lofting is circumvented.

But I am getting ahead of myself. We should get flat transoms out of the way first. For a flat transom, the best approach is to build a female mould just like the station moulds, the aft face of which is at the aft face of the transom. If the transom is raked, the mould should be expanded and picked up just as you would pick up the raked transom, and set up at the rake, too. Carry all of the hull mold stringers to this transom mould, and saw them off flush with its aft face. Then install the hull mold's bottom and topside lining, and trim it off flush too. After the hull is lined, you can fasten a piece (or pieces) of lining against the transom mould's aft face, and fasten some stringers or horizontal stiffeners across on the outside of it. Also, because shrinkage causes flat surfaces in fiberglass to "dish in," or become concave, you should saw or plane a faint curve into the forward face of the stiffeners athwart the transom to give the lining a slight outward bow as it is fastened to them.

Now, for the curved transom, whether raked or plumb. You should, as I said, extend the long lines of the boat to a mould at or abaft the aftermost transom point. Carry the stringers to this mould, but not the lining, yet. Make up some boards longer than the width of the transom with the transom radius cut into one edge as a concave curve. These boards will be horizontal moulds on the outside of the mold's transom. If the transom has a strong curve, they are best cut from plywood. For a mold transom center post, select a straight piece of common lumber that is, depending on the size of the boat, from 1 to 3 inches thick in the proportions of a 2 x 3; and notch the center of the forward, curved edge of each mould board so that the post fits flush into it.

Set up the center post, cleating it to the centerline member of the mold (horn timber or keel) at the proper rake; and fit its top into the notch in one of the mould boards laid across the sheer of the mold. The flat of the mould board should be normal (at right angles) to the center post; that is, one edge of the board should be tipped up by two wedges on the sheer, because of the rake, so that its curved edge is flush and parallel with the forward face of the center post. Now, plumb the top of the center post with a plumb bob to the center of the keel member, horn the ends of the curved mould board (or measure them equidistant from the nearest mould), and recheck the rake of the center post. When all of these adjustments are satisfactory, fasten the ends of the mould board to the sheer. This will give you a true skeleton of your mold's transom. Put more bones in the skeleton in the form of mould boards as needed. Fit their ends between or against stringers with wedges or cleats to hold them normal to the rake, and horn each board before fastening it. You can also notch in more vertical stiffeners if the transom is very wide, or just fit and fasten vertical blocks between the mould boards, especially near the sides. You will find, however, that sheet lining material tends to stay straight vertically when curved athwartships except at its very outboard edges.

When you line the transom, you should be sure that the lining extends well above the sheer. Due to the crown of the deck, the center of the transom is always higher than the sheer, and much higher than you might think when the transom is very curved, or well raked aft, with the sheer sweeping up at the stern.

After the lining is in place, when you have something on which to draw a line, you can find the shape of the top of the transom using three temporary deck beams. Fit one of these as close to the transom as possible, and fit the other two spaced 12 to 24 inches apart forward of it. All of the beams' outboard ends should be flush with the top of the mold. Lay a moderately stiff batten with a chisel point at its bottom aft edge on the beams; and, holding it parallel with the boat's centerline, slide it against the transom lining. The point of contact, when the batten is resting on all three beams, is a point on the transom at the top of the deck, bulwark, or whatever height the top of the mold represents. If for some reason the top of the transom is to be a different height than the top of the mold, you can mark off that height with a block fitted to the batten. If, for instance, you want your deck or its bulwarks to end *against* the forward face of the transom, so no joints show on its aft face, the top of your hull mold's transom must extend up to the railcap. But at any height, it will always be parallel to the line that you draw with temporary deck beams fitted to the top of the mold.

The Hull Mold Lining

It is now time to consider the lining of your mold. Should your boat have a "developable" flat or V-bottomed shape, which in boatbuilding language means a shape to which continuous sheet material will bend without buckling or, to put it another way, a shape you could form with sheet plywood as the skin or planking—

then you don't *have* to line the mold. Rather than fit sheets of Masonite into the mold and then, in effect, build sheets of fiberglass on top of them, you can line the mold with sheets of fiberglass that will be the outside layers of the boat and simply add the rest of the laminate to them. This approach is ideal for small boats for which you can make up full-length side and bottom pieces, so the only joints are at the chine, keel, and ends of the boat. With bigger boats, you have to put up with joints on the hull's surface as the panels of fiberglass get larger and less practical to make and install in one piece. However, some tabbing to join the pieces on the inside and some cosmetic work at the joints on the outside are still far less costly than lining the mold and preparing the lining to make a more or less unblemished exterior. Also, it is much easier to polish, apply gelcoat, and lay up the boat's first few layers as sheets on a table than it is to lay them up in the mold.

So, rather than cut and fit a lining material, you can make up prefabricated sheets of outer skin. It would be nice if you could purchase some thin sheets of gelcoated fiberglass off the shelf somewhere. This would eliminate the whole step of setting up a table and laminating these parts. Perhaps such products will be available in the future. The last time I surveyed the market for sheet materials, I found that many were available, but that most were frangible with a low glass content and none was suitable for the outside of a boat. Further, by the time these materials were marked up in the distribution process, they were very expensive for what you received, not counting what you would waste later when you cut pieces to fit the mold.

In making up your own sheets, as in almost all one-off work, it is best to use no-wax, or very low-wax, resin to maintain a bondable surface. Wax mixed into resin floats to the surface and keeps the air away from it. When air remains in contact with the surface of a laminate, it inhibits the cure, and the surface doesn't harden completely. In fact, it may stay tacky for days or even weeks. This is advantageous when you want to "hook" onto that surface with more fiberglass. It saves going all over previous work that has become hard and glassy with a sander so that the next layer can get a good grip on it.

It is also best to keep the thickness of prefabricated sheets on a single-skin boat to a small percentage of the total laminate thickness. If you don't, you will have to use a wide "butt strap" of fiberglass tabbing across the joints that is as thick or thicker than the prefabricated portion. Such tabbing is unsightly and wastes enough time and materials to negate in large part the advantage of adding any layers after the panels are sufficiently thick to lie fair as a lining in the mold. If the hull is a sandwich construction, you might prefabricate most of the outside skin; join it with tabbing of equal thickness; rabbet, or taper, the core material to accommodate the thickness of the tabbing; and, to ensure good contact , double the wet mat it is set in over the lumpy area. You would then lay up a continuous inner skin about half as thick as the outside skin.

It is possible to construct less wasteful and neater-looking joints, however. After you lay up the first two layers of prefabricated panels, you step subsequent layers back from the edges to be joined, not less than 3 inches per layer. This creates a tapered, actually stepped, edge on each panel where it butts another. If you make uniform steps, cut strips of tabbing the right width to fill in each step, and fill in all the steps, you will bring the shallow V where the panels meet about flush. Then you must add at least two more layers, each extending 3 inches farther out onto the panels, in order to get a lamination across the joint equal in strength to the rest of the panel, the first two layers of which are butted.

Of course, you can't indulge in such fancy stuff as tapered joints and avoid a lot of unpleasant grinding if you don't have more or less the exact shape of each panel marked out on the table before you lay it up. But then, it is quite wasteful to make oversized sheets and trim them to shape no matter the type of joint. So you are better off making a pattern of each panel in any case. Unless you have done a very bad job of mold making, the same pattern will do for both sides of the boat with little or no adjustment. On little boats a paper pattern suffices. Pasteboard is better; yet it is trickier to cut and fit because it won't crease along the line. But strips of ¼-inch plywood about 4 inches wide screwed together with ½-inch screws make the most accurate and durable patterns for any size piece of prefabricated fiberglass you would care to attempt to make.

The trick to quick and easy pattern-making with any material but paper is to avoid fitting any one piece of the pattern material to more than one edge, and, if a long edge is very curved, to make it up with several pieces. When you have fitted pieces of plywood to the perimeter of the panel and tacked them in place, you cleat them together, bracing any long spans. You can then drag the whole pattern over the rail and lay it on the table.

To trace the panel's outline on the slick surface of the table, you can use masking tape, stuck down with its edge along the contours of the pattern. The tape shows you where to apply the gelcoat; and if you pull it up before the gelcoat dries too much, it leaves a clean, sharp line that you can follow while laminating and trim to when finished. Alternatively, to eliminate the chore of trimming the panel, you can hot-glue some light sticks about the size of a kite stick to the table around the pattern as stops for the laminate. They give the panel a clean, true edge. Before you take the pattern apart, don't forget to use it to cut the fiberglass mat and roving for the panel.

For fastening prefabricated panels to the mold, small copper, brass, or bronze nails are best. They are easily clipped off and ground or drilled back from the surface after the mold parts are pulled off the completed boat. And, after patching over with gelcoat, they won't bleed rust. On a little boat you may be able to hold the panels in position with hot glue, but I wouldn't chance it with heavy panels, or in areas where walking might loosen them. You can also pull panels into place with long, thin stainless-steel tapping screws applied through clearance holes in the stringers from the outside and snipped off where they come through on the inside. I say stainless screws because they are quite strong, less likely to break off when going in or being removed, and less likely to bleed if a piece is left in the laminate. I say clearance holes in the stringers because a screw threaded in the stringer is not going to pull the panel a bit closer to the mold until you turn it hard enough in the wood to strip the threads. Also, such needlessly tight screws are difficult to remove.

Each panel should be backed well in the mold around its perimeter to avoid undulating edges and wavy-looking joints as a result. You should place one stringer with its top edge at the sheer, two more-or-less meeting along the chine to back up the juncture of the topside and bottom panels, and whatever number necessary in the keel/garboard area to keep edges evenly butted. Chine corners almost always form an obtuse angle. Thus, if you shove one of the chine stringers right into the corner of the section moulds and push the other up to it, you won't get a close joint without beveling either of them. However, their edges will touch at their top corners if you hold them both a certain distance away from the corner. You can quickly determine this distance at each mould with two small blocks of the stringer material. It's not really all that important that the panels be backed up precisely to their edges; but it's nice to know how to do things just right—isn't it? To keep even any vertical joints, which run across the stringers, you can slip well-waxed strips of sheet metal behind them or install small blocks of wood between and flush with the stringers.

Plenty of wax or some waxed paper or masking tape behind joints helps keep resin from oozing through and messing up the exterior of the joints, and a coat of wax on the gelcoat side around the joints makes any that does get through easier to remove. At the same time, a narrow smear of polyester putty or a tape of presaturated mat on the inside very nearly prevents such drips.

Many V-bottom designs today, the deep Vs in particular, have a very shapely bow that doesn't lend itself to forming with sheet material. Many others, and even some flat- or radius-bottomed boat designs, have at least a small area of compound curvature around which sheet material won't quite fit. You can often get a panel to take the shape of a small area by cutting "darts" in its edges. Darts, as every dressmaker knows, are V-shaped cuts that let the segments of material between them come together to form a spherical type of compound curve. Or it could be that you need a series of straight cuts, which open out to Vs as you stretch the segments between them around the flare at the sheer. But if there is more than a very slight compound curvature, you have to strip up your sheet material and apply it diagonally to the shapely area. When 3 to 6 inches wide—depending, as I so often say, on boat size and shape—any material not too thick to take the bends without breaking will fit best on the compound curves of a boat (or mold) in a diagonal direction. In this direction, the curves are relatively gentle, there is little angularity at the seams of the strips, and the strakes are often short enough to be made in one piece. Whether you are planking the boat's skin with fiberglass strips in the mold or lining the mold with a material on which you will lay up the whole laminate, diagonal is the way to go.

The angle of diagonal planking can be adjusted to fit the shape. There is no reason to use 45 degrees if the planking winds more comfortably over the stringers at a shallower or steeper angle. In fact, as the form of the boat changes, you can change the angle of the strips by putting in some wedge-shaped pieces. Hold a strip down over the area containing the worst bends and swivel it to different angles. It will soon tell you what angle it likes best. If you want, you can start right there, at that angle, and work in both directions. On some shapes you might get two or three narrow strips fitted before you have to "spile" one, that is, to mark and cut the edge of a strip to fit against the previous strip. You must spile a strip when it won't fit without being bent edgewise so much that it buckles up along one edge. It doesn't pay to force strips into place, for they may break even if you can fasten the buckled edge down. One way to spile a strip is to tack it so that it overlaps the previous strip and then mark it from underneath. Another way, which is necessary on a second layer, or when you can't reach underneath, is to place the strip adjacent to the last strip using pencil dividers or a rabbeted block of wood. The curve of the spiled line is usually very gentle. Generally, I get a fairer, more even line cutting it freehand on a table saw with the blade set just peeping through the material.

Now that's a big no-no! You can slice up some fingers and catch the end of the strip in the stomach all in one split second if you don't know what you're doing. So why do I mention it at all? Because somebody's going to think of it anyway; and if he or she is going to be a damned fool like me, I might as well explain how (aside from good luck) I've kept all of my fingers for over 40 years of using table saws.

1. It's safer with a weak motor or a slipping belt, which is to say, a saw blade that stops when jammed.

2. It's safer with a sharp blade, which is less likely to kick the material back at you.

3. It's safer when only enough blade is above the table to cut through the material, which could make the difference between slicing the flesh and cutting off the fingers.

4. There should always be a back table behind and flush with the saw table to take the weight of the material. Then you aren't tempted to reach behind the saw to hold up the piece. Nor are you struggling to hold it down flat on the table with your hand alongside the blade when, at the end, the weight of the piece hanging off the table tries to bow it up. At this point, the back teeth of the blade coming up can catch the uplifted piece and catapult it toward you like a bullet. Worse, if the piece has sideways pressure on it, the blade will spin it right around horizontally; and your hand, which you thought was safely off to one side, albeit behind or opposite the blade, will be pulled around into it.

5. Never reach behind or alongside the blade. Use a notched pusher stick for the last of the cut.

6. Rig a spring hold-down to keep the material flat to the table.

7. Never stand in line with the blade. Keep head and body to one side, and wear glasses.

8. Maintain a wary respect for all power tools. As an old friend remarked when his son received a cut finger, "The hide don't bother them machines."

When you complete fastening an outer skin into a mold and patching its joints one way or another against resin leakage, you can go right ahead with the rest of the laminate. But, when you complete a mold lining in which you are going to mold a hull, or hulls, you have to decide how far to go with cosmetic work before you start the laminate. If you have had to cut many darts in sheets, or apply an area of the lining in diagonal strips, your concern is with how much filling and fairing you want to do in the mold versus how much on the outside of the boat. Since working on the hull's exterior is generally easier than working inside a mold, this decision usually hinges on the number of hulls to be built. Work done once in the mold is more attractive than work repeated on two or more hulls. For a one-off, however, it is usually better simply to tape over the many joints in the mold lining with household-type Scotch tape, lay up the hull, and fix up the outside. Should there be few sizable areas that will come out smooth and fair, you might even lay up the hull without gelcoat and do a complete finishing job on the exterior. Conversely, if there are only a few widely spaced joints in the mold lining, it would be foolish even with a one-off not to fill and polish them neatly and pull out the best possible hull.

Hull Details

Not as many details can be molded into hulls as in decks, but the labor savings in those that can are just as great. When possible, it is most important to mold in whatever convolution is needed to support and connect with the deck. This might be one of the deck joints described earlier in this chapter, provided you are going to have a molded deck. Otherwise, it can be whatever goes best with the type of built-on-the-boat deck you choose. There are two basic ways to support a built-on deck: with an inturned flange that is part of the hull, or with a "clamp," like those in wooden boats, that is built either of fiberglass on the inside of the hull or of wood and bolted to the hull. If you want to use the mold again, any inturned flange requires a removable piece along the sheer to release the hull (unless the mold is split).

One detail in your mold you would be quite sorry to be without is the slot in the keel for a centerboard. It's a ridiculously tough chore to cut a slot through a thick keel, whereas a waxed-up stick in the mold does the job painlessly and better. You can, of course, mold the entire trunk integral with the hull; but in most cases this causes more trouble than it saves. First, it's much handier to work around a trunk mold standing on the floor than in the bilge of most boats. Then, to avoid a violent struggle when it's time to remove the deep male mold from the trunk, you must build it either with two wedge-shaped pieces, one of which can be driven out first, or, if solid, with very pronounced draft. But draft on the inside of the trunk results in more clearance at the bottom than at the top, which can result in a rattling centerboard. In Chapter 11, some quick and easy methods of building parallel-sided centerboard trunks off the boat are discussed. For now, it suffices to make the point that a slot in the keel should be a part of any one-off laminate, but that usually the trunk itself is most conveniently built off the boat and installed either during or after the main hull lamination.

The best shaft log for any fiberglass boat is a fiberglass tube. Being of the same material, it can be made virtually one piece with the hull. But I doubt that it is to your advantage to install the tube in the mold and lay up the hull laminate against it. The most trouble-free, practical approach to shaft logs is to provide a hole in the hull by means of a block in the mold, and let it go at that. After the engine is in place, with the propeller shaft fitted through the hole, you can center the tube on the shaft with wedges and glass it to the hull, knowing that the alignment couldn't be better. The ideal time, by the way, to figure out the location and shape of the hole-forming block is when your mold is a "basket" of section moulds and stringers. At this time, when you have a see-through and reach-through three-dimensional boat, it is easy to pick up the shaft centerline from the loft or plans and rig a wire or a chalk line through the mold. This gives you an opportunity to check the location, clearance, and angle of engine and propeller, as well as to install the block.

The hole for an outboard well is another feature you shouldn't leave out of the mold. But this time, since a well is usually just a box-shaped structure, you can probably mount a male mold for the entire well in the hull mold and turn the hull laminate right up onto the sides of it. This ensures a neat, integral, watertight structure, to which only some plywood and more fiberglass need be added to beef up the motor-mount side.

The rudder port, like the shaft log, is another feature that should have a hole formed in the hull to make its location and installation easier. However, like the shaft log, the alignment of the actual tube should await the time when you can install the rudder with its shaft projecting through the hole, since the tube will be either a close-fitting metal tube that doubles as a bearing or a fiberglass tube that contains a bearing at its lower end. There is also likely to be a close-fitting stuffing box at the upper end. Meanwhile, when a sailboat calls for a rudder-heel fitting and perhaps some intermediate strap or gudgeon and pintle bearings along the "sternpost," you can eliminate a lot of mean fiberglass chopping by hot-gluing some slabs of wood to the inside of the "deadwood" area to make recesses for these fittings. In the hollow keel of a motorboat, you can form a recess to accept a skeg the same way. Don't fret unduly about the exact outline of a recess if you don't have the fitting in hand or haven't made a pattern for it yet. Just make sure that the recess is as big or bigger than the fitting will be. It's much easier to fill in an oversized recess than it is to chop the laminate. It is also stronger to have the layers of the whole laminate formed around the recess than to chop some of them away to make it; and that's important in this most vulnerable area of the boat.

Perhaps you can incorporate other details in your hull mold, like a cove stripe, hawseholes, or holes for freeing ports, dockline chocks, deadlights, or portlights in the topsides. Any detail that can be turned out with clean lines and gelcoated edges through the relatively simple application of wood to the mold with hot glue or removable screws and a bit of radius wax or modeling clay is more than worth the effort. Naturally, the holes for cockpit scupper drains and various other through-hulls would be good things to have molded in, if only to get neat recesses backed by the whole laminate to bring them flush on the exterior. Yet it's almost a waste of time to mention these, because the precise, handiest location for through-hulls so often can't be visualized until the interior joinerwork has been set up. If you should incorporate some detail in your mold that doesn't work out, however, cheer up. A nice thing about fiberglass is the way you can repair it so that it doesn't show, and, at the same time, bring it back to its original or greater strength. There's a really reparable material for you!

This has been a long chapter. No doubt it is the longest in the book, not because molding is a particularly involved way to build a one-off, but because it is the first one-off method described, and so requires fuller explanation. Fortunately, my comments on basic procedures and materials won't need repetition, except in variations. Thus, although the ensuing chapters are shorter, I wouldn't want you to get the impression there is any less thinking or doing associated with the one-off systems described therein. Each system has its stages easily come by and its hard parts. In the chapters ahead you are likely to find a method of building your one-off that is more suitable, more appealing to you, or both, than using a mold. If that be the case, much of what has been described here will nevertheless be useful to you. Moreover, every boat, except the simplest open dinghy, has some part or parts that you can build best in a mold.

3

PVC Foam

Once you select PVC (polyvinyl chloride) foam to enhance the physical properties of your hull or deck, the opportunity to use it as the starting layer of the laminate is a nice bonus. PVC-foam sandwich is so good at resisting bending and impact without delamination or fracture, and without significantly increased total weight, that it is unquestionably the most effective fiberglass construction for high-performance boats now known. As mentioned in Chapter 2, PVC foam has other superior qualities that are highly desirable in almost any boat: its excellent insulation value, its all-but-unshakable bond with resin, and its closed-cell (waterproof), tough, elastic, relatively inert composition. Due to its light weight, any sandwich made with it will float unless the total thickness of the fiberglass exceeds that of the core. It is truly great stuff; and although I'd be the last to say that all boats should have it, I do think that the use of it in one place or another could improve most boats. Unfortunately, PVC seems relatively expensive compared to other cores, which causes builders to avoid it. But to one-off builders who use it for the starting material on which to lay up fiberglass as well as for a core, the price has double justification.

"Rigid" PVC foam, as used in boatbuilding, actually includes two types of material, the manufacturing processes of both of which were the invention of a Professor Lindemann. The earliest was cross-linked PVC, which is a blend of PVC and polyurethane. This process was sold in the late 1930s to Kleber-Colombe of France, who licensed a number of other companies to produce it under such trade names as Klegecell, Conticell, Divinycell, and Plasticell. In the 1940s the professor came out with the Airex process for manufacturing pure PVC foam, the production of which Airex AG, a subsidiary of Lonza AG, both of Switzerland, began in the mid-1950s. The production of a new generation of improved, pure PVC foam called R6280 began in 1978. It is better suited for decks, being unaffected by heat up to approximately 160 degrees, and seems even tougher than its predecessor.

According to tests I have made, a test Lonza made, and seemingly the general opinion of designers and boatbuilders, a balsa-core sandwich is much stiffer than one cored with either Airex or a cross-linked foam. It carries a heavier load without bending as far. However, it ultimately fails with drastic rupture and delamination or shearing of the core. In contrast, Airex can suffer much greater bending and still recover in perfectly serviceable condition. In fact, you can slowly bend a piece of Airex itself (without fiberglass skins) 180 degrees around a mandrel with a diameter three or four times the thickness of the foam without breaking it. Klegecell, as an example of cross-linked foam, has properties somewhere in between balsa and Airex. Those who would like a more scientific description can get industry reports on the results of lab tests.*

My own tests were crude and simple. One consisted of an A-frame pivoted on the wall of the building with an 11-pound weight behind a 2-by-3-inch anvil that was hoisted to 8 feet above the floor and let go by pulling a pin. Laminate samples were placed bridging two cement blocks and rated by the number of blows it took to break through them. I suppose you'd call that an impact test, which I thought was quite important at the time, being deep into the building of C. Raymond Hunt–designed deep-V powerboats as well as cruising and racing sailboats. What stands out in my mind from memory was that the anvil went through plywood- and mahogany-planking samples with one blow; three-layered cold-molded samples—two layers cedar, one mahogany—in 25 or more blows; various single-skin and sandwich fiberglass laminates, including balsa core and polyurethane foam with ribs, at up to 50 blows. But when we tested an Airex foam sandwich, Wally Greene (who has his own boatshop now) came to me and said, "I'm through the outer skin of the Airex at 100 blows; but my arms are killing me from hoisting that thing up. Can't we let it go at that?"

We ended the test, knowing that the owner would be satisfied. R and D is not only expensive, it can be a pain in the elbow; but I'll bet nobody has a better feeling for the impact resistance of Airex sandwich than Wally Greene. Another thing

---

* *For product information about Airex, write to Torin Inc., 125 Sheridan Terrace, Ridgewood, NJ 07450. See also Thomas J. Johannsen,* One-off Airex Fiberglass Sandwich Construction. *Available from Torin and from International Marine Publishing Company.*

For product information about Klegecell, write to American Klegecell Corporation, 204 N. Dooley Street, Grapevine, TX 76051. See also Christopher G. Hart et al., Klegecell Composite Structures *(Grapevine, TX: Klegecell, 1981). Also available from International Marine Publishing Company.*

that impressed me was that although the outer skin was broken, it was only delaminated from the Airex at the break, the delamination hadn't spread, nor was the Airex itself holed yet. If in the real world a boat built with this material hit something, it would not be leaking.

Sheets of PVC foam are stiff enough to bend around a few section moulds as you would wood or plywood, if you want to build a little flat-surfaced pram or skiff. They are also flexible enough, depending on thickness, to bend over the curves of a form for a round-bottomed hull; but scored sheets are also sold that fit such curves cold and can be pressed against the outer skin of a shapely boat being built in a mold. There are innumerable other handy one-off boatbuilding uses for PVC foam due to its ease of cutting, fitting, and gluing with resin and its other unique qualities. But before discussing such uses, I should describe the processes of building yourself a one-off hull or deck with PVC foam.

A PVC-FOAM ONE-OFF HULL

A one-off hull with solid PVC foam as the starting material requires a form consisting of section moulds, stem and keel pieces, a transom form, and fore-and-aft stringers (also called ribbands) over the whole thing. The sandwich is then begun from the core outward as you: (1) cover the form with cut and fitted sheets of PVC foam; (2) lay up the outer skin on the foam; (3) pull the hull off the form and turn it over, or turn it right side up and tear the form out of it; and (4) lay up the inner skin.

In fitting the sheets on the form, the athwartship or curved edges are stiff enough to lie evenly butted against each other without continuous back-up. But the fore-and-aft joints must be made along a stringer so that the edge of each sheet can be fastened down. Fairly wide, not too thick stringers are better than a deep, narrow section for this reason. All fastening must be of a temporary nature to allow separation of the part from the form. Several methods have been tried over the years. One is sewing or lashing the sheets to the stringers with twine, which can be cut to release the part. Another is nailing the foam with small-headed nails, which will pull right through the foam as the part is removed. Both of these methods are more suitable to easy curves than hard bends. A third method that we used in the mid-1960s, still probably the most popular today, is to hold the sheets on with round- or pan-head tapping screws applied through the stringers into the foam from inside the form. Preboring the stringers with a slip-fit hole for the screws every 6 inches or so saves most of the drilling from inside. When drilling any extra screw holes around the edges with the foam in place, a stop on the drill bit prevents overrunning into the foam, which doesn't need a hole.

In practice, the sheets are first nailed to the stringers with small flathead nails like box nails through a thin plywood washer. If a number of sheets are nailed to the form about where they will be fitted and left for a while, they will take a set, or "get the habit" of conforming to the shape. Then, after they are scribed, trimmed,

66 BOATBUILDING ONE-OFF IN FIBERGLASS

The one-off form for the 50-foot ketch Carib Owl, *designed by Sparkman and Stephens and built by Joseph Conboy with Airex. (Courtesy Torin Inc.)*

Welded angle for station on an I-beam strongback, as set up by P-Squared Boats, Anaheim, California. (Courtesy Torin Inc.)

and fitted, there will be less resistance to the screws holding them in place and less likelihood of curled-up edges. If the bends are too hard or too compound in curvature for the full-width sheets, you should cut them into narrower pieces and put them on diagonally. Otherwise, the athwartship seams may pucker.

It is important to get the sheets as flush and fair as possible, because PVC foam is too tough, elastic, and readily heat softened to grind easily. If you have to sand it, a circular sander with 24 or 16 grit on a foam pad at 7,500 r.p.m. and a light touch will do it. But if there is a lot of material to be cut away, I prefer sharp cutting tools. For slight discrepancies, putty is good, but be careful that to fair raw foam you use a tough, resin-based putty like microballoons that won't defeat the purpose of the sandwich by cracking up and delaminating when the hull flexes. Also, you should do all the sanding before you apply putty to raw foam; otherwise, the putty, being harder, will project above the surface as the foam is cut away faster around it. The best way to prevent such problems is to keep the puttied areas minimal, not to smear putty all over the boat, plastering over every little dimple. In

Airex sheets fitted on the form for the 50-foot ketch Carib Owl. *(Courtesy Torin Inc.)*

Airex foam applied to a form diagonally.

practice, you will find that overly meticulous smoothing at this stage is largely defeated by new lumps and hollows created when you laminate the outer skin, whereas modest imperfections in the surface at the start tend to be wiped out as layers are added.

In the early years of their manufacture, PVC foam sheets did not always come out a uniform thickness when sliced from the "bun" or "log" of raw product. Some sheets used on the first one-off racing sailboat built in my shop had one edge up to ⅛ inch thicker than the supposed thickness; others had an edge as much as ⅛ inch thinner. The fairing problems this uneven material caused were traumatic for all concerned. I guess you'd call it the high cost of pioneering in a new material. Fortunately, the Airex people helped me with the expense of working the hull over until it was, well, fair enough to win the Southern Circuit, anyway. (The other day, by the way, I read in the paper that this same boat, entered in the Southern Circuit 11 years later, had the fleet whipped until it had to withdraw from the last two races with mechanical problems.) Unfortunately, one reporter's comment that it was the roughest hull he's seen in all his years of covering yacht races was probably no exaggeration. So now you know why I stress the difficulty of fairing the material, and the importance of getting the sheets flush in the first place. You should feel fortunate that the thickness of Airex sheets today is so accurate that you can achieve a surface with no more than $1/16$-inch offset at any joint.

An early technique, now remembered only as a good trick to know if you have to make an especially hard bend in forming Airex, was heat soaking the sheets. When softened in an oven, they could be formed in tight curves; and we did this to all the sheets on our first boat that had to go around the hard turn of the bilge. But now Airex is supplied "contoured," meaning sliced or scored partly through in a checkerboard pattern. This configuration conforms to the tightest bends you'll find in most boats built with a given thickness without a bit of trouble. All you have to do is to provide closely spaced stringers, for this material cannot span as great a distance as the solid sheets can.

In a sailboat with a lead ballast keel, PVC foam is not used in way of the lead, if external, nor in way of internal ballast. Nor is it or any other soft core material recommended in the grounding surface of any keel. Due to the compressibility of low-density materials, the weight of the boat and/or the weight of a ballast keel distorts or crunches a sandwich laminate made with them. An additional danger with cores other than PVC is that if the outer skin of the keel is holed by grounding, the core entraps water, which makes repair more difficult. Generally it is recommended that a core be ended before the deadrise turns down into the keel and that the keel itself be an extra-heavy single skin.

I agree that PVC foam should not be used in way of a ballast keel, whether internal or bolted on, or under plates or floors to which a ballast keel is bolted. I also wouldn't carry most other core materials into any keel. But as long as there is a heavy single skin capable of taking the weight of the boat locally, I would rather see the more vulnerable lower portions of a keel filled with PVC foam than left hollow. PVC will not hamper repair by absorbing water; in fact, it will serve as backing already in place against which you can build up fiberglass patches. More important, it will be there as a secondary barrier against flooding. For these reasons, nothing could be better than to fill this vulnerable area with the stuff, unless you fill it with a more solid material, as I suggest in Chapter 11.

Attaching Airex sheets so that they will take the shape of the form. Note the wood strip planking on the keel, where Airex won't be wanted as a core. Joseph Conboy, builder. (Courtesy Torin Inc.)

To terminate the foam core on the form for your one-off, you could first continue it on over the keel, coating the area with mold release or taped-on Mylar, and then remove that section of foam later. You could also use a mold lining material (mold covering in this case) so that the part of the form where there will be a single skin becomes a male mold on which to lay it up. But a more direct approach is to cover the single-skin area of the form with a starting layer of C-Flex, CVC, or Str-r-etch Mesh. All of these materials are described in Chapters 4 through 6. When they are used as a starting layer, you can lay up your outer skin on them and leave them in the keel as part of it. C-Flex and CVC become added layers of fiberglass, whereas Str-r-etch Mesh becomes a steel core.

Rather than create a joggle in the exterior lines of the hull, you can shim the surface of the starting material for the keel's single skin up flush with the outboard surface of the PVC foam so that the outer skin passes smoothly from one to the other. However, there is an easier way to put additional layers into the keel to beef up the single layer that the combined inner and outer skins of the sandwich form, which is hardly enough for most keels. To do this, you install your starting material over shims on the stringers that are below the level of the foam's surface by just the thickness of the layers you want to add. Then you can laminate the added material on the outside of the boat, where it is easier to work, and run the outer skin over them.

Should your one-off be a small boat or a multihull, which is likely to rest too lightly on its centerline or keel to compress the PVC sandwich, you can probably forget about switching to a single skin. This will simplify the building process considerably; and if you have any doubts, you can add some extra layers of mat over the bearing points for extra stiffness and wear. Such extra layers should start with a narrow tape, and each should be wider than the last so that the buildup tapers off. It helps to place them between or beneath the layers of the outer skin so that their edges blend better. But even if you added such layers to the outside, anytime in the life of the boat, it would be all right.

It is also customary not to use a PVC core in way of a bolted deck joint, or where a clamp for deckbeams will be bolted in. In molded boats, the builder sometimes stops the foam in the topsides, bevels it with a sharp knife, or builds a ramp of putty, and turns the inner skin down onto the outer skin to make a single skin from that point upward. In order to keep the outer skin fair, either part of the foam on the form has to have release so that it can be removed, or a waxed substitute for it installed in that area. However, in this critical area it is good to install a permanent replacement for the core, a harder material that can withstand the compression of bolting, yet at the same time continue to provide the stiffness of a core. I like fir plywood for this because it has ample resistance to compression, it is light enough for all but the most ultrahigh-performance boats, it is obtainable in a variety of thicknesses, and several thin layers can be laminated in place to accommodate curves. The notion, by the way, that a plywood core in fiberglass will rot away is just that—a notion. The cause of the notion is real enough, however. Plywood or natural wood that is inadequately sealed by thin coverings of fiberglass and similar materials eventually lets in air and water. This seepage, especially when the water is fresh water, certainly rots wood. But there have been hundreds of thousands if not millions of boats built with plywood cores in their transoms; and not one I ever saw with a well-buried core showed a trace of rot. Natural wood is stronger and stiffer than plywood; so if you want to take the trouble to fit it, one of the harder woods can only make a better sheer core, and softwood a lighter one. If you are a purist (of the new breed) and want only fiberglass and PVC foam in your hull, you can accommodate through-bolting with a small block of fiberglass cut into the core where each bolt will be, using a strip, for instance, in way of a chainplate. The blocks can be cut from a sheet of fiberglass prefabricated at the same thickness as the core. You can also build such inserts in place by routing or boring out the core down to, but not through, the outer skin after you have turned over the hull and before you lay up the inner skin. With a hole saw, chisel, and a pot of putty made of glass fibers in resin, or a package of little disks of mat, you can prepare a number of these very quickly.

Again, only those decks that rest on a clamp or those built off the boat need a row of bolts; and of the latter, only those like the "shoe box" and the "coffee can," which involve the topsides, require that you leave off or replace the PVC core. If you build your hull with an inturned flange along the sheer to accept a deck built off the boat, the PVC can stop against the flange, the inner and outer skins can join to form the flange as a single skin, and the deck can be bolted through it.

If you build a PVC-cored hull on top of a deck that is still in its deck mold, you don't have to worry about any of the aforementioned, for you turn the deck laminate down over the side of its mold as a bulwark, or up as a vertical flange in the topsides, which the outer skin of the hull will join. In either of these one-piece boat configurations, the inner skin of the hull should be turned onto the underside of the molded deck; and to avoid overhead work, you might want to go inside the one-piece boat before it is turned upright and lay up this angle or knee tapering the leg that is against the hull, which the inner skin of the hull will join after the boat is upright. You will have to tear out the form and pass it down through deck openings if you do, but in some cases this may be worthwhile.

If you wish to make a one-piece boat of a PVC-cored hull, the deck of which is built in place on the upright boat, you can do it with a taper in the topsides of the hull to accept down-turned layers of the deck laminate when there is no bulwark. When there is a bulwark, you should leave off the hull's core at the underside of the deck and turn the deck's laminate up alongside the outer skin for a nice, long join. If you want a sandwich bulwark, it is best to add its core and its inner skin above the top of the completed deck; which is to say, boats that are traditionally associated with bulwarks should not have their decks hanging off the inner skin of the hull only.

Although it is tempting to make a "showing" by hanging full sheets of PVC foam on your form, you should remember what I mentioned before: on some hulls or parts of hulls, the work will actually go faster and the stuff lie fairer if you cut it into strips and apply it at an angle. You can't tell what angle without bending some

Turning an Airex-cored hull. Doug Petersen–designed 2-ton yacht, built by P-Squared Boats. Note the "receiving cradle" to help the hull hold its shape until the inner skin has been applied and bulkheads have been installed. (Courtesy Torin Inc.)

pieces on your form, but you might save yourself a lot of needless struggling with wide pieces of foam that are tricky to handle. I have always wanted to try lapstrake planking a small boat with PVC foam over section moulds only, which amounts to running the material horizontally. It should be a handy way to put a traditionally lapstrake boat together, not that I want lapstrake just because it is traditional. It is well known that laps stiffen a boat, dampen roll, and hold down spray; and reverse laps (looking up) in a fast powerboat's bottom make it perform better, too.

Although applying solid (unscored) sheets to stringers on a form has been the most popular one-off building procedure to date, the advent of scored sheets has made a slightly different process quite worthy of consideration. Rather than start with the core and lay up the outer skin on it, the newly popular method is to plank over the stringers with a thin, temporary skin of wood, hardboard, or other suitable material, lay up the inner fiberglass skin of the laminate on this lining material, weight scored PVC sheets down on the inner skin, and, finally, lay up the outer skin.

The trade-offs between the two methods are:

1. The form for solid sheets is only stringers on moulds, whereas the form for scored sheets must be planked over entirely, at a much greater cost in labor and materials.

2. The inner skin is laid up much more easily over the outside of a form than within the hull, and the difference in difficulty increases with the size of the boat.

3. The partially completed laminate of solid PVC core and outer skin only is distorted easily while it is turned over and receiving its inner skin. It thus requires good support, as with a "receiving cradle." Again the magnitude of this problem increases with size. The completed laminate built with the scored core is quite stiff, however, and is distorted less easily.

A PVC-FOAM ONE-OFF DECK

To build a complete one-off PVC-cored deck in place on the boat, you must build a temporary male mold surface there. In other words, you must set up temporary deck moulds or deckbeams, or fit longitudinal stringers between the bulkheads, spaced close enough to support a mold lining material. This material can be thin plywood or hardboard if you intend to put some sort of applied finish on the underside of the deck later, or one of the slick materials, such as melamine-coated Masonite or Formica, if you want the slickest surface possible or intend to use gelcoat. You can also use wood left in place (WLP) as the mold surface if you prefer to have wood showing in the finished overhead. In that case it might help to read Chapter 7, in which I discuss the WLP one-off building method. However, you can screw a decorative wood lining to the overhead with relative ease after the deck is built.

You should cut a temporary mold surface material athwartships and butt it atop each bulkhead so that you can readily extract it from between the top of the bulkhead and the inner skin of the deck. This chore is also expedited if you have at least one butt in the sheets between any two bulkheads in which you can get your pry bar started without chopping a hole. After you remove the mold surface, you can stuff the gap between the inner skin and the bulkhead with a strip of PVC foam before you tab the bulkhead to the deck.

Should you use gelcoat in molding the deck, you will save a lot of grinding of the margins along bulkheads and the deck at side by taping off these areas, wide enough for the tabbing, before applying the gelcoat. However, with the paints, vinyl lining materials, and other finishes available today, I doubt that most one-off builders will attempt to use gelcoat. Even production builders seem to be drifting into alternative finishing processes because of the large amount of rework involved when gelcoat is chipped or scratched along the way from molding to delivery. It should be mentioned that high-pressure phenolic laminates like Formica and Micarta not only glue well to the overhead, but also will stick well with resin to the inner skin of the laminate if you want to install a patch of one of them upside down on the deck mold surface prior to laying up the inner skin. Again, you should leave a margin for tabbing.

The neatest solution to the fiberglass tabbing problem in the overhead, when it is to be exposed to view, is to place a strip of hardboard at least as wide and thick as the tabbing's overhead leg on the mold surface above each bulkhead. This creates a recess in which to build up the tabbing. After tabbing, you can bring the recess flush with the overhead surface, using resin-based putty. However, the strip placed on the mold surface at the same time creates a bump in the inner skin on which you must install a strip of the PVC core, which is that much thinner, to keep the outer skin or deck surface fair. Nevertheless, in cases where the surface of the overhead is to be the finished surface, it's quite worthwhile to eliminate the unsightly lumps and problems fitting joinerwork over the lumps that tabbing is bound to cause when it is substantial enough to ensure a durable connection. Naturally, you can also eliminate the lump tabbing causes on bulkheads by rabbeting their margins for it before installing them.

When it is too inconvenient to build a foam-cored deck in place on the hull, perhaps due to the lack of headroom in a building or of scaffolding equipment out of doors, and when you consider a full deck mold too complex or expensive, you can build it on a plain form of station moulds and stringers on the floor. The form can be either a female form, like an unlined mold, or a male form, like a right-side-up deck. The treatment is essentially the same. It begins with your covering the form with PVC foam temporarily fastened to the stringers in the same way as on the hull form. Then you lay up the inner skin in the moldlike form, or the outer skin on the right-side-up form. When you have brought either of these to a finished state, you turn over the deck so that you can lay up the other skin and finish it off.

The cost of labor and materials to construct either form is almost identical and the difference in results not too great, for the skins of each are laid up and hand finished in the same way. You do have the option to build a male mold for the cockpit in (actually on top of) the mold-type form, giving you a slick or gelcoated finish in an area difficult to smooth and polish. The boxlike nature of most cockpits all but demands that it be built as a box of sheet materials anyway, which is in effect a male mold, but you can also build the cockpit on a separate male mold and install it in the deck of the right-side-up form later. With its outer skin built first, the deck built right side up is stiffer and less fragile to turn over; but it also has to be turned back again to be installed on the boat. Meanwhile, some stiffeners temporarily fastened to the inner skin of the upside-down deck will hold its shape until it is turned and the outer skin laid up. Although this comparison seems to balance the choice of forms, the human element tips the scales heavily in favor of the male form; for most of us would prefer to deal with a right-side-up, right-side-out building project than one in which everything is reversed. Therefore, I imagine that most one-off builders will choose the upright-deck form, and perhaps rightly so. It only slows down building to undertake a method that is harder to visualize, unless it offers substantial advantages.

If you have a hankering, and the headroom, for deckbeams in your boat, there is another approach to building a PVC-foam-cored deck in place. On the beams you can install sheets of foam with the inner skin already laid up on them and lay up the outer skin over them. You should space the beams so that there are no fewer than three of them to the width of a sheet and run the sheets athwartships with their long edges butted on beams. For instance, using a standard-size Airex sheet, which is 3 feet by 6 feet, a 9-, 12-, or 18-inch center would give you a beam at each edge of a (3-foot-wide) sheet with three, two, or one beam, respectively, between them. To glue the inner skin together across its joints atop the beams, lay up a two-to-four-layer laminate on the top face of each beam. Before you install the sheets, sand the laminate on the beam and along the line of contact on the sheets; then screw the sheets down in resin, wet mat, 3M's Scotch Seal #5200, or epoxy glue. Needless to say, fairly wide deckbeams are a help in this. The fastenings should be short round- or pan-head screws countersunk right down through the foam, if you want to make the most of their holding power. But if you trust the glue and want the fastenings mostly to secure the sheets until the glue sets up, you can sink flathead nails or screws only a little way into the foam. Fastening heads should not be left flush with the surface of the foam. They can cause bumps in the outer skin someday, if not now.

With wooden beams to hide the athwartship joints, it is not difficult to lay out the biggest deck so that very few fore-and-aft joints of the inner skin need to be hidden by carlings, overhead grab rails, light wire moldings, or blended fiberglass tabbing. But it is also possible to make up lengths more than one sheet long to cover the full width in one piece. You should make sure that the pieces of Airex with the inner skin on them will bend easily over the crown. When the crown is very round or the inner skin too thick to make the bend, you should prebend the sheet into a concave form, which might be as simple as propping up its ends with blocks of wood. Alternatively, if the inner skin is slick surfaced, you can lay it up on a convex or arched piece of waxed, slick material and weight the foam down on it in wet mat, using the contoured (scored) type if necessary to make the bends.

I'm not trying to confuse you by suggesting so many alternatives. However, I do want to mention every procedure that might help you work out the best combination of methods, materials, and results for the boat you envision, under the circumstances that you have to build it, given your own know-how, abilities, or predilections. Much as both of us might prefer it, I cannot simply say that this or that is absolutely the best way. There is no such thing for all boats, all builders, or all times and places. So bear with me; "you ain't heard nuthin' yet."

You have probably noticed that when you build with PVC foam as the starting material on a form, or use a male-mold technique, the outer skin's finish is bound to be "as laid up." This is not the end of the world for a walking surface. All boat laminates should have no fewer than two layers of mat on the exterior surface to make them watertight; and a neatly rolled mat finish is an acceptable deck surface. It has a good nonskid texture and is fair enough if you carefully butt all seams in the laminate. You can use pigmented resin the color you want in the final two

Plywood core replacements in position along the edge of Centennial's *raised deck, Airex foam weighted down on deck, and Airex being fitted to the raised-deck side. The plywood is set in wet mat. Note the blocks representing portlights in the form, and the corresponding cutouts in the Airex. Photographs in Chapter 2 show further details of the laying up of* Centennial's *deck in its mold. (Loy photo)*

layers, or you can paint it. If you don't want the texture along waterways and next to deck structures where dirt collects, you can tape off the areas and fill them smooth.

OTHER PVC-FOAM ONE-OFF STRUCTURES

No material intrigues the one-off or custom fiberglass boatbuilder more than PVC foam. Aside from building straight hulls and decks, the material has many potential uses. It is easily marked, cut, glued with resin, or pinned together with finish nails or small wooden dowels; then it is readily transformed into as rugged an item as you need with a fiberglass laminate. In small, open boats I have used it as a one-off form that remains in place to build seats, flotation tanks, self-bailing soles, half decks, and coamings. The larger the boat the more items you will find to fabricate this way—for example, stringers, floors, a dam in the keel when you are filling part of it solid, a sump tank, an engine drip pan, a tight locker for compressed-gas bottles, a fish well, almost an entire flying bridge, and a built-in cooler, freezer, or refrigerator. When refrigeration is involved, PVC foam not only provides good insulation, but when glued, puttied, or sealed over with fiberglass, it forms a vapor barrier, too. When used in the engine room, it is vibration and sound dampening and oil and gasoline resistant as well as waterproof; however, it should not be subjected to extreme heat (see manufacturer's recommendations).

If you are installing partial bulkheads of PVC foam, their edges can be glued to the hull with resin, which beats a lot of temporary screws or braces. If one side will become difficult or impossible to reach, that side can be precovered with a fiberglass skin to stiffen it before it is installed.

If you want to use PVC foam for a light, thin-skinned sandwich and you are worried about its stiffness, you can stiffen it by building ribs within it, using a method we developed at my shop for such a construction with 2-pound-density polyurethane core. In Star boat decks, we got that construction down to 1.1 pounds per square foot, or about the weight of ½-inch cedar. And we regularly built 37-foot Meadow Lark cruising ketches with hull, deck, and trunk laminates ranging from 3½ pounds down to 2 pounds per square foot, depending on the specific area. With pure PVC, like Airex, you won't need glass ribs often; but there are times when it's nice to know how to maximize stiffness without adding significant weight or without adding frames or stringers to the interior surface of the structure. To construct a ribbed sandwich, you build the ribs on the edges of foam planks as you apply the planks consecutively to one skin; then you cover the whole with the opposite skin. The width of the planks you use determines the rib spacing. Beveling the edges of the planks helps you turn the flanges of the ribs horizontal, where they attach to the two skins, without lumps or bubbles. Obviously, you must have either a male or female mold surface, or a table for flat panels like bulkheads, on which to lay up the first skin and fabricate the ribbed core. Thus, wherever you build ribs into the foam, it is no longer the starting material. But you can back special ribbed areas in a form-built hull, such as in way of the mast, with thin mold lining material on your form.

The methods described in this chapter are applicable to the tops of cabin trunks or deckhouses and for the soles of cockpits; which is to say, for all "down" surfaces. Some of them can be applied to the vertical surfaces of these structures, too. On production boats, the vertical parts of the deck are usually single-skin laminates, but you don't have to copy that. Manufacturers reason that the handling of window areas, or of a number of portlights, around which a core must be cut and the inner and outer skins brought together, and the extra moves of tilting the mold to facilitate pressing the core to vertical surfaces, make a sandwich too labor intensive. It is quicker for them to bring the inner and outer skins together around the corners, off the cored horizontal surfaces, onto the vertical. It should be obvious that they then would be wise to add a few stiffening layers to the single-skin sides of the structures, and some of them do. Anyway, PVC-foam-cored-sandwich house, trunk, and cockpit sides are certainly worth having to insulate against heat and sound and, in offshore boats, to protect against impact, including that of breaking seas.

You can build the forms for these structures as parts of the main deck form or leave holes and set up their forms after laminating the deck. But if you find it awkward to work on the forms aboard the boat, as when the housetops are too close to the overhead or a cockpit tub is too cramped, then you might decide to build them on the floor. In that event, their attachment to the deck must be very strong. There are at least three ways to make the connection. The continuous fiberglass way is to leave a taper or rabbet at the edges of both the deck and the part to allow for a sturdy tabbing, both inside and out. Two mechanical ways are: (1) to build a flange on the structure that sits on the deck, or that will fit into a rabbet in the deck; and (2) to turn a flange up on the deck edge, as I mentioned in Chapter 2, and fit a house or trunk down over it. All such mechanical joints should be bolted together in a resin and glass-fiber mush, often called applesauce. For myself, I like joint and bolts sealed over with fiberglass tabbing on at least the inside or outside of the boat. A cockpit built on the floor cries out for a male mold to save finishing work. But, especially when it is a boxy affair, you can save a significant cash outlay for materials by building the part with PVC sheets fitted over a sketchy form. You can also prelaminate one skin to these sheets on a table. Make sure, though, that where there are curves, you don't stiffen the sheet so much with the laminate that you get into a hassle trying to bend it into position.

I am very fond of PVC foam. I have used it to build a 9-foot Chapelle-designed Squall dinghy, the 60-foot Newick-designed trimaran *Gulf Streamer*, and dozens of sail- and powerboats between these sizes, and it has never let me down. Nevertheless, I do not consider it the only, or quite the best, starting material for all fiberglass one-offs that are PVC-foam cored. Indeed, I have often built both hull and deck with other methods and put the PVC-foam core in afterward. So read on.

4

C-Flex

When the question is, Which form-built one-off system for round-bottomed boats is the fairest of them all?, my experience prompts the unequivocal answer—C-Flex. In the early 1970s, Bill Seemann worked out a special fiberglass material that bends over (or into) the compound curves of a form without wrinkling. It is, simply put, a continuous 12-inch-wide "plank" made up of small fiberglass rods and strand roving running lengthwise, held together with a lightweight fiberglass cloth. The rods provide the stiffness to bend fair along the length of the hull, and the cloth provides a smooth surface that will stretch on the bias to accommodate transverse curves as well.

Available in rolls up to 250 feet in a single length, C-Flex is applied in one-piece strakes, adjusted and held in place with ice picks, then lightly stapled to the form. While conforming to the shape, the planks can also be curved edgewise considerably so that they can be kept butted together along their "seams" without spiling on most hulls. Nor is the most difficult hull to plank likely to require spiling and cutting more than one strake per side, as long as some judgment is used as to whether to start at the sheer, the keel, along the turn of the bilge, or, in chine boats, with a strake centered on the chine. Only the ends need trimming where they run off the edges of the form at sheer or centerline. To cut C-Flex when raw, you can use tin snips, but when saturated and hardened, an abrasive wheel on a hand power saw or grinder is best.

Once you have laid out, stapled, and trimmed the C-Flex on the form, you wet it out with resin. When this has cured, you lay up additional layers over it. These

Generally, stapling starts in the midsection and proceeds to each end of the hull. It is easiest to have one worker hold the C-Flex in place and help pull it fair around the framework while another comes along to staple the plank to the frames. (All photos and captions in this chapter from the C-Flex manual, courtesy Seemann Fiberglass, Inc.)

might make up the balance of the entire laminate, or they might be either the inner or the outer skin of a sandwich, depending on your construction and laminate schedules. The great advantage of C-Flex is that if you have done a neat job, following the advice given in Seemann Plastics' excellent manual, you will have very quickly gotten the hull off to a beautifully fair start.

The C-Flex manual is an in-depth discussion of one-off building with C-Flex. Written by Barry Kennedy, it is available from Seemann Plastics, Inc., P.O. Box 13704, New Orleans, Louisiana 70185. Its contents are as explicit, but not as formidable, as its title: *Construction Manual for Custom GRP Fabrication with C-Flex Fiberglass Planking.* In a way, it makes this chapter unnecessary; but then, I would like to express my opinions and to draw comparisons with other systems.

Due to C-Flex's longitudinal stiffness and lateral floppiness, it does not set well on stringers. Rather, it needs athwartship supports: not more than 18 inches apart for the heavier-weight CF 65, nor more than 14 inches for the lightweight CF 39, the two weights supplied for building heavy or light boats. This requires either that you apply C-Flex directly on moulds (or ribs) set up as closely spaced as needed, or that you bend over a stringered form thin hooplike battens spaced as needed. The difference essentially is whether you'd rather loft and build more moulds and not have to use stringers at all or whether you'd rather build fewer moulds, fill in the shape with stringers, and then cross them with hoops to support the C-Flex. Some considerations that might affect your decision are:

1. Stringers and hoops give you a good opportunity to see and correct unfairness in the form in both directions before you commit the C-Flex to it.

2. The greater number of moulds—usually about twice as many if you don't use stringers—need meticulously accurate lofting and setting up if you are to avoid a tedious session of trying battens all over them and adjusting their shapes.

3. Although you might have little trouble reaching the entire surface of smaller forms, you could be hampered by scaffolding problems trying to reach the upper parts of a big form consisting of moulds only. In contrast, you can climb

The ribband/batten approach to framing. In this method, the transverse frames are set on relatively wide spacings (normally the designed station spacing). Temporary wooden longitudinals (ribbands), spaced about 18 inches apart, span the framework, and temporary transverse battens are then attached to the ribbands to support the C-Flex. This framework also includes the permanent fiberglass longitudinal stiffeners.

substantial stringers like a ladder and walk on them with impunity, even during lamination.

No matter which way you provide the lateral supports, it is worthwhile to make them as fair as you can get them, because C-Flex will surely translate whatever shape it's on into a smooth surface. You check fairness by bending a batten over the supports here, there, and just about everywhere. You also get a last chance to see how fair the surface is and to correct it when the raw C-Flex is installed on the form, before you wet it out. You can shore up sags from below and pull down humps with wires on the inside of the form, tied off to the moulds or the building jig. However, if you have been careful, there should be little of this last-minute adjustment.

Wetting out the C-Flex is not difficult. A fuzzy paint roller holds more resin than the harder types, so it is better for this phase. Here you are just transferring the resin from the bucket to the surface and spreading it around until it soaks in. Nor is it important to saturate every bit of glass on the underside of the C-Flex. After the hull is turned over, the inside can be wet out. Actually, it facilitates the attachment of additional fiberglass on the interior if some of the C-Flex glass there is not yet saturated. Be careful that you don't bear down so hard with the roller that you dislodge the C-Flex from the form. Also, don't load it up with resin, for this only weakens the bond of ensuing layers and might cause excessive shrinkage. Shrinkage is one very real danger to a C-Flex one-off. It is caused by too-rapid curing of the resin, which, in turn, is caused by a heavy buildup and/or overcatalyzing (a "hot mix"). What shrinkage does to your one-off is to pull the C-Flex so tight over the form where the hull is round that the C-Flex flattens out between the supports. Now you have a series of flats from one support to the other instead of sleek convex curves. Such flats can be built back up to the lines with a generous application of putty, but you don't need that job. Due to this danger of radical shrinkage, the manual advises that you use a slow-curing resin for saturating the C-Flex. I can remember at least one nice hull that was wet out with a "slow mix" of general-purpose resin at my former boatshop, so I know it can be

A framework with fiberglass longitudinal stiffeners included, ready for C-Flex. The framework consists of the permanent bulkheads (marked by tape) with temporary intermediate framing providing the maximum recommended spacing of 18 inches for CF 65.

done. But that was during the 1974 resin shortage when we were lucky to get any kind of resin, and we had some very experienced glass men, who probably could have made it with road tar and window curtains. Anyway, it would be prudent to get the Seemann company's recommendation as to which currently produced resins are best for this stage.

An entirely different way to go about putting together a one-off with C-Flex is to use it over the wooden framing on which you would plank up a wooden boat. This can be done even with a frame built right side up by tipping the hull onto each bilge while you laminate. You should use stout, permanent fastenings through the skin into the wood, unless you intend to use the wood only as a form, fabricating fiberglass ribs or stringers around it.

However, you can build fiberglass framing on the inside of a C-Flex hull, using foam, pasteboard, or softwood formers. To supplement the longitudinally oriented strength of C-Flex, ribs would seem to be the most logical choice of framing to use; but stringers are all right as long as the C-Flex is crossed by enough strands in other layers to give the laminate strength athwartships. You have to be careful not to distort the hull when you build an unreinforced single skin, pull it off the form, and then build framing or install the core of a sandwich in it afterward.

Hollow fiberglass hat sections, to be used as permanent longitudinal stringers, are fabricated by laying C-Flex and conventional glass reinforcements over a shaped wooden form that is covered with a release agent (wax paper or cellophane). Although the C-Flex is not used here to develop shape, it gives excellent unidirectional reinforcement to this lightweight yet very strong structural member.

The empty hull should be set up level and true and well supported in enough places to hold its shape while you work on the interior. This problem can be avoided if you leave the form in when you turn the hull over and then take out only a section at a time to build the reinforcements in that area. Nor will there be a serious problem if you build an unreinforced hull skin onto a deck in its mold. Not only will that hull's sheer be fast to the deck all around, but you will probably include several permanent bulkheads in the setup as well. You'll have fun maneuvering big ones down the hatch if you don't. Nor do you need to worry about the bulkheads poking out through the thin skin if you set them up with a piece of PVC foam fitted around their edges, to cushion their contact with it. Another scheme, not unlike setting up a cold-molded wooden boat, is to let prefabricated hat-shaped fiberglass stringers into your moulds so that when you lay up the C-Flex over them and wet it out, you have an already stiffened shell. Because C-Flex is so limp laterally, it is, by the way, an excellent first skin for building fiberglass angle bars, channels, or stringers. You can fold it quite easily into and over the angles of the form for such members.

To avoid the problem of keeping the outer skin of a sandwich hull from being distorted while installing the core in it, some builders use C-Flex to start the inner skin on the form and build the entire sandwich from there outward. If the core is end-grain balsa, which sands quite easily, I don't suppose that's a bad idea. You could give her a good grinding and filling to restore fairness before laying up the outer skin. Still, C-Flex can yield such a beautiful surface that I would rather have it close to the outermost layers of my boat. Not only does a core tend to negate this fairness, but every fiberglass layer added to a good C-Flex start must be butted (not overlapped), carefully rolled, squeegeed, and possibly sanded and puttied here and there if you don't want it to be a step backward toward roughness. C-Flex

A proper job of planking the hull and saturating the C-Flex with marble casting resin yields top-quality results and saves time and money on fairing the hull.

is also very rugged stuff, which is another good reason to have it "up front" in the laminate where it can help resist impacts best.

Basically, there are two peculiarities of C-Flex, mentioned before but worth repeating, that must be kept in mind as you formulate your construction schedule. First, it is impractical within a reasonable effort to saturate C-Flex all the way through, all over. In recognition of this fact, you are well advised to plan to wet out the interior surface after the hull is turned. Concomitantly, C-Flex is better with at least one layer of mat on the reverse side, to seal it and to enhance the attachment of anything tabbed to that side. This ground rule means that no matter how much glass you build up on one side, you are not finished properly until you apply resin and, it is hoped, mat to the other side.

The second peculiarity is that C-Flex's great strength is all longitudinal, due to its exclusively unidirectional rods and strands. Laterally it has practically no strength. Therefore, you should not fail to supply athwartship strength to your laminate in the form of either woven roving or a unidirectional material the strands of which cross those of the C-Flex. At the same time, layers of woven roving or unidirectional roving should, properly, be alternated with mat, which binds the long-stranded layers together. Savvy glass men have long recognized that the best laminate schedule for building up strength while retaining resistance to delamination is alternate layers of long-strand and short-strand materials. To facilitate building such laminates, both woven and unidirectional roving are supplied with a mat backing bonded to them with a resin-soluble binder. These are sold under trade names like Fab-mat (woven roving and mat) and Lyasil (unidirectional roving and mat).

Of course, the chopped strands of CSM add some strength in all directions, too. However, short strands do not reach nearly the high bending and tensile strength that long strands do until built up much thicker and heavier. The most important functions of mat are its adhesiveness, due to its strands' more intimate involvement with the glass in adjoining layers (or with other surfaces), and its ability to seal out water, due to its multidirectional reinforcement of the resin against seepage cracks. Anyway, if you keep its peculiarities in mind, you can build a superb one-off hull with C-Flex.

C-Flex has been used to start a deck on an upright hull over both permanent and temporary deckbeams. I also think it would work well if applied athwartships over longitudinal deck stringers. However, when used to start a right-side-up deck, the builder must always deal with C-Flex's raw underside. A minimum sealing treatment for the underside would be a coat of resin, perhaps thickened with short milled fibers. A layer of mat would be better. Either of these, not to mention any cosmetic application, is obviously an unpleasant, low-efficiency operation, working overhead. It also wastes material on any but the heaviest sandwich decks to use C-Flex in the inner skin. By the time you add enough glass at 90 degrees to the C-Flex to balance the laminate's strength orientation, you have enough glass for the outer skin of most decks, and too much for the inner skin. Usually an inner skin one-third to one-half the outer skin's thickness is sufficient. You lose the beautiful fairness of C-Flex too, after you have buried it under an entire sandwich.

For these reasons, it is more practical to build a C-Flex deck from the outside or top of the deck inward on an upside-down form, like an unlined mold. Here, you're standing on the floor and everything is working for you. The fairness of the C-Flex and its strength are at the top of the deck laminate, and the underside of the deck can be given a handsome finish while the deck is still upside down. This method of C-Flex deck building is, in effect, building a deck in a mold with C-Flex taking the place of the mold lining and the first few layers of glass materials, all in one quick operation. A tremendous amount of labor is saved. The costs of materials, however, aren't significantly less, for the added cost per foot of C-Flex over that of standard glass reinforcements more than equals that of mold lining.

Temporary deck framing, 18 inches on centers, ready for C-Flex. This deck will be constructed upside down, then turned over for the exterior surface finish.

If you haven't already thought of it, setting up the hull atop a C-Flex deck that is built upside down in a mold-form like this works just as well as it does on a molded deck. Many of the features mentioned in Chapter 2 that you can build into a molded deck can also be built into the C-Flex deck. You can install male cockpit and seat molds before applying C-Flex, fitting the C-Flex around them. Or, after the C-Flex is cured, you can set them right on top of it and cut out the C-Flex after the deck is turned over. You can include a cabin trunk as part of the C-Flex form or line its sides with something slick, leaving its top open for C-Flex. The latter arrangement would give you smoothly molded trunk sides while avoiding the chore of fitting a mold lining into the crown of the top. You can brace up other, smaller features that are depressions in a mold, like hatch coamings or mast collars, flush with the deck surface, run over them with the C-Flex, and cut holes out of the C-Flex after it has cured so that the rest of the laminate can be turned down into them.

Once a C-Flex deck has been turned right side up, it should get a sealing (and wear) surface of mat. I prefer no fewer than two layers. They can be lightweight mat if the boat is light, but there should be two so that you can butt all the pieces to keep the surface smooth yet completely watertight. When rolled out with a nubbly roller, a mat finish is just about the right nonskid texture; and if you have put pigment in the resin used with the mat, your deck is finished. Should you prefer to paint the deck, the texture might still have a fair amount of tooth the first time you paint it. Eventually, though, it will get filled up. If you would like a more formal nonskid pattern, you can make it up in pieces as described in Chapter 2 and weight them down in wet mat.

Once you have built a one-off with C-Flex, I think you will agree that it is a remarkably apt solution to the problem of starting the laminate. It's a truly quick and easy system, requiring the simplest sort of form work and an incredibly short "planking" time. These are great advantages, but the greatest, in my opinion, is the fairness of the surface when it is spread on a true form. Not everyone might see C-Flex this way. I happen to enjoy lofting and setting up, and I tend to get bored with filling and sanding. I'm filled with admiration when the C-Flex is wetted out, and I worry about mussing up the lines with too many additional layers. Despite these foibles, I am forced to admit that C-Flex is worth using to start off any number of layers, with proper care in putting them on.

No way will you come to the outer surface of any form-built one-off system without some amount of filling and sanding. It's the nature of laminated fiberglass not to be smooth on the working surface. It's also the nature of its continuous surface, unbroken by lines that distract the eye, as do the seams of wooden planking, to accentuate imperfections. Every imperfection is the despair of the conscientious finisher, who is in danger of succumbing to "flawphobia." When exasperated by this situation, you should remember that it takes many hours to outboard-join a carvel wooden boat properly and also that the job is never finished: the wood will still be moving around a century later. Once you have faired fiberglass, only cosmetic treatments will interrupt an indefinite future of continuous use. But one way to minimize that fairing, which is described in Chapter 10, is to use C-Flex on a fair form.

5

CVC

CVC is another system of building one-off in fiberglass. The letters refer to the two John Collamores of Hulls Unlimited–East whose brainstorm it was, and to myself, who developed it with them. We thought it was a brand-new idea in the late 1960s, but it turned out that Charles Bell had described it in an article 15 years before. Bill Seemann told me recently that he too was building boats the CVC way, while he was inventing C-Flex.

CVC is a simple system. It amounts to nothing more than covering a form with very thin planks of mostly cured fiberglass. The form is built in the usual way, with moulds and stringers, and the fiberglass is lightly stapled over it. This layer of fiberglass then becomes the starting material on which the rest of the laminate is laid up. When the outside of the hull is finished, the form is ripped out and the tacks or staples clipped or ground off. From this point on, interior work depends on your construction schedule. You might want only a sealing and smoothing plaster of lightweight putty or a layer or two of mat on a small boat. On a bigger boat, it may be time to install ribs, or bilge stringers, or the core and inner skin of a sandwich laminate.

We found that the best fiberglass planks for round-bottomed CVC one-offs are single-layer strips of roving, usually 4 to 8 inches wide—whatever fits the curvature in a given area best. We made these strips by wetting out a large piece of woven roving on a table and cutting it into strips with a knife and straightedge at the leather-hard stage. We found that it is best to put the strips on the form while fairly green. Not only is it much easier for staples to penetrate them, but continued shrinkage in place seems to improve the fit also. Needless to say, diagonal is the best direction to lay the strips on most round-bottomed boats, but any direction and quite large strips or sheets work on flatter areas such as the deck, transom, or fin keel.

One might think that sheet fiberglass suitable for this work could be bought, but all we found in a brief survey were relatively low-strength, brittle machine-made products. These were also not cheap and certainly not worth sanding all over, which is what you would have to do to any fully cured fiberglass to ensure a good bond. So we made our own. Making up the strips of CVC takes at least four times as long as fitting and fastening them on the boat. For instance, when we built the 52-foot headboat *Albatross* that Dave Howes operates out of Suisit Harbor in Dennis, Massachusetts, it took four fiberglass men to supply one carpenter who was fitting and stapling the strips on the form. But if I remember correctly, it took less than two days to cover the whole boat. I also remember that we were able to start laying up the next two layers as soon as part of one side was planked. Strips of CVC, unlike wooden diagonal planking or any sort of mold lining, do not have to be butted against each other. One layer of roving is so thin that you can let each strip lap over the last a bit (like lapstrake planking) without fear that the resulting ridges will show after you have covered them with several more layers. Only the ends of the strips need trimming, at the keel and on any stringers where they might be butted. At the sheer they can be left long and all be trimmed at once. That's why you can put them on very quickly.

One thing generally disliked about CVC is that the entire interior of the hull must be sanded to get a good bond for whatever fiberglassing takes place there. Nobody likes sanding fiberglass, but it is a particularly important step when the strips are made on a waxed table and/or with a resin high in wax. Had we known about melamine-coated wallboard for the table, and had we used no-wax resin, we would not have had to grind so heavily on our early boats. However, other arrangements for cutting the sheets into strips are necessary to save the melamine from the knife. A table saw with large extensions of the table and a carbide-tipped blade or an abrasive wheel is one way. A small hand power saw with such a blade is another.

An interesting extension of the CVC system is that you can build a rugged sandwich construction with it that is well insulated, yet downright cheap in materials, although not particularly in labor. What you do, in essence, is to leave the stringers in as part of the hull, cover each of them with fiberglass mat, fill between them with 2-pound-density polyurethane foam of a thickness equal to their height, and then cover the whole interior with an inner skin.

We used this system to build the hull of Miner Brotherton's *Integrity*, which he sailed along the New England coast for about eight summers and has now taken south on a yearlong sabbatical. *Integrity*'s hull was built atop her deck in its mold, her bulwarks consisting of the overlap of both laminates, to make her a truly one-piece boat. Then Miner took over the removal of the moulds and the building of the sandwich on the interior—not the easiest sort of job with the deck in place! Yet, in

On the following pages:
Integrity is a Thomas Colvin–designed schooner that I built for Miner Brotherton, a college professor, in the winter of 1972–73. Colvin had designed her for steel but adapted her for round-bilged construction. Her deck was built in a female mold, and the hull moulds were then set up on the upside-down deck and the hull built using the CVC method. The boat is thus all one piece. Sailing her every summer and through most of a one-year sabbatical, Brotherton has ranged from Schoodic Point, Maine, to Key West. She has been a successful boat. (Photos courtesy Miner Brotherton)

in boatbuilding, everything is a compromise. *Integrity* was built with good features for a reasonable cost—the hard way.

Before setting up this stringered sandwich construction, you want to deduct in the loft the depth of the stringers plus the thickness of the outer skin from the sections and build your moulds to that line so that you can fasten the stringers on the outside of the moulds, rather than notch them into the moulds. This is important if you want to be able to extract the moulds from the hull without hacking them to bits or wrenching the stringers loose. Fastenings that you can take out from inside the boat, like toe screws fastened from underneath the moulds into the stringers, also help with removing the moulds. Of course, if you set up your form with the interior's bulkheads in place, you can notch the stringers into them. You then have bulkheads that can never work loose. This is not necessary; you can tab your bulkheads to the inner skin as well. It's just a nice strengthening feature if it fits your building schedule.

Since the fastenings of the CVC strips to the stringers in this sandwich construction will be permanent, it won't hurt a bit if they are plentiful and sturdy. However, covering the stringers with fiberglass mat on the interior locks them securely to the outer skin. It also adds to their stiffness, seals them from the possibility of rot, and links the inner skin to the outer skin along the length of each stringer. To sum it up, the layers of mat over the stringers are the heart and soul of this construction. By itself, 2-pound-density polyurethane foam an inch or so in thickness has almost no strength; and a sandwich of it without stringers (or ribs) to provide stiffness and to hold the two skins apart and together would be just about worthless. However, the foam is useful in its own way: it provides insulation with minimal weight, excludes water from the space, and supports the inner skin until it hardens. All of these things it does very well, if it is good-quality closed-cell polyurethane foam—not Styrofoam, which is resin soluble. Polyurethane foam is generally available in sheets or planks of many sizes at a much lower cost per board foot than PVC foam.

The moulds for the deck mold are set up.

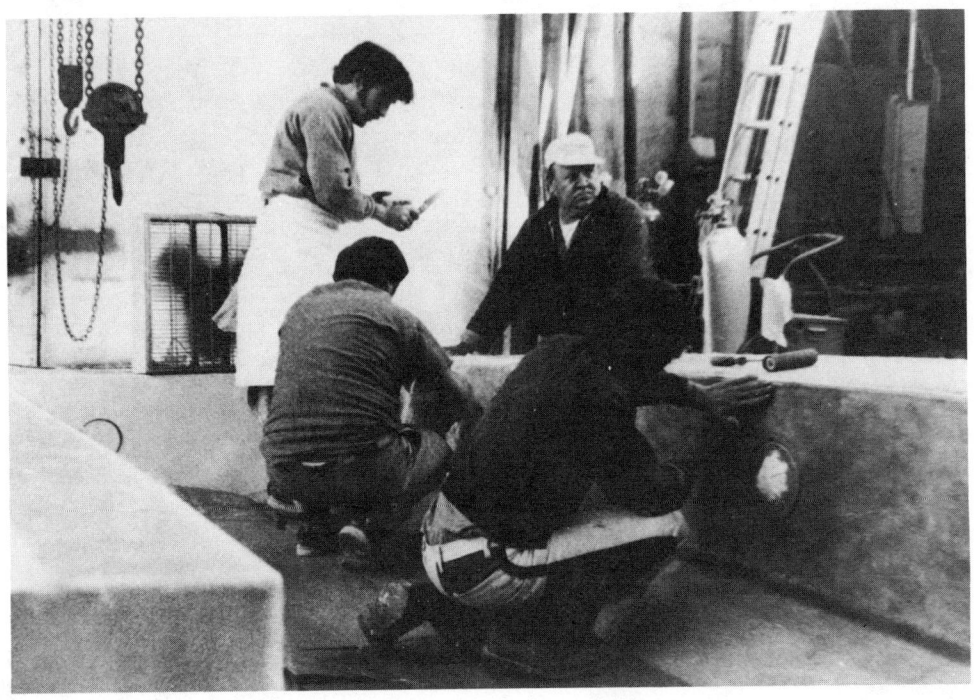

Laminating the deck in its mold. The laying up of a deck upside down in a mold is detailed in a series of photographs in Chapter 2.

The hull moulds are set up on the completed deck, still in its mold. Note the setback from the bulwark to allow for the thickness of the hull form stringers. The fiberglass of the hull will pass over the stringers right onto the bulwarks.

Stringering the hull form.

Hull form almost ready for the CVC "planking." The hard bilges show where Colvin adapted Integrity's *lines from his hard-chine steel design (and aluminum) to a round bottom for wood or fiberglass.*

Applying the CVC planks to the hull form. The keel is already covered. The workman is Walter Greene, learning the trade.

Lamination of the hull progresses.

Integrity's *molded deck and form-built hull after turning.*

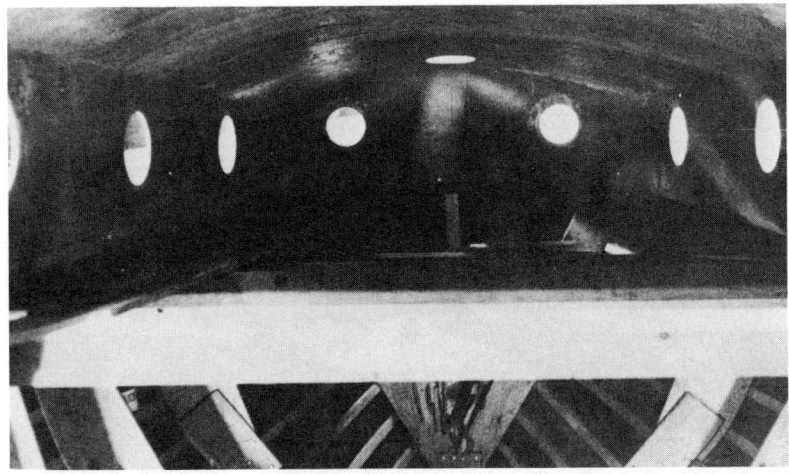

A view on the inside of Integrity's *molded deck and form-built hull after turning but before taking out the moulds.*

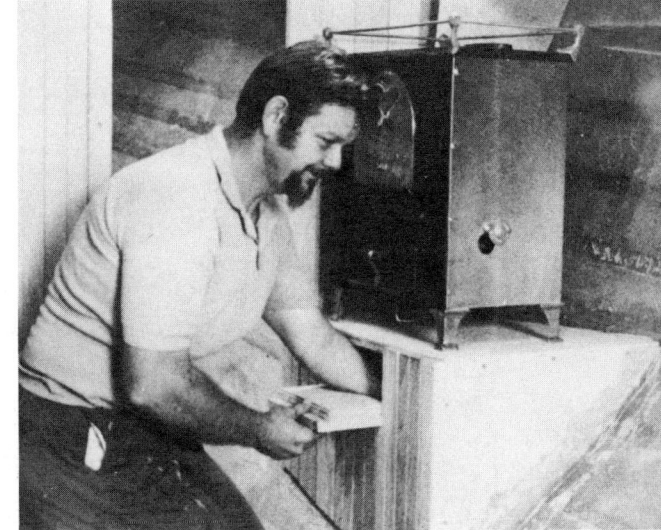

Left: *Fitting foam between the stringers, which have been covered with fiberglass since the hull was turned upright.* **Right:** *Fitting* Integrity's *stove locker. Note stringers showing through inner skin, and the tabbing of locker to skin.*

Integrity *sailing in Narragansett Bay.*

Fitting foam into the bays between the stringers in a round-bottomed boat is made easier if you taper the stringers inboard to lessen the tendency of the bays to be wider at the bottom than at the top. This truncated triangle section is also easier to cover with the mat because of its obtuse angles or corners.

In fastening joinerwork to this construction you have the opportunity to use screws, short tapping screws into the inner skin and long ones into the stringers, as well as fiberglass tabbing. I always advocate the use of screws into wooden bulkheads to help hold tabbing on, and I would, while doing so, put some into the hull side of this construction at each stringer, too. One of the most common flaws in fiberglass boats I have surveyed is tabbing that has worked loose; so why not "pour" a few screws into the first few layers, cover them with a layer or two more, and play it safe?

Needless to say, all bolting areas should have a firm replacement for the polyurethane core, as described in Chapter 3 on PVC foam. But you can install through-hulls in a recess where you have cut away the foam—with sloping sides—to expose the outer skin and lined the hole with fiberglass that turns onto the inner skin. This lining both reinforces the area around the through-hull and seals off the surrounding foam. Like other sandwich constructions, this one should not be carried into a hollow keel. However, in a canoe-bodied boat with a bolted-on keel, it might be carried down to a stringer at each side of a central bay in which a solid-core replacement, a steel backing plate, or a heavier laminate will receive the keelbolts.

This unusual construction has gotten more space than I intended, but it is a relatively inexpensive way to insulate and stiffen the hull. It can be used with other systems built on a form with stringers, not just CVC. Anyway, like the glass ribs and foam construction described in Chapter 3, it's worth keeping in mind; because you never know when you'll find a use for it, or for something of your own devising it suggests. That's what makes one-off in fiberglass stimulating. You have many options; yet thinking about them is sure to develop more. CVC itself is good to remember as a way to start parts other than the hull. There is nothing to prevent you from tacking prefabricated strips or sheets of fiberglass to a form for any part of a boat as the beginning of a laminate. They can also be permanently fastened to wooden deckbeams or to the framing of deckhouses. The inside of sheets can be made to look good cosmetically, but strips would look rough on the inside and would probably be suitable only when they would be covered from view. If you were to start a fiberglass outer skin on a wooden boat frame this way, as described in Chapter 4, you should use substantial fastenings, closely spaced, and apply them through two or more layers of the laminate for greater holding power in the fiberglass. These can be flathead stainless steel screws, Anchorfast nails, heavy power-driven staples, or even plain galvanized roofing nails. When they are covered by not less than two layers of mat, they'll be well protected from the marine environment.

When it is colder on the outside than in, the fiberglass might "sweat," particularly if insulation is not used. Thus, in a construction like this, there is some danger that condensation collecting between it and the wooden frame might rot the wood. You can prevent this by treating the wood with a good wood preservative and/or using a bedding compound in the interface, like 3M's Scotch Seal #5200.

The advantage of the CVC system is that it saves the labor and material costs of applying something to the form other than the first layer of the laminate itself. On a round-bottomed hull it's a bit rough and ready with the strips; but anywhere you can use sizable panels or sheets it's as good a form-built method as any. All things considered, it's about as inexpensive as a one-off can be, since the only items you have to spring for, which are not parts of the boat, are the form and the surface on which to wet out strips for the first layer. For that reason, I think it will always appeal to the impecunious home builder and to the person who needs to put a plain, rugged boat together with little special knowledge, preparation, tools, or equipment "right now!"

6

Str-r-etch Mesh and Fer-a-lite

Amid the proliferating technological advances of our time, learning the boatbuilding trade is a career-long process that begins and ends in midstream. One piece of unfinished business that has nagged me since I undertook to write this book is that I have yet to try Platt Monfort's one-off in fiberglass inventions, Str-r-etch Mesh and Fer-a-lite. Platt came by the shop to show us his wares after I had sold the place and had decided to retire from managing it. He was cartopping a round-bottomed dinghy that had been left in the translucent, plain resin state so that the observer could see the wire mesh that is at the heart of the process. I was impressed with the fairness of the little boat, with the way Str-r-etch Mesh lies in a fair compound curve over a form, and with the low cost of the material. Despite the fact that I haven't actually handled the materials on the job, it is obvious to me that the method is straightforward, in fact simplicity itself—easy, fast, and inexpensive. Therefore, I must tell you about it with apologies in advance for any inaccuracies. If it turns you on as it did me, you can write for more information to: Aladdin Products, Inc., RFD 2, Wiscasset, Maine 04578.

Str-r-etch Mesh is a woven wire cloth of 19-gauge hard-drawn steel wire with ½-inch spacing. It is welded only along the selvage edge, and that's just to keep you from going mad trying to handle it. The individual woven wires are free to slip by each other a little at their crossings, which makes it possible for the mesh to bias or conform to round-bottomed boat shapes without wrinkles requiring darts cut in it. If the welded selvage wires are cut off, the mesh becomes completely free forming; but if one edge is snipped every couple of inches, the mesh becomes limber enough for all practical purposes without creating unraveling problems. Meanwhile, being of hard-drawn wire, the mesh is "springy" and tends to form fair curves from one support to another.

Now, when you can buy a product with these characteristics in 3- and 4-foot widths by the 100-foot roll, when you can cut off a piece as long as the form and staple it to the stringers, then you know you're into a *fast* one-off starting material. The cost of Str-r-etch Mesh at this writing is 55 cents per square foot, so it's inexpensive, too.

To build with Str-r-etch Mesh, you set up the same sort of one-off form of station moulds, backbone or centerline pieces, and stringers that you would use for PVC foam or CVC. The mesh is stiff in both directions, so you don't need athwartship support specifically, as you do with C-Flex. At the same time, the mesh requires too closely spaced support to be laid directly over moulds as you can do with C-Flex. Rather small stringers spaced about 6 inches apart amidships (they'll naturally gather closer toward the ends of the boat) seem to be enough to support Str-r-etch Mesh, which is stapled to them with the small, light variety of staples used in such jobs as putting up insulating materials. You begin to get a feel for the fairness of Str-r-etch Mesh when Platt advises applying the staples close to a crossing wire so that it won't make a "bump." You are also warned not to drive the staples too hard, which will cause a "dimple."

In laying out the stringers you must plan to have one of each fall under each seam. By seam I mean the line where the selvage edges of the planks or widths of mesh that it takes to cover one side of the boat meet. If, for instance, the maximum half-girth of your boat is about 6 feet, then you would need two 3-foot widths to cover it; and you would want to run a stringer roughly along the center of each side, a little less than 3 feet from the sheer at the greatest girth, on which you could butt and staple the selvage edges of the widths of mesh. When you actually install the mesh, you should cut and fit the piece that covers the bottom part of the side first, shaping it about 2 inches bigger than the profile everywhere, and staple it on with its lower selvage edge centered on the butt-stringer. Then you can butt the topside piece against the bottom piece and staple it along that same stringer, which can be made a little wider than the rest to take the double row of staples. The reason for working from the keel, or from the top of the form, down is to avoid disrupting or denting the lower wire while installing that above it. If your boat has close to 9 feet half-girth, you could cover each side with three widths of 3-foot mesh with two seams butted on stringers. For 8 or 12 feet of half-girth you could use two or three widths of 4-foot mesh. Transoms are said to be better formed with plywood than with open work, because the mesh is so slippery that a back-up surface helps with hanging up the fiberglass.

You snip off the overhanging wire around the edges of the form with heavy-duty wire cutters, and—that's it; you're ready to lay up your one-off hull. There are various approaches to getting started with fiberglass on the mesh, an operation that the slipperiness of the bright, hard steel makes a bit tricky. Apparently, if you walk up to the wire-covered form and throw on a piece of mat or roving, wet or dry,

Workboat hull ready for application of Str-r-etch Mesh at North End Marine, Rockland, Maine. (Courtesy Aladdin Products)

Typical construction is used at the transom when building with the mesh. (Courtesy Aladdin Products)

The mesh lays fair on highly contoured shapes. (Courtesy Aladdin Products)

In this hull, selvage edges of two mesh "planks" meet on a stringer. (Courtesy Aladdin Products)

Resin is applied to fiberglass over the mesh. (Courtesy Aladdin Products)

it simply slides off onto the floor. The most obvious way to prevent this is to balance the weight of the material by cutting strips that reach from the sheer on one side over the keel to the sheer on the other side. Platt favors this in combination with cutting and fitting the entire laminate of several layers of mat on a small boat, with each piece butted to the next and the butts of each layer staggered relative to the other layers. When the layers are assembled on the boat, they can all be wet out at once. Wetting out a number of layers at once is an advantage not often enjoyed in fiberglass work. In this case, because the mesh is open, there is no air entrapment to form bubbles, which have to be forced out through the top layers when you laminate against a solid backing. With careful fitting and a temporary cover of 18-inch strips of cheesecloth or similar material, or a final layer of fiberglass cloth, Platt claims you can roll out a beautifully fair surface that will need minimal cosmetic treatment. I tend to believe it, for we have done the same thing with a gauzelike mat called finishing mat.

Another method of preventing the glass materials from sliding off the mesh is to lay on athwartship pieces of woven roving as described for the mat above, but in a single layer, and wet them out with resin. Once the resin has cured, it's a normal fiberglass laminating procedure from then on. Due to the much greater area of surface to which the fiberglass can adhere, the material stays in place better than on the bare wire. As with any form-built laminate, some grinding of lumps and bumps between layers would be in order. Those who have gone this route forewarn that the roving will try to bridge hollow garboards, as the lower portion tries to slip down and pull the part over the hollow up off it. Careful attention with the roller until the resin gels will keep the hollow shape. Those who have used the mesh also admit candidly that it does not always wish to conform or lie fairly in

A slick layer of fiberglass woven roving over the mesh. (Courtesy Aladdin Products)

strong concave curves like the flaring bows of some powerboats. Sometimes it helps to have a piece of wire running vertically, stapled in over the mesh, and closer-spaced stringers, too.

Platt's other product, Fer-a-lite, is a mixture of polyester resin with a light aggregate—so light that the cured product floats. Platt developed it back in the 1960s as a more suitable material with which to plaster wire than the cement and heavy aggregates used in ferrocement hulls. When you know that, you finally realize how this particular inventor came to develop a one-off-in-fiberglass system based on wire mesh. Anyhow, Fer-a-lite is used to flush up the mesh on the inside when you leave the mesh in the hull. It is troweled over the interior and "scratch coated fair with the wires." The wire and Fer-a-lite thus become a steel-reinforced, medium-weight core backing up the outer layers. You can then add as many or as few inner-skin layers of fiberglass as the particular hull requires. The end result is a sandwich laminate with an extremely rugged core. "Steel-belted fiberglass," Platt likes to call it. What with its contribution of 105,000 to 150,000 psi (pounds per square inch) tensile strength and much greater stiffness to the structure, that's a good name for it.

However, you don't have to leave the Str-r-etch Mesh in the hull. If you prefer, you can use it only to shape the hull, then rip it out with the rest of the form; and, as uneconomical as that seems, there is a school of thought that holds that you should, indeed, do that. The day Platt visited me he was a bit down in the mouth, having just called on a nearby prestigious fiberglass production plant where, he said, "What's-his-name threw me out."

"No kidding. Why?"

"He said steel and glass have different coefficients of expansion, and they shouldn't be mixed."

"Wow! How does he explain the old safety window glass with the wire inside of it?"

"Don't know. Anyhow, we've built a fair number of boats with Wire Plank,* Str-r-etch Mesh, Fer-a-lite, and fiberglass; and they're all standing up very well."

Time, of course, will arbitrate that difference of opinion. I, personally, wouldn't worry too much about the expansion and contraction of wires that are woven rather than straight. Nor do I worry much about the only other objection I've heard—that in time the mesh might rust. Sure, if it were close to the exterior under a porous coating, it might soon erupt with rust. But if well captured in Fer-a-lite and armored with at least two layers of chopped-strand mat on the other, I think it will be a long, long time before it begins to rust. What I might worry about, if anything, is the adhesion of the Fer-a-lite and/or the fiberglass layers to the wire. In other words, how well does the sandwich resist delamination under stress or bending or impact? Does the delamination tend to propagate (spread out), or is it confined to the locality ruptured? Here, Platt says, "Because of the rough texture (tooth) of Fer-a-lite, fiberglass bonds to it with no tendency to delaminate."

To that I would add the opinion that if chopped-strand mat is used against the Str-r-etch Mesh on the one side and against the Fer-a-lite on the other, you would optimize the grip of the inner and outer skins on their core. I think that Str-r-etch Mesh compares favorably with many other cores in general. Some of its physical properties are superior to those of others, and it is cheaper than all cores except perhaps wood. For these reasons, I sure hope to use it in a one-off or two someday.

As with other one-off systems, you can leave in the wooden stringers of the form as part of a Str-r-etch Mesh hull. After you trowel Fer-a-lite into the mesh between stringers, you cover both it and the stringers with the inner skin. This is easiest to do with longitudinal strips of the fiberglass materials that are narrow enough to include but one stringer. Otherwise, pushing the material into the corner against one stringer tends to pull it away from the stringer on the opposite side of the bay. Except on large stringers with softened corners, woven roving is difficult to use in the inner skin. Stringers add great strength and stiffness for the weight and the amount of material involved. There's also considerably less waste when you

---

Wire Plank is an earlier Aladdin product used to plank a form with 3½-inch-wide strips of mesh similar to Str-r-etch Mesh.

leave stringers in, not just because the material and labor in them are retained, but also because the hull strength they provide eliminates the additional materials and labor required to provide that strength another way.

Because it is necessary to cover its underside, I don't think there is much point in using Str-r-etch Mesh to start a one-off deck in place on any boat too big to turn upside down to do the inside work. On a small, open boat there should be no problem. But there are certainly better ways to build a deck in place on a big boat, although, here again, you could use Str-r-etch Mesh and Fer-a-lite to build a rugged core in a deck after you put down the inner skin another way. I'm also sure it would be an excellent material for starting a deck plug, for the interior of a plug is of no importance. But that's a matter for production, not one-off builders. No doubt, you could use it in the same way that you might use C-Flex or CVC, as the starting material in the unlined framework of a one-off deck mold. Although a molded deck built this way can't yield anywhere near the detail or the finish that a lined mold does, using Str-r-etch Mesh would be very quick and cheap. Therefore, it is probably worth considering in an uncomplicated deck.

To summarize the reports of those who have used it, Str-r-etch Mesh is a product with the truly unique ability to conform to compound curves while covering 3- or 4-foot wide swaths of a hull's sides in one piece. It is applied over a simple form quickly and it is inexpensive. When embedded in Fer-a-lite (or a similar filled or reinforced resin), it can be used to build a very rugged sandwich laminate as well.

The techniques of using Str-r-etch Mesh and Fer-a-lite to build one-offs are still being developed. However, the ways it is employed at present are efficient and competitive enough to make it a very attractive starting material on a form for a shapely one-off up to 30 or 40 feet.

7

WLP (Wood Left in Place)

A fiberglass one-off built over wood that is left in place combines a tough shell on the outside with the warmth and charm of wood on the inside. No other one-off system can satisfy as easily both the functional and aesthetic requirements of an owner fond of wood as this straightforward approach. The system is a natural for the builder more at home with wood than fiberglass; and some of its variations are lower in cost than any other system for a particular type of boat.

A variety of constructions is included under the designation WLP, if you'll pardon my acronym. The wood that is left in place can range from an entire wooden boat to a thin shell of planking or decking limited to certain areas. Also, wood can be left in and covered with an inner skin to become the core of a sandwich construction. A great number of one-offs, and a scatter of production models, too, have been built with WLP over the past 30 years. The popularity of the method peaked in the latter half of the 1960s and receded to a rather low ebb by the end of the 1970s. In my opinion, the system fell from grace because time and the marine environment revealed a serious mistake many builders made: the imposition of an inadequate fiberglass laminate on an often more than adequate wooden structure. Perhaps because they were wooden-boat oriented and unfamiliar with fiberglass, builders tended to build a self-supporting wooden structure covered with only a thin fiberglass skin. They simply didn't realize that a thin skin on a relatively heavy wooden boat is doomed to eventual failure. In 5 to 10 years, you could find most of these skins fractured and weeping somewhere on the boat, and too many of them actually split open or peeling off.

WLP (Wood Left in Place) 107

A Frers-designed WLP ocean racer. WLP is often a good choice for a one-off ocean racer. This one had a triple-diagonal cedar hull and double-diagonal deck, fiberglass covered. With neither enough glass nor fastenings—per owner instructions—the glass came off and had to be replaced within a year! The company that gave the owner those instructions made good, thank goodness! (Milton Sylvia photo)

At this point, I could launch into an entire book about how to cover what is essentially a complete wooden boat with fiberglass; but you are spared, because I have already done so. *Covering Wooden Boats with Fiberglass*, published by International Marine, tells how to cover old boats as well as new ones with a shell that will stay in place indefinitely. Throughout the book, the reader is implored not to use too little fiberglass, not to expect a layer or two of fiberglass cloth to do anything worthwhile for any boat weighing over a few hundred pounds, and always to fasten fiberglass and wood together mechanically. These concepts are crucial to an enduring union of the two materials, and you will find them stressed in this book, too. But since this chapter has to include an overview of all of the variations of WLP, a reader interested in building mostly with wood can find many more useful details, including a step-by-step description of how to cover a boat that is right side up, in *Covering Wooden Boats*.

WLP-LINED, SINGLE-SKIN FIBERGLASS CONSTRUCTION

One WLP one-off construction that is quite the opposite of the mostly wooden boat is a boat in which only a wooden skin is left on the interior for livability, but not for structural reasons. To build a hull with such a wood-lined interior, you would need only a set of moulds, a male transom mold, and suitable centerline or backbone members. You would plank these with the lining wood, over which you would lay up the fiberglass hull. Nonferrous nails hammered into the moulds make the quickest fastenings for WLP, because you can clip them off and grind them down or lay them over with a nail-set after you remove the moulds. However, screws into the lining through cleats on the moulds from inside the hull make the neatest job; for if you bore only the cleats, the wood will close up after the screws are removed, leaving barely a trace. For this, small-gauge screws with sharp threads are best. I have never tried it, but I think that if the lining were not too recalcitrant it might be banded into place with some strong nylon packaging tape. It sure would be a pleasure to release moulds from the hull with nothing more than a sharp knife. Anyway, the number of temporary fastenings needed is reduced the more bulkheads you set up in lieu of moulds. Putting in the bulkheads when you set up the form saves labor by eliminating mould construction. It has the additional dual advantage that you can fasten the bulkheads to the hull as you fasten its lining to them and you can add fastenings through a number of layers of the laminate into the bulkheads, or, better, into cheekpieces around their edges.

The spacing or number of moulds and bulkheads needed depends on the thickness or stiffness of the WLP and is best determined by trial. If still in doubt after trying a piece on two blocks, you can nail four blocks to the floor at the station spacing of the plan and fasten a plank or two over them. Pushing (for small boats) or treading on the planks (for big boats) between the middle blocks quickly tells whether or not the spacing is viable. For a fair test, you should fasten the planks and make the middle blocks an inch or so higher than the end blocks to give the planks a little curve, such as most of them will have on the boat.

A way to get around changing the mould spacing is to adjust the thickness of the lining stock so that it is not too limber. Still another is to use an occasional cleat or short piece of temporary rib in the middle of a bay where the planks' edges tend to get out of alignment.

It is not a good idea to use very wide pieces of lining or to jam them too tightly together. If you do, and they get damp (or wet) and swell up, they will have nowhere to go and will surely buckle out into the interior. In an extreme case, like prolonged flooding of the interior, some of them might tear themselves off the fiberglass despite the mechanical fastening to it that I am about to urge on you. The harder woods are more prone to do this than softwoods; for although they shrink and swell more slowly, their width changes more, and being less compressible, they build up tremendous pressure. One provision for the possibility of swelling, which also makes the interior better looking, is to V the joints by beveling the edges and rounding the inboard corners of the planks so that only the outboard edges are touching. The other provision, implied above, is to use relatively narrow planking, which minimizes the amount each piece will move and increases the number of seams to take up that movement.

Aside from swelling, a good reason for using relatively narrow planks is to avoid some of the labor of spiling and fitting. Not that there's anything wrong with planking the boat just as you would any wooden boat. Such properly lined and spiled planking looks right because it is right. However, narrow strakes can be edge set (bent edgewise) more, which allows much quicker and easier fitting. After all, these planks are not structural, and any method of "hanging" them on the form that comes out looking good is fair play. If you make up a standard pattern for narrow strakes with one straight edge and the "diminution curve" on the other edge, you can use it to lay out most of the strakes between the sheer and the sole, be it cockpit or cabin. Diminution is the amount that the width of the strakes diminishes toward each end of the boat, where there is less girth to cover than amidships. You find it by dividing the side of the hull into a number of full-length strakes of the width wanted amidships. For example, if you decide to use 20 planks 4 inches wide to plank in 80 inches of the boat's side (sheer to sole) amidships, you might find that halfway to the bow the width of the area to be covered is 60 inches, calling for each of the 20 planks to be 3 inches at that point. If the area's width at the last place where you can measure it vertically toward the bow is 50 inches, the planks should each be 2½ inches wide there. In normal planking procedure, you would spile one edge of each plank to fit against the preceding plank, then set off the diminution widths from the spiled edge, and run a batten through the points to mark out the other edge of the plank.

The shortcut I proposed above, making a pattern with one straight edge and the diminution curve on the other, is one often used to shape the ceiling in wooden boats; and I have used it on the strips of strip-built boats, too, when I didn't want the strips running off the boat at the sheer. If the hull's lines are reasonably easy, you can cover large fractions of its girth with identical planks like this, sometimes the whole side. But obviously, this capability depends upon their width, as width determines how much you can bend the planks, and their pattern, to fit the curves that develop on the working edge as you go. To take full advantage of your pattern, you should flop it over on your planks so that either the curved side will fit into a hollow situation or the straight side will bend around a bulging edge. Further, as the curve in the working edge gets more hollow or bulging, you can bend the pattern edgewise to favor the shape the plank must take, before tracing it on the plank. You should start at the sheer of most hulls and work toward the bottom. When the shape of the sheer strake is extreme, as in the flaring, round bow of some motorboats, you may have to work out of the wild "powderhorn" shape before you can use a pattern to advantage. Anyway, because you certainly will not want this wood lining below the sole and will not see much of it at one time below berth or locker tops in most interiors, you need only a handsome plank line partway down the hull. Once out of the highly visible topside area, you can use "stealers" (wedge-shaped planks), "half-moons," or "hourglasses" to straighten out the plank line. And when you get to the areas that won't be WLP, you won't have to be told, I'm sure, not to worry about anything but getting them "boarded up," as long as the surface is fair. You should wax these planks that are coming out heavily. You should not fasten the fiberglass to them, of course, as I will insist you do to the WLP portion.

Except in the shortest boats, you are going to have to make up each strake with two or more lengths of planking. A butt joint is the simplest, and if V'd slightly on the interior, probably the best looking. You should hold the butts with temporary butt blocks, using screws from the inside through the block into the planks. Butting planks on moulds is not a good idea, as it usually results in the surfaces meeting at an angle. The fore-and-aft length of the butt block and its fastenings are what keep the ends of the planks meeting in a fair line. Of course, you can get a fair joint with glued scarfs, made up on or off the boat. However, scarfs take a lot more time, even when made with power tools, and they are hardly necessary when the wood is not structural.

The seams of the planking can be puttied to keep resin from drooling through them; but it is much quicker to cover them with narrow masking tape or Scotch tape. As mentioned above, any planks that you want to remove should be heavily waxed, including all wood from some point below the sole down, under the engine and its beds, and possibly a strake or two at the sheer if there is a deck joint in the topsides or if interior tabbing of the deck at side is called for. It is also an excellent precaution to coat the wood that will be left in place with a wood preservative like clear Cuprinol on the outside or all over. But where the wood is open to the air on one side and can "breathe," there is no more reason for it to rot than any wood inside a boat. In the long run, the most important precautions are to provide good ventilation and to prevent freshwater (deck) leaks.

I haven't mentioned which varieties of wood might be most appropriate for WLP because it is mainly a matter of personal taste. If the wood is to be painted, fine-grained woods are best. If left bright, it's a matter of what grain you like to look at, what's available, and its cost. The illumination of the interior is also an important consideration when choosing a wood finish. One venerable belief is that after hours in the brilliant light of seascapes, a dark interior is restful to the eyes. The opposite viewpoint is that a light interior is more cheerful and less claustrophobic. There's no question that a preponderance of dark wood like African mahogany absorbs so much light that it makes a dark interior, that lighter woods like pine and cedar bounce the light around a little more before absorbing it, or that white paint makes the most of whatever light there is. The question is what combination of these factors makes you most comfortable. And I'm glad to leave it up to you with but a few of my own opinions tossed in.

I think "satin-finish" or "rubbed-effect" varnishes show wood off better than hard, glossy types and protect it better than plain oil. I find off-whites much more compatible with wood than plain white. Having been involved with the building of hundreds of custom boats and having spent time in hundreds more, both before and after the advent of the all-teak look-alikes, I remember being just as charmed by some interiors finished in eastern pine, cedar, Philippine or Honduras mahogany as I have been by some finished in butternut, walnut, bird's-eye maple, African mahogany, or teak. I've seen a number of delightful interiors, mostly on big, old power workboats or schooners, done in fir (staving, not plywood) and yellow pine, too. From these observations, I am led to believe that it's not so much what wood you use as how you use it. I am also sorely tempted to question who knows how to use lumber anymore, but it wouldn't be fair. After all, when I first started working in boatyards, a boatbuilder didn't have to be a gentleman and a scholar, but he did have to be a judge of good lumber, because in most boats that was the whole ball game.

While you are laying up the fiberglass hull, you should not forget to fasten the wood and fiberglass together mechanically. Sure, the resin will stick the first layer to the wood. It's also true that most of the wood couldn't move far if it did break loose, being held in place by the bulkheads and all the joinerwork. If the wood extends to the ends of the boat, it is also locked in by the "toggle effect" of being bent around against the inside of the hull. As the middle of a plank tries to move inboard, it straightens out and tries to grow longer; so if neither end can move, the middle won't go far. Still, despite the most favorable conditions, the wise approach to every union of wood and fiberglass is to add mechanical fastenings. On all but the smallest boats you should make the first two layers of the laminate a layer of 1½-ounce mat and a layer of 18- or 24-ounce roving and mechanically fasten these layers to the WLP. This will give the laminate an excellent hold on the wood. Staples are the best fastening for this, as they are cheap and can be quickly applied in great numbers, especially with a power stapler. But flathead nails or screws are good, too, as long as they are applied fairly close together. Galvanized fastenings are all right; since they are totally buried in wood and fiberglass, they should last indefinitely. Yet stainless-steel fastenings of all kinds are very cheap today and well worth the slight difference in cost. I do not recommend nonferrous fastenings with smooth shanks in this use because they slide out of the wood too easily; but bronze screws and ring nails (like Anchorfast) have excellent holding power. Due to the flexibility of fiberglass, you should space the fastenings no farther than 2½ inches apart in a small boat and 5 inches apart in a big boat.

You should not forget to put some fastenings of appropriate size and length into the bulkheads, too. These will hold better the more layers of laminate lie under their heads. At the same time, you don't want fewer than two layers of mat over the heads of such fastenings, which penetrate all of the other layers. Perhaps you are wondering why I don't also recommend more layers under the fastenings of the inner skin to the WLP. I would just as soon see that. Experience has shown, however, that with the closely spaced fastenings for laminates thinner than ¼ inch on heavy wood, or for wood thinner than ¾ inch on heavy laminates, two layers, one of mat and one of roving, are enough. Two layers are also the most you can expect to lay up before they turn too hard to fasten without drilling. Not only does drilling for so many fastenings mean an exponential increase in man hours, but any other fastenings with holding power equal to that of staples are more expensive.

Admittedly, it is not especially dangerous for this particular kind of WLP and the fiberglass to part company. By definition, you would still have a sound fiberglass boat around you if all of the WLP got loose from it. Nevertheless, any plank that someday got detached would be an annoyance; and living with a number of them would be downright depressing until they were reglued with epoxy, 3M's Scotch Seal #5200, or some other high-grade product. So why not head off the possibility with mechanical fastenings?

As long as this ceiling or lining type of WLP is nonstructural, you should follow the same laminate schedule you would if it wasn't there. But to back down just a bit from this position, it is obvious that relatively thick WLP adds considerable stiffness and strength to the hull (or deck). You might wish to use thick WLP because it doesn't require spacing moulds closer than the stations, it makes the attachment of interior joinerwork easier, it increases heat and sound insulation, or simply because it is sometimes less trouble, cheaper, and less wasteful to use an available thickness than to mill it to an arbitrary dimension. When such practical factors indicate relatively stout WLP, then you might also want to adjust your boat's total weight (and expense) by deducting some layers of fiberglass from the laminate in the WLP area. To get a handle on how many, I would compare the thickness of the planking of a similar carvel-planked wooden boat to the thickness of the WLP. Then, if the WLP exceeded half the thickness of wooden planking, I would feel secure removing up to one-fourth of the fiberglass reinforcement by weight. I would not remove more than one-third of the glass in any case where there were neither the ribs nor the frames of a wooden version, but only a few bulkheads doing the work of ribs. I would also be inclined to substitute unidirectional roving aligned normal (at 90 degrees) to the planking seams for some of the woven roving in the remaining laminate. This glass orientation would provide a greater proportion of fiberglass strands acting as ribs. There you have a boatbuilder's approach to such questions—somewhat unscientific, of course. But I always say, "First come the designers and builders; then come the graphs and tables explaining them."

In a single-skin fiberglass hull with a WLP interior, it is a bit tricky to give joinerwork a good grip on the wood, or, through it, on the fiberglass hull. You must depend on relatively short screws into the WLP only, for such screws cannot be expected to take hold of the single skin of any boat less than 45 to 50 feet long without protruding too far out into the outer surface layers. Nor would you want to use through-fastenings (bolts or rivets) except for an item as local and important as a chainplate. But if the WLP is at least ½ inch thick, screws that go just about through it will hold well enough. You can also use glue behind any wood screwed to the WLP.

Should the WLP be too thin for screws, you can resort to fiberglass tabbing the joinerwork after setting it up with whatever tacking, hot glue, or shoring you need to hold it there. Although tabbing runs counter to the philosophy of WLP, you can often place the majority of it where it will not be seen without opening doors or hatches. In exposed areas you can cover it with wood trim, which, if done right, gives the WLP and joinerwork a paneled effect. As you might know, I'm going to advise you to fasten the tabbing to the wood mechanically. Put on some layers, fasten them, and cover the fasteners' heads with another layer or two. If you worried that the WLP is too thin for fastening the tabbing securely, you can bore an occasional hole through it with a hole saw to expose the fiberglass of the hull, fill these holes up flush with disks of saturated mat or a putty of resin and glass fibers, then lay up your tabbing over them. Hooked to the hull with these fiberglass buttons, it won't be inclined to let go. Similarly, I have also bored holes right through the "half bulkheads" of the joinerwork, and main bulkheads too, and filled them with fiberglass to anchor their tabbing, in lieu of using mechanical fastenings. When tabbing on both sides of a bulkhead is fastened right through it with fiberglass buttons, the bulkhead is locked to the hull as well as if you had used a chain and chain binder.

Anyway, in the long run, a good connection of interior joinerwork right through to the outer skin could make the difference between an interior that begins to loosen up or come apart in a decade or so and one that remains sound as a nut for the indefinite future. Fiberglass is a relatively flexible material, and it is always "working" on anything more rigid that is attached to it, like a dog on a leash. Your job as a builder is to see that it doesn't get away. As a surveyor, I can tell you that on innumerable production boats it has.

WLP–FIBERGLASS SANDWICH CONSTRUCTION

I would not want to give the impression that WLP is for single-skin hulls or decks only. If you want wood on the interior of a sandwich construction, there are good reasons to use WLP as starting material on the form, just as you would for a single-skin one-off. Fitting and installing the wood is no more difficult on the outside of the form than it is working in the interior of the upright boat. The fastenings into it from the laminate will not show. WLP takes the place of the stringers needed on the form to support the core material; and you save time laying up the inner skin directly on the outside of the WLP, rather than on the interior of the core after turning the hull.

The schedule of a WLP fiberglass sandwich one-off is a straightforward building procedure:

1. Install WLP planking on the moulds and bulkheads.
2. Lay up the inner skin of the sandwich.
3. Cut and fit the core, and set it in wet mat.
4. Lay up the outer skin.
5. Pull out the moulds and any temporary sections of the WLP.

It should be obvious that this procedure is not only good for building hulls, but even more attractive for building a sandwich deck or trunk top in place on an upright hull. Here, everything is happening with the full cooperation of gravity and with a minimum of wasted time and materials. What you get is a wood-lined overhead, with deckbeams left in place if you wish, that is light in weight, strong as a mill floor, well insulated, watertight, and just about maintenance free for long, long periods. What more could anyone ask?

Whereas it is very simple to weight down almost any type of core material on a deck, the weights on an upside-down hull want to slide off or cause the core to slip down. You can get around this problem when the core is a floppy type, like balsa blocks on scrim or scored PVC, by draping chain or "saddlebags" of weights strung on light line over the keel. Pieces of thin board or plywood (well waxed or set in Mylar) can be used to distribute the pressure of the weights. However, the weights can be eliminated, if you want to fasten these "pressure plates" right through the core into the inner skin and WLP with temporary screws. You can also fasten stiffer core and core replacement materials directly this way, and there is little reason to remove the fastenings from them. This is another advantage of WLP in a one-off; you have it everywhere under the laminate to accept or at least hide the tips of any fastenings you wish to use.

Whatever the means you contrive to put pressure on the core, be assured that what you are doing is of utmost importance. Delaminated core is the most common fault found in fiberglass sandwich construction, and is very often caused by poor contact of the underside of the core with the layers on which it is placed. In moulded boats, the underside is the side toward the mold or against the outer skin; whereas in form-built boats, the laminate of which starts with the inner skin, it is the side toward the form or against the inner skin. Equally important to pressure is ample resin—well laced with glass fibers—to glue the core to the underlying laminate. This requirement is best fulfilled by pressing the core into a layer of mat freshly wet out. Pressure forces the resin into the surface of the core and at the same time brings the fibers of the mat into close contact with both laminate and core. If the surface on which you're fitting the core is very uneven, you can make it two layers of wet mat; but there should not be much unevenness in the inner skin of your sandwich one-off at this early stage. It is still another advantage of WLP that you can outboard join it to near perfection, if you want, before laying up the inner skin. Any bumps related to fiberglassing are easily knocked off with a grinder before setting the core.

One last word of caution about setting core materials: you should watch out for excessive heat buildup. The high insulation or R factor of balsa and PVC, especially of PVC, combined with that of the WLP on the other side of the curing resin slows the dissipation of its "exothermic" heat. This heat (given off by curing resin) can build up to the point where the resin "cooks" itself. Resin that has cooked from overheating has the look and strength of butterscotch candy (but hardly its taste; in fact, it has a very acrid odor). In other words, it becomes so brittle it is worthless. You should, therefore, use a "cool" or slow-curing "shot" of catalyst in the resin wherever insulating materials will trap the exothermic heat of cure. The likelihood of overheating a single layer of saturated mat over a cured inner skin that has gone cold, in normal ambient temperatures and with moderate resin catalysis, is not great. But some combination of an extraheavy wet mat bedding, an inner skin that is still giving off heat, a hot day (or strong sunlight on the boat), and/or a "hot mix" could get you in trouble.

So much is said elsewhere in this book about laying up and finishing off the outer skin, which is like the outside layers of all form-built one-offs, that we will skip the subject here. Likewise, installing joinerwork against WLP in a sandwich fiberglass hull should be no problem. Here, tapping screws of generous length through the WLP and inner skin will anchor the work securely.

OTHER WLP ONE-OFF CONSTRUCTIONS

There seem to be few WLP one-off constructions that lie between those in which the WLP is virtually a lining in a fiberglass hull and those in which it is virtually a complete wooden boat with a fiberglass covering. Most builders seem to lean toward one or the other. However, there is one WLP system that in its most common form could be called either a one-off wood-core fiberglass sandwich or a fiberglass-covered wooden construction. According to this system, you build the hull and/or deck with strip planking on moulds, or within them, then cover the resulting shell on both sides with fiberglass. At one time, this was thought to be a stunning breakthrough: a low-cost way to build a "composite" wood/fiberglass boat that is strong, durable, and easily maintained. It is well suited to one-off building in that a minimum of form construction is required; semi-production is simply a matter of reusing the moulds and full production is a matter of tying the form together so that it remains in one piece while a succession of parts are built on

On the following pages:
Centennial's *hull is built atop her deck, which is still upside down in its mold. (Centennial's deck construction is illustrated in a series of photographs in Chapter 2.) The hull of this leeboard ketch was built with fiberglass laminations over a WLP plywood core, which had to have darts cut out of it to achieve the hull's compound curves. The boat's shallow keel and hull shape and her heavy construction enable her to take the beach with ease. She has performed without incident since 1980. (Loy photos)*

Lofting Centennial. *The lofting took place on the floor of an unfinished shed.*

Hull form moulds sit on the loft floor. The stock used was ship-lap pine obtained at a bargain price from the local lumber yard.

A hull mould inside the upside-down doghouse.

Inside the hull form. Shown are the moulds, the stringers, and the inner of two ¼-inch layers of plywood fastened to the stringers. The inner face of the plywood is precovered with fiberglass mat that is pigmented white to save interior work.

Inside the hull form. Those stringers will have to be pulled out from between the bulkhead and the bottom. Then a strip of Airex foam can be inserted into the gap before tabbing the joint with fiberglass.

Looking up into the keel recess inside the hull form. Note the sticks around the upright piece. These will make disassembly easier when the moulds are taken out. They represent the thickness of the stringers, which, it was decided, were not needed to support the three straight panels of the box-shaped keel.

The prefabricated, WLP, boxlike outboard well was fitted up into the hull form through the deck mold, so that the hull's WLP bottom could be fitted and fastened over it. The crack visible in the rim of the circular opening is the centerline joint of the first layer of the hull's WLP plywood.

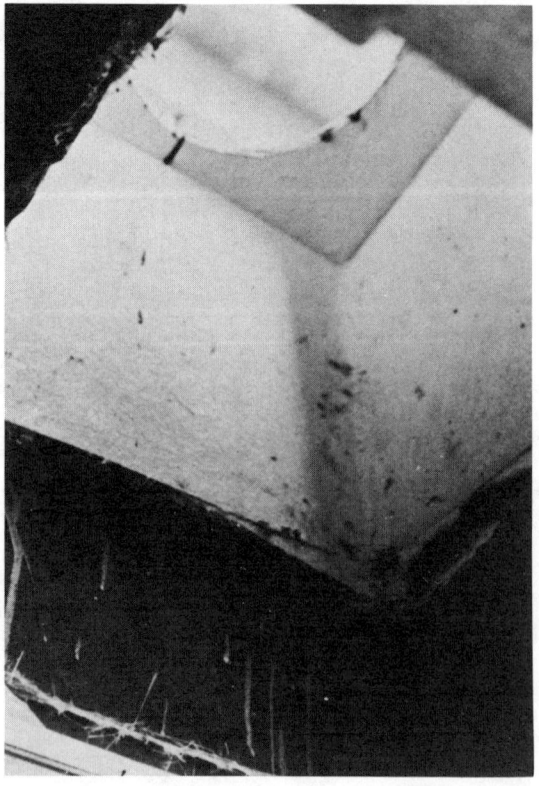

WLP (Wood Left in Place) 119

The bottom in the raw, showing the keel, outboard well, and skeg. Not readily apparent are the hull's compound curves, which required that darts be cut in the plywood.

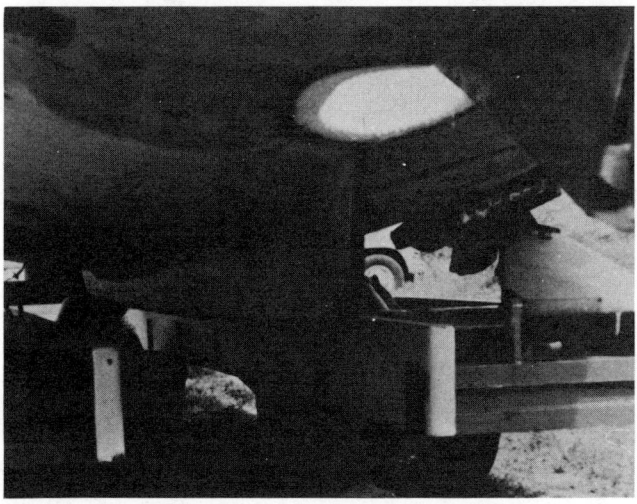

The bottom after turning the boat right side up.

The outboard well, after turning the boat upright. Reinforced with wood, it is covered around the top with fiberglass. It has been tabbed to the bottom around its outside, but not yet on the inside.

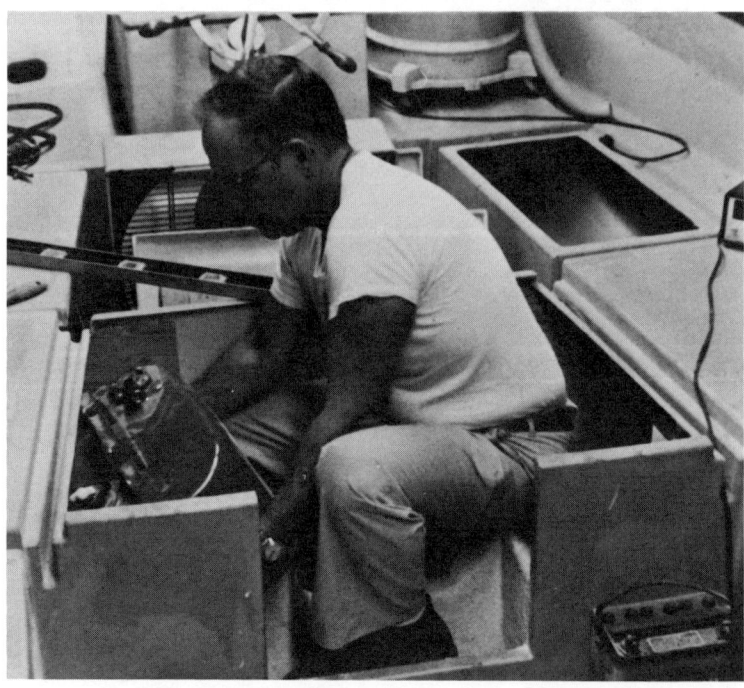

The plan called for a gas tank stored each side of the outboard-motor well. The gentleman has his right foot in the motor well and his left foot in the slop well. To his left and right are the forward and after cockpit tubs.

Covering over the keel, which was solid-filled with a layer of reinforcing rods, then lead pigs, surrounded by resin and chopped glass fibers (see Chapter 11).

Interior fiberglassing of the hull to seal the pre-covered plywood sheets and add more strength to the inner skin. Cover the sides first, lapping over onto the bottom to strengthen the chine.

it. Such a permanent form, sometimes shod with metal at its wear points, is traditionally called a mandrel in wooden-boat building.

The theory was at one time that relatively inexperienced, lower-paid workers could edge nail and glue together strips of less-than-top-grade lumber to create what has long proven a stout structure. This core was then "sheathed" on both sides with a minimal laminate of "the expensive stuff" to make it still stronger, watertight, and easy to maintain. Unfortunately, it seems that many boats so built did not stand up long in service. In those I have seen, the troubles were due to water penetration of the thin sheathing, which was sometimes fiberglass-reinforced polyester resin, but often polypropylene, Xynol, or even Dynel; and the resin was often epoxy rather than polyester.

In the heyday of this construction, I found myself one of the few dissenters from its practice, although not from the general idea. Today, paradoxically, I find myself again among the minority who advocate essentially similar systems, although I must add that I only recommend such when combined with the practice of using a relatively thicker laminate that is mechanically fastened to the wood.

Certainly no known construction is more rugged and durable for its cost of materials than nailed and glued strip planking, especially with fiberglass on both sides. But when the cost of highly skilled professional boatbuilding labor is reckoned in, any number of other constructions yield as good or better boats for the money. If you have ever built with strips, you'll know what prompts that statement. Strip building is slow, slow, probably the most tedious method devised since log canoes were hollowed out by burning. Down east, where eastern pine and "casual" labor are plentiful and reasonably priced, there is still some strip building as I write this. If these builders give their boats stout skins of mechanically fastened-on fiberglass, it could go on for the indefinite future. But if a poor grade of lumber laced with untreated incipient rot is used and/or the boats are only thinly covered, then history could easily repeat itself.

Akin to strip-built is double-diagonal WLP. The main differences are that double diagonal requires stringers on the form, but fewer hours spent planking, and much fewer spent outboard joining or smoothing the surface before applying the fiberglass laminate. When plywood is used for the diagonal planking, the amount of outboard joining is reduced to nothing more than superficial sanding of "proud" seams. Due to its greater stability, plywood doesn't "cup" or "hump" as much as natural wood does when subject to changes of ambient moisture. For that reason we took to using plywood almost exclusively for the double-diagonal planking of temporary, or short-run, female molds at my shop.

Let me interject that I do not recommend the planking of cold-molded wooden boats with stripped-up plywood when they are not reinforced with fiberglass. Years ago I checked that out by making up some cold-molded samples with plywood and some with natural wood, which I tested by dropping weights on them. Not only was the natural wood much more resistant to impact, but those samples with only two or three layers of natural wood, as few as the bends of the

Above: Scoter, *a WLP, double-cabin, tandem-centerboard, diesel auxiliary, round-bottomed Alden ketch. The only uncovered wood was in the trim and spars.* **Left:** *The photo shows a layer or two of laminate over Scoter's double-diagonal fir-plywood planking.*

hull would allow, were stronger for their weight than those with many thin layers. As I remember, my demonstration didn't convince some designers, who were, to my horror, specifying triple-layer plywood planking on some big, high-speed craft; but I expect a collision with something solid may have swayed them by now.

Despite my belief that stripped-up plywood is inferior to natural wood in that use, I do not hesitate to recommend it, especially in sheet form, as a core between substantial skins of fiberglass that are mechanically fastened to it. Plywood is certainly much stronger and less problem prone than balsa core. It isn't as much heavier as you might think either, for it takes a heavy saturation of balsa with resin to develop an enduring bond to fiberglass. The secret of longevity for all wood-product cores in fiberglass is to encapsulate them thoroughly to keep air and water from them. There are literally hundreds of thousands of fiberglass boats of all sizes and ages around that have transoms, if not several other parts like engine beds, with plywood cores. I have never seen one such item in any trouble, except when the surrounding fiberglass had lost its watertight—and therefore air-, or more specifically, oxygen-tight—integrity.

Anyway, the most common practice is to fasten the planking to some or all of the stringers permanently and leave them in place in a cold-molded boat. Because this makes covering the inside an onerous job, you will probably prefer to cover only the outside. That's just fine, as long as you use a relatively thick, mechanically fastened outer skin. You can do the same with a strip-built boat, or any other self-sufficient wooden construction. Here, we have come full circle to the boat that is built as a wooden boat and fiberglass covered. As mentioned at the outset, a number of production builders and some custom builders, too, have specialized in building wooden boats of various traditional constructions covered with fiberglass. Many of these were plywood-planked chine boats, for it was discovered early on that sheet plywood was stable enough to retain the thin coverings then in vogue fairly well. Most of these builders used but a layer or two of glass cloth because it could be easily filled and quickly brought to a slick finish. Had they used the thicker, rougher mat and roving laminate their boats really needed, the cost of finishing would have been several times greater. However, the repair-free life expectancy of the covering, and therefore of the boats, would have increased in proportion to the increased thickness of the laminate, if not faster.

Should you prefer to build a one-off wooden boat and then make it a WLP fiberglass one-off with a stout covering, you can do it with just about any known wooden construction. No one is likely to object if you continue to call it a wooden boat, either, despite its fiberglass clothing. Just a few more words of advice for those who don't care to read yet another book, the one I wrote on the subject:

1. Carvel planking, particularly if it is one of the harder woods, should not be too wide, too tightly fitted, or drier than (outdoor) air dried. Despite the fact that a good laminate will not let water into it, the planking is bound to get wet sooner or later, or at least very, very damp, in the marine environment. This is to say that it is bound to swell and must have somewhere to go. It should also have seams, and

The owner of this Colvin-designed ketch wanted us to finish her, starting with the strip-built hull. After a look at the work his house carpenter pick-up crew had done, I told him she should be a WLP fiberglass boat if he wanted her to be fit for extended cruising, and he agreed. Heavily covered with fiberglass, she has been a fine boat since the 1960s.

they should be puttied only with a compressible material at the outside surface so that they are not prevented from closing.

2. The best protection for the wooden boat left in place is a continuous laminate, one with no breaks or gaps. The fiberglass on the trunk top should overlap or blend with that on the trunk sides, the sides with the deck, and the deck with the hull. That way, you have a wooden boat in a completely watertight envelope, and maintenance is minimized.

3. You can either carry your fiberglass around the wooden keel of an auxiliary and bolt the ballast on over it, or take the fiberglass right around the ballast, too. In the first case, the ballast keel will take the abuse of grounding, but its bolts will be exposed to corrosion. In the second, the bolts will be protected and their holding power will be supplemented by the fiberglass to the point where they become unnecessary, depending on its thickness; but the fiberglass itself will be more vulnerable in a grounding.

4. All through-hulls, bolted-on metalwork, guardrails, hardware, and trim should be installed *over* the fiberglass. There is no excuse for ending the laminate *at* any fitting on a new boat. Doing so is looking for future trouble. This means that when any fittings are to be installed flush with the surface, you should provide generous recesses in the wood that allow for the thickness of the laminate.

I could go on and on about WLP in all its variations, about my earliest fiberglass-sheathed cedar-on-oak dinghy, my most recent 32-foot sheet-plywood-cored sharpie hull, and other wood-lined, wood-cored, traditionally constructed or cold-molded WLPs built during the intervening 25 years. There were cruising boats to 47 feet and ocean racers to 45 feet, all built with some WLP arrangement. Then there were existing wooden boats, some with planks and ribs broken and bulging out, with tired fastenings, and with rusted-off boltheads lying in the bilge.

Now they enjoy reincarnation within a stout fiberglass outer skin. That's stretching the definition of a fiberglass WLP one-off, I know. It might give you an idea of how to get a good boat at a reasonable cost, however, so it's worth the reminder. Obviously, I have always been enthusiastic about WLP boats of all types. As one who spent the first half of his working days building wooden boats, I come by it naturally. I also happen to think that with the steady increase in the cost of petroleum products, it's a logical solution to combine wood with the expensive stuff. If you agree, please heed the lesson I learned the hard way: use enough fiberglass, well fastened to the wood, to withstand both the rough and tumble and the sneaky, seeping aspects of water. Water is the same stuff, you know, that has been eating mountains of solid rock for lunch since the Earth began.

8

A Boat From an Existing Boat

Just about the easiest way to build a one-off boat is to take it off an existing boat. If a boat of the model you want to build is available, it might be feasible to use that boat either as a male mold, or form, or as a plug for a female mold. Admittedly, having just the right boat for your intended use at hand is hardly the most common situation. More often there's something about an existing boat that's not quite the way a particular boatman would like to have it. Were it otherwise, the only use of this book would be to guide production builders in building prototypes. There are also built-in obstacles of size and complexity that make many boats, particularly sophisticated powerboats and auxiliaries, unsuitable subjects for this method. Nevertheless, you might indeed find a boat the lines and size of which are right for you, but one that is not laid out or rigged the way you want her, one that you can't buy because it's not for sale, or perhaps too derelict to resurrect.

If she still has her shape, or can be pulled together temporarily, a derelict is the ideal subject for this kind of one-off building. She should be obtainable for little or nothing, and once you own her you have complete freedom of action. However, getting a one-off from a boat in current use can be a rocky road, if not an impassable one. First, there's the matter of negotiating the use of her. I have rented the use of boats or have bartered with labor, such as a free refinishing job on the boat in question. Once or twice, covering the boat with fiberglass gave its owner a nice return, while it created an excellent surface for the female mold we took off his boat. Occasionally an owner bursting with enthusiasm for his boat has approached me and offered the use of it as a plug or male mold. So, although it might be impossible to arrange the use of some boats, it's surprisingly easy with others.

Obviously, as intimated above, the size and complexity of the subject boat influence both the likelihood of making a deal and the practicality of attempting to build a one-off from it. Even if you are willing to go so far as to drain tanks or remove engines, or to drain the oil, fuel, and water from them in order to turn her bottom up, the owner may quite understandably not want any part of it. Then there's the ballast keel on large sailboats, which makes turning them upside down tricky business at best and nearly impossible without powered equipment.

Under ordinary circumstances, the male-mold method—laying up the new boat directly on the outside of the existing one—is the most efficient. When you use this method, the one-off is bigger all over by the thickness of its skin than the boat over which it is laid up. This slight increase in size means nothing unless the boat is to be a racing boat, which must measure into a class. If the original boat is a one-design, the one-off must be identical to it to race in the class; thus the male-mold method is out. With other racing types, you can determine the effect of the difference in size only by running the one-off's measurements through the formula of the rule under which it would race. Anyway, if you must have an identical boat, you have to use the female-mold method.

Another reason to use a female mold is to transfer an exquisite finish to the one-off. Given a fine finish on a small existing boat, it might be cheaper, and for most of us more pleasant, to build a light mold than to try to re-create that finish. In addition, the mold has some value. I have never known a mold for a small boat to lie around long before somebody wanted to buy or rent it.

However, as the subject boat gets bigger, the cost of building a mold on it increases very rapidly. The mold for a boat twice as long as a given boat doesn't cost twice as much. It costs several times as much. The difficulty of recouping one's investment in a mold also seems to increase radically with its size. The bigger the mold, the fewer potential customers there are to be found with sufficient resources to tackle it. At some size or other, then, building a mold for a single boat becomes an exorbitant investment, despite the availability of a ready-made plug in the form of an existing boat. At that point, if you can't use the existing boat as a male mold either, you are better off not using it at all and going to another method. Nevertheless, "back molding," taking a mold off an existing boat, can yield the fairest, most accurate result, complete with a gelcoat finish, whenever it's affordable. A little farther on, I take up how to go about it. First, though, let's consider laying up the one-off directly over an existing boat.

THE MALE-MOLD METHOD

Done properly, laying up fiberglass over a boat, whether built of wood, fiberglass, or metal, will not harm the boat physically. There is a chance, however, that polyester resin will attack an applied finish. Some paints and varnishes, including some epoxy finishes, react with the resin or are dissolved by it. If this happens, the interface, the inner surface of your laminate and the outside of the existing boat, can become a gooey mess. Worse, the resin can cure after joining with the paint and become stuck to the existing boat—forever. It has happened, and it's a sorry business. Of course, it's also possible for a laminate to become stuck to a bare, unpainted surface, due to resin penetrating the protective coats of wax and/or sprayed-on release agent. But that is preventable with simple, well-known precautions. I don't wish to turn you away from considering the use of an existing boat, I only want to forewarn you that these things have happened when proper procedures were ignored.

The best test for the resin's reaction with the finish or possible sticking is to lay up a test patch of fiberglass on each surface that has a different finish. I can tell you now that most antifouling bottom paints have to be removed immediately either by washing with a solvent or by sanding, for they are quite soluble in resin. You can quickly check that by merely painting the bottom with some catalyzed resin, which will immediately blend with the paint through its porous surface. A less susceptible test area should be prepared with several coats of release wax, and perhaps a coat of PVA (polyvinyl alcohol), applied just as you would in preparing the entire mold. Then a 12-inch-square patch of fiberglass consisting of three or four layers of 1½-ounce or 1-ounce mat should be laid up on it, using generously catalyzed resin. The idea here is to simulate the worst condition likely to develop while laying up the whole laminate, that is, to build up as much concentration of resin, thickness of uncured laminate, and consequent heat of cure as is likely to occur during lamination. If this doesn't melt the wax and allow the resin to attack the underlying finish, it is not likely to happen when you apply a layer or two at a time and allow them to cure before you apply more, which is the proper way to start a laminate.

When the patch has cured, it should pop off the boat with a little light prying up at one edge. You can then see whether the laminate took anything more than mold release with it, or whether the boat's finish was affected in any way. If the finish tends to get involved with the resin, the wisest course of action is to remove it entirely.

There are other preparations of the existing boat and possible problems to solve that vary with its type and size. You may have hull appendages, struts, or a skeg and stern bearing, a rudder, and rudder hardware to remove. You may have through-hulls and strainers, too, although if the through-hulls are not too prominent, you could simply plug each with a flush plug, surround it with a tapered fillet of wax or putty, lay up your laminate over it, and fill in the shallow dent on the inside of your one-off hull later. You must remove spray rails and guardrails on the hull lest they lock the one-off hull to the existing hull. But you can leave a guardrail or rub strip along the sheer in place and mold it into the one-off as long as its configuration contains no undercuts. If, for instance, the rail is half round or half oval, you cannot carry your laminate past the most outboard point, for, from there up it returns inboard and loses its draft, making it impossible to part the one-off from the hull. However, you can build out the top half with a wedge of putty, or

When an existing boat is used as a plug for a one-off, it is best that the boat be upside down. If a boat is not stiff enough to rotate on pivots attached to stem and stern, you can build wooden wheels to fit around the hull and rotate them in greased troughs. Boats are turned in slings, too, but wheels require no lifting from overhead.

with wood hot-glued to the rail, making it straight faced from the middle up. Once off the existing boat, you can build up the inside of the rail and grind it to any shape you want.

The force of gravity and the fluidity of resin make it all but mandatory to lay up your one-off on an upside-down boat. Sure, if you are as stubborn and fascinated with "problem solving" as I have sometimes been, you can roll a boat down on one bilge and then the other and lay up each side of the one-off separately. Then you can prop up the two halves and join them down the middle. Done with a widespread, sufficiently thick joining laminate, there is nothing wrong with a boat so built. I have surveyed boats joined on the centerline, like the old American Boats' Block Island 40, more than 20 years after they were built and have found no trace of trouble in that area. Admittedly, I have found serious trouble along the centerline joint of boats half as old, too, but invariably these were badly built boats with trouble in other areas as well.

To build a boat joined on the centerline, you install a fence or stop of wood with one edge on the centerline of the hull, lay up the first half-hull against that fence, roll the boat the other way, remove the fence, and lay up the second half against the edge of the first along the centerline. You can screw the fence to a wooden boat or hot-glue it to fiberglass or metal. The fence should be well waxed, as well as the edge of the first half-hull, so that things don't stick together prematurely.

Of course, if the boat has draft, and if it is feasible to lift it clear of the one-off, you *can* build the one-off in one piece by overlapping and intermingling the layers from both sides. You can do this everywhere except areas where the blocking under the keel interferes, which you can fill in later.

Because it is relatively difficult to lay up fiberglass on a heeled-over boat, you don't need to complete the laminate. You need only to build up as much laminate thickness as can be propped up without distortion while being completed. The outer skin of a sandwich construction or not over one-half the total fiberglass thickness necessary in a single skin should be stiff enough to stand alone with supports judiciously located. Whenever the laminate is done in two stages, it is best to use the layers laid up on the male mold as the outer skin of the one-off, working on the principle that layers close to the mold are always fairer than the succeeding layers. The balance of the laminate can then be laid up on the inside with relative abandon. A one-off built that way is only bigger than the existing boat by the thickness of the outer layers laid up on it. You might therefore feel free to use a thicker sandwich core, or to add more bulky reinforcing layers to the outer skin, because they won't affect the lines of the one-off. The extra burden of building a one-off over an upright boat, then, is both alleviated and sweetened a little by laying up the more accurate outer skin only.

A one-off built over an upside-down existing boat is also fairest and most accurate if you lay up only the outer skin while on the boat and add on the balance of the laminate on the inside. For most boats, though, I do not think it worth the trouble, unless the subject model is a fine-lined, fine-tuned, high-performance craft. As I said before, you probably would not be able to detect the difference in performance between the original and a boat that is ½ inch bigger all over if a small boat, and not over 2 to 3 inches bigger if 30 to 40 feet in length.

How much fairing of the existing boat you should do, how much surface detail (or lack of it) will actually "telegraph" through to affect the fairness of your one-off's surface, is a matter you largely determine by your choice among the procedures discussed above. If you build a female mold, every bit of preparation of the existing boat is going to improve the one-off. Also, if you want a nicely prefinished interior on a one-off that is male molded from the innermost skin out, then you must fair and polish the existing boat's surface nicely. No doubt you will mess up the interior when tabbing joinerwork to it, especially in bigger boats. In spite of that, if large areas of the interior are to be left exposed in the finished boat, it is well worth your while to get them in shape on the male mold and apply gelcoat to them before starting the laminate. The more work of this nature you can avoid doing inside the boat, the better, always.

As far as the exterior surface of a male-molded one-off goes, only gross irregularities in the existing boat's surface will print through to it. In the laminating process, small depressions fill while projections are buried; and a sandwich construction obscures almost as much as a blanket of snow. This is to say that although a fair mold—the absence of extensive flat spots, angularity, or bulges—is still important, local roughness, smoothness, and any degree of polish all mean nothing after you lay up the first few layers. Just as with form building, in the end you have to create your own final exterior finish on a male-molded one-off. Aside from fairness and reasonable smoothness, how you come out on the one-off depends mostly on laminating techniques, which are discussed in Chapter 9 on hand layup procedure.

If the existing boat is an older boat with some shape problems—for instance, if the ends of a powerboat have fallen, giving it a hogged keel and bottom—you should adjust the shape before you mold your one-off. If you own the boat and she is all dry and loosened up, it may be possible to jack the hog out of her. Otherwise, you should fill it in. The quickest way to fill in a large hollow is to fill it in with glued-on lifts of polyurethane-foam board. The polyurethane variety of foam, widely sold as insulation board, is not attacked by resin; and its most common (2-pound) density is easily sawn, sliced with sharp cutting tools, and hand sanded into shape with coarse sandpaper on a block. You can hot-glue it on if you'd rather not make fastening holes in the existing boat. When any hollow or unfairness is shallow, building it up with a fairly stiff putty of filled resin is quicker.

When the existing boat is a derelict, it is best to do all of the fairing work right on the boat. Then, after you have restored the proper shape, you can cover any big, soft patches of foam with a binding coat of filled resin, a layer of fiberglass cloth, or, if you will be stepping on it, one of mat and one of cloth. Where other faired surfaces are porous, you can use a sealing coat or two of resin. When the surface of the existing boat must be protected, it is wiser to wax it up as it is, spray on mold release, put on the first two layers of the one-off's laminate, and, when these have cured, apply fairing putty over them. Because this fairing putty will become a part of the one-off's laminate, it should be made of chopped glass fibers and resin, or, if that is too heavy for the particular boat, of a light, tough putty like microballoons or microspheres. For very thick fairing without too much additional weight to the laminate, you can build in some PVC foam. Sometimes, where the unfairness is only faint hollows, raised plank edges, or angularity at plank seams associated with either broken ribs or loose fastenings, it is sufficient to build back fairness with patches of fiberglass mat during lamination. You can apply these at any stage of the lamination after the first two layers have cured. It is easier to see where a patch is needed early on, but less thickness is necessary as the laminate fills in the faults somewhat, especially when they are small in area. You should tear or comb the edges of the pieces of mat so that they taper out to nothing and shape the pieces to fit the contour of the depression in progressive larger or smaller sizes as required. Four or five layers at a time are enough. After these are cured and shrunk, and perhaps covered with ongoing layers of the laminate, you can tell whether and where more are needed. Thick putty also shrinks quite noticeably, often requiring a second application.

When the sheer of the existing boat is hogged, a common fault in older sailboats, you can either pad up the ends by adding wedge-shaped strips of wood or foam, or, if the boat can spare a bit of freeboard, glue on a stop that subtends the amidships hump to fair the sheerline. You should check the transom of a hogged wooden sailboat, for very often when the stern sags, the long, curved planks along the bottom of the stern, straightening out as the stern comes down, push the bottom of the transom out while the side planks hold its middle in, causing the transom to develop a hollow in profile. This is a sure sign that the stern has fallen. Typically, the shrinkage of your one-off laminate tends to assume a similar hollow; so you are well advised to build the existing transom out with a faint round in profile. One-sixteenth of an inch to the foot should come out just about right.

While on the subject, I should mention that a hollow entrance at the bow also tends to become more hungry in a one-off. This may be partly due to shrinkage, but it is accentuated by the good fiberglass boatbuilding practice of overlapping the layers from one side around the stem onto the other side. Such a doubling of the laminate thickness around the stem is important in the event of collision or striking submerged objects; and, of course, it doesn't affect the lines of a bow made in a female mold. Neither is it very noticeable on a full bow that is male molded or form built as long as each layer is overlapped 4 to 6 inches farther than the last. But on a bow with hollow lines abaft the stem, the overlap of each layer should be carried at least twice as far, lest the stem become bulbous and the hollow exaggerated.

The extra thickness may also cause a fine entrance to be too blunt at the stem. If you see this happening, you can run narrow strips of mat down the stem, keeping them narrower than its face, to draw it out finer. It is good to add on such layers between the layers that go around the stem, or to cap them with a couple of layers at the end. It is better if you can remember to anticipate too much width at the face of the stem before starting the one-off. Then you can glue on a piece of wood or foam that extends its taper to a very narrow face, which you will build back to the original width with the lamination. That will lengthen the boat a tiny percentage of its original length. So? It's already a tiny bit wider and deeper, too.

Another way to avoid ending up with a too-wide stem is to butt each layer to its counterpart on one side or the other, carrying alternate layers around the stem to a different location for each butt, then build up the extra thickness you need for strength on the inside of the one-off later. If you do elect to do that, lay up the internal reinforcing layers a few at a time and let them cure before adding more; for heavy shrinkage of this "breast hook" can pull the cheeks of the bow in, too.

Having hopped from transom to stem, let's skip aft again to the sternpost. As with the stem, the width added by the laminate can make the afterface of the sternpost too gross, both for the eye of the beholder and for the smooth flow of water. Once more, it would be nice to be working on a derelict. Then you could pick up your adz, or more likely nowadays a high-speed grinder with a very coarse disk on it, and work these parts down to the size and shape that, with the laminate added, would come out just right on the one-off. When the existing boat cannot be attacked like that, there is often enough room in the boat for you to rearrange the position of the one-off's rudder and/or propeller in order to extend the post aft some inches with a temporary fairing piece tapered to the needed fineness. When extending the post aft is not practicable, the hard way to get the right-sized post on the one-off is to lay up but a few layers on the post and the area just forward of it, then build up the thickness of the laminate desired on the inside after you remove the one-off from the existing boat. This is a mean area in which to work when the keel is deep and narrow, requiring long arms or long-handled tools, all sorts of contortions, and great patience to do it right. But if you build up enough wall thickness, you can even grind off some of the outside layers, until your one-off's trailing edges are as fine or finer than the original's.

Thick though a sandwich construction is, retaining the original shape of the stem with it is hardly more difficult than with a single skin. To switch from sandwich to a massive single skin around the stem, you stop the core just abaft the stem, then grind the forward end of it so that it tapers from full thickness a foot or two abaft the stem down to nothing along a line parallel to the face of it. You then build up alternate mat and roving around the stem and onto this tapered area until it fairs in as a continuation of the core's outboard surface. The inner skin plus more fiberglass as thick as the core material make an extremely rugged stem piece when the outer skin is added to it. Needless to say, you can butt all the layers of the outer skin to each other, rather than overlap them, and you might want to drop off some of them as they overlap this buildup.

For a lighter stem on a light sandwich-construction boat, you can build the core material right out past the stem, using the unscored sheet form of PVC foam, or softwood. It should be carried far enough to ensure a fine-enough entrance when you add the outer skin to it, whether you overlap or butt it.

Because the core of a sandwich construction should not be carried into the keel, you want to stop it at the "garboard seam" of your one-off, where the planking meets the keel of a wooden boat. If the keel is of the straight-sided, plank-on-edge type, you can simply butt the core against it. You should stop the core far enough away from a deep fin keel so that you can build up a solid laminate that carries the bending strains out into the hull, and you should taper the core in the changeover to a single skin. If the boat has "hollow garboards," the hull fairing down into the keel, you can stop the core just above that hollow curve, grind a long taper to a feather edge, build up a single skin from there down, which beefs up the area while fairing it, and then bring the outer skin down over the whole area onto the keel. The sternpost will not have an extra thickness problem due to the core. It can still be treated as for a single-skin one-off.

To keep the core of a sandwich-construction one-off out of the area along the sheer where you want to attach the deck to a single skin, you have to install a temporary, waxed batten or plank of wood or foam as thick as the core on the existing boat. You should bevel down the lower edge of this waxed sheer plank to the existing boat's hull, so that you can turn the inner skin out onto it smoothly. Then you can stop the core against the bevel, when its outer surface should come out flush with that of the inner skin–covered batten, so that the outer skin continues smoothly over all as it joins with the inner skin.

THE FEMALE-MOLD METHOD

Ordinarily, the plug on which a female mold is to be built should have all the careful fairing and polishing the builder can afford. A fine finishing job done here produces a fine finish almost automatically on each of the many boats that can be taken from a mold. But when you're making a mold essentially to get one boat, there are limits to the amount of labor you are wise to invest in the surface of an existing boat.

Sure, if you are starting with a smooth fiberglass or metal boat, you should polish it up and go for a highly polished mold and one-off. But if, for instance, the existing boat is an older wooden boat, its surface is likely to be quite unstable with seams cracking as it dries, puffing out as it swells, and the planks either rolling or curling. It is very difficult to get a mold from such a boat in which some imprint of the planking is not evident. The only sure way is to stabilize its surface with a layer or two of fiberglass. If you remember my mention of bartering a fiberglass-covering job for permission to take a mold off the boat so covered, you will note that the choice of payment was not entirely altruistic. Anyway, only if you have other paying customers for boats from your mold to share its cost is it justifiable to try for a perfect finish on an existing wooden boat. Better to take the mold from her after any needed fairing only, and do the fine cosmetic work on the stable surface of your one-off and perhaps some in the mold, too.

After you take a mold off an existing boat with surface flaws, you will save some labor if you sand down any bumps or protrusions in the mold. This is easier to do than filling up and/or sanding out the hollows or pits that protrusions leave in the one-off. Conversely, depressions in the mold are more difficult to deal with than the protrusions they create on the one-off, so it is better to leave them alone until they are reversed and can be sanded down.

Whether or not the existing boat is highly polished, it is worthwhile to use gelcoat for building the one-off, because gelcoat sands and polishes better than plain resin or most filled resin putties. I would not use it for the mold. It is expensive and will be wasted unless many boats are to be built. In fact, I still have a crude mold built off an old existing boat without gelcoat about 20 years ago. Although built specifically to make just four replicas, about 10 boats have been built in that mold over the years. Except for a rash of pits in the mold's surface, which makes a rash of tiny bumps to be sanded off on the ever-one-more-offs, it continues to make good boats. You only have to make sure that the gelcoat fills up the pits and then some, so you won't sand through it at the base of the bumps on the boat.

When you intend to build but one boat, or very few at most, it is most important to remember that you don't need a thick, strong mold. It's easy to get carried away with visions of entrepreneurial success and to put too much into a mold. Believe me, few people are going to beat a path to your door because you happen to have a mold for a lovely boat. The thickness of production molds ranges from half again to several times the thickness of a single-skin boat of that model. The mold of your one-off can be thinner than a boat—about three-fourths the thickness of its

Cardboard tubes were used to form the longitudinal reinforcing stringers on this mold taken off an existing boat. Yard goods are shipped on such tubes, and long, easily damaged items of hardware are shipped inside them, which means that store owners, who throw them away, are a good source. Note the rocker moulds.

topsides all over, not built up with extra layers on the lower hull and keel like the boat. Special "tooling" materials are used in production molds; general-purpose boat resin and fiberglass are good enough for a one-off mold.

You should build the thinnest mold you dare in order to minimize the cost of labor and materials. Then you should install some longitudinal stringers on the outside while it is still on the existing boat to stiffen it against distortion. There should always be one such stringer close to the sheer. Another stringer might run through the center of the topsides and a third through the center of the deadrise. On a transom, a layer or two of thin plywood laminated as a sandwich is better than stringers, although you might need two or three if the transom is large and not too strongly curved. A plywood-sandwich reinforcement also works well on the flat areas of flat- and V-bottomed boats. Due to the flexibility of fiberglass, you may need reinforcement on the flattest "panels" of the boat, which are likely to flex or distort. Curved areas are naturally stiff; the more curved, the stiffer. Anyway, a stringer around the sheer, the unsupported edge of the structure, is by far the most important place for reinforcement. On small, quite round boats, it is often all that is needed; and it is remarkable how one of ample dimensions stiffens up the whole boat.

It is customary to build fiberglass stringers over formers made of foam, of ordinary cardboard tubes cut in half, or of softwood with many crosscuts most of the way through it to eliminate stiffness. The former is hot-glued in place, and strips of mat are laid up over it and out onto the boat, making a stringer with a hat-shaped section. Two layers of 1-ounce or 1½-ounce mat on a 1-by-1-inch or 1½-by-1½-inch stringer are enough on a small boat mold. As the mold and the stringer get bigger, more mat and/or roving is in order. But even on the biggest one-off mold, it is better to use additional stringers than to build up more than about $3/16$ inch of thickness, because its effect on the thin skin of the mold becomes too localized.

Two other useful items to add before the mold is pulled from the existing boat are some sort of stand and a set of attachment points for lifting it off the existing boat, for rocking it, turning it over, or tying it down when pulling the one-off from it. You can meet both requirements by boring holes in the stand for rope or wire lifting straps, provided that the stand is well braced and glassed to the mold. The most popular stand consists of two rocker bulkheads. They are simple to build, useful in rocking and turning the mold over, and add stiffness to the mold. To make the stand, you scribe sheet plywood to fit the bottom shape, cut it to fit loosely, and tab it to the mold. Its opposite edge should have flats on which the mold can rest in different positions, as described in Chapter 2. To keep the plywood rockers from swaying or collapsing, you should brace them to the mold and/or to each other. Finally, as suggested, you can bore four holes in each bulkhead about 1 to 1½ inches in diameter for attaching rope straps, one near the top on each side and one near each end of the bottom flat. But if you don't think your rockers can stand the strains of hoisting and turning the mold, you can build some fiberglass eye straps directly onto the mold's surface at strategic points. These are quickly made by laying up a number of alternate pieces of mat and roving over a short pipe nipple or length of cardboard tubing, say, 4 to 6 inches long with not less than a 1¼-inch inside diameter. When each layer is extended a little farther, up to 6 inches out onto the mold, the strap will have extraordinary strength.

Now there is one rule to bear in mind about fiberglassing any hard object, such as a wooden stringer, bulkhead, brace, or steel pipe, to a mold. You should always provide a cushion, a strip of corrugated pasteboard or perhaps a thin strip of foam, between that item and the mold's skin. If you fail to, the shrinkage of the fiberglass attachment squeezes the object against the skin, which is likely to create a bump or ridge on the inside of the mold.

I might mention that fiberglass molds can be, and often are, reinforced with any of the usual core materials rather than with stringers. A sandwich is built either over the entire exterior surface or in patches as needed over the flatter, more flexible areas. I am not enthusiastic about this use of core materials because their insulating effect inhibits the dissipation of exothermic heat. Heat might melt the wax and cause release problems, it is hard on the surface of the mold, excessive heat might cook the one-off laminate, and balsa blocks have been known to print through a mold if put on over too few layers or before the inside layers have fully cured. But stating my objections may be unnecessary, for I think you will prefer stringers to sandwich reinforcement on a one-off mold anyway when you figure out how much more expensive the core material is.

LAMINATING AND RELEASING THE ONE-OFF OR ONE-OFF MOLD

Although the subject of laminating is discussed in Chapter 10, there are some matters peculiar to laying up a mold or one-off over an existing boat, or a one-off in a one-off mold, that ought to be mentioned here. Shrinkage causes any parts built over a male mold to grip it tightly. The more shrinkage, the more trouble getting the part, the one-off or the one-off mold, off the existing boat, and the more danger of damaging the part or the boat. Shrinkage also tends to emboss the surface of the part with the weaknesses or imperfections of an existing wooden boat. The plugs or putty over fastenings, seams, and loose planks and the hard and soft grain of wood that were invisible on the existing boat often appear, nevertheless, in a part made on it. It is relatively easy to avoid such problems; yet in the enthusiasm of rushing on with construction, the following simple but crucial rules are sometimes forgotten:

1. The existing boat should be well waxed: four or five coats, an hour or two apart.

2. Safer than just wax is PVA mold release on top of the wax. Polyvinyl alcohol is a thin, water-soluble, volatile liquid with which you can build up a coat or skin over the waxed mold. It is applied with an ordinary paint sprayer. You should use PVA wherever you have the faintest doubt about release. It is particularly important to use it on tall, narrow places like keels and skegs where you must release a large surface area from the surrounding laminate.

3. You ought to proceed *slowly* with the lamination of the one-off or mold.

   a. Apply the gelcoat, if you're going to use it, with a generous portion of catalyst stirred into it *well*. (See manufacturer's recommendations as to percentage.)

   b. When the gelcoat is cured—when it is dry and firm to the touch, perhaps a bit tacky because it has no wax—lay up one or two layers of 1-ounce or 1½-ounce mat and let them cure very well. Overnight is a good period of time to allow for this. Experts disagree as to whether one or two layers are best, but they all agree on the importance of complete cure before adding more layers. When you are working in uncontrolled conditions of ambient temperature and humidity, two layers are more sure to cure completely within a reasonable time.

   c. Proceed with the rest of the laminate, applying two layers at a time, and allowing each to cure hard and dry before adding the next pair. Use moderate catalyzing, not hot, fast-curing mixes.

The above procedure is calculated to minimize shrinkage and to give you a part that is neither clutching the existing boat in a death grip, nor distorted and imprinted by excessive pressure against it.

To release the completed part, drive thin wooden wedges between the part and the existing boat around the sheer. Nylon wedges are sold for this, but wood wedges work fine for one time, and their supply is as inexhaustible as your willingness to make them. When the sheer is parted all the way around, you can cause the separation to spread toward the keel by pounding on the part with a rubber hammer. I'm sorry that I can't tell you how hard you can beat on each particular part without cracking the fiberglass. In each case, it's possible to belt it harder than you might think; yet there is a point at which the fiberglass cracks no matter how heavy the laminate. Worse, you may not know that you're cracking the inner face until you get the part off and see the "star cracks" there. Anyway, mighty wallops won't loosen the part appreciably more than just good, solid thumps. While you are separating the part, your lifting straps are hooked up to it, keeping an upward strain on it. Yes, you can build some eye straps on the one-off hull (if built below the waterline, you have less work to restore the finish), which can be ground off later. Alternatively, you can use jacks against the sheer or against blocks glassed to the topsides near it on a one-off, or against the sheer stringer of a mold.

If the part doesn't pop off the existing boat right away, don't get excited. There's a sort of frantic tension that seems to build when a part is stuck in the mold. I have witnessed, and have been drawn into against my better judgment, some real mob scenes: people running back and forth for ever-bigger pry bars, hammers, and wedges. Soon everybody is attacking the part in a different way in a different place according to his individual theory. The result of this frenzied anarchy is usually some unnecessary damage to part or mold. Keep your cool. No matter how many volunteers arrive, or how plausible their suggestions seem, keep control and don't rush into anything. It's your hard work they're itching to attack. Often, in the midst of a debate about what to do next, the part lets go with a final groan and thump, proving that it was only necessary to get it started, to keep the mold's weight hanging from it an inch or two off the floor, and to be patient.

Two gentle and very effective ways to apply pressure between a stubborn part and the mold are with air and water. To use air, bore two or three small holes through the keel of the part or mold until you reach the surface of the other. If you can't get results holding an air nozzle against the hole, which has been chamfered with a countersink, you can fiberglass a threaded nipple or a quick-connect fitting over the hole. Production builders often incorporate air fittings in molds where release could be a problem.

The easy way to use water is to turn part and mold with sheer up and simply pour water between the two wedged-apart top edges. As the water finds its way down, it applies pressure proportional to its head and literally floats the inside part out of the one around it. Another advantage of water is that PVA is water soluble.

Although it is entirely possible to build a one-off deck on most existing decks, it is often not worth the trouble. When you tote up the labor required to strip off hardware and projecting wooden trim, to remove handrails, wooden coamings, and railcaps, and to fill in recessed portlights or wedge out any features the rake of

Building a mold on an existing boat, a Watch Hill Class Herreshoff 15½-footer. One must be careful with a class boat: The main reason this was legal was because no patent or copyright has the longevity these boats have had. Besides, the new boat wouldn't be the same; in fiberglass, it couldn't be.

which would lock the one-off to the deck, another method might be more attractive. To build a deck, even more than a hull, you are better off with a derelict, for you are free to do anything and everything necessary to acquire the one-off you envision without worrying about rehabilitating the existing deck. The preparation and refitting of a molded fiberglass deck are likely to be much less onerous than of a wooden deck. At least you are starting with a basic configuration that was molded and is therefore shaped for the process.

When parts of a deck are too cluttered, it might still be worthwhile to build one-off pieces off the remaining areas, to be incorporated with the cluttered part built by another method. Main or side decks are hardly worth fighting for from an existing boat; they are built with any method so easily. But you might save yourself a tidy number of hours if you could get a one-off part from the cockpit area or cabin trunk of the existing boat. Even the bow deck of a small, open boat or the cockpit sole is worth going after, when you compare the labor it takes to build them in place. If the part is curved or convoluted but clean, it's probably worth trying for. If it's straight, plain, and cluttered, it probably isn't.

This chapter has run on in length, but perhaps it's worth the space to discuss what, with the right existing boat, can be the easiest of all one-offs to build. It's done with little boats almost every day, and it's not uncommon for professional custom and production builders to take one off the biggest.

Just one word of warning before we move on: Check out the legal rights to a design. I hope you won't be so reckless as to take a mold off a currently produced boat and build one or more identical boats without getting the permission of the owner of the design. The owner is either the builder or the designer, and you may be able to get permission for a fee. It might just turn out that you can buy a raw hull and deck almost as cheaply as you could build them, or there may be a mold that you can rent, if the model has been discontinued. Whether or not the boat is being built, the designer may have the right to a fee. This also applies to the plans or lines of a boat that you build with any of the other one-off methods.

If you change the shape or size of a boat, it is not the same boat. Thus, a suit against you would probably not stand up in court, as in the case of *O'Day* v. *Sailstar*, where it seems the Sailstar Company had taken a mold off an O'Day hull and altered its stern. However, if the design of your boat is close enough to stir him up, the designer or builder could at least cause you considerable aggravation and legal expense. Therefore, the sensible thing to do is to find out where you stand legally before, not after, you build your one-off.

Part II

Techniques and Finishing

9

Hand Layup Procedure

It is wonderful how much can be accomplished in fiberglass with a few simple tools and only modest physical exertion. No other hand-fabricated boat construction in any material is comparable to hand-laid-up fiberglass for ease and speed. With nothing more than resin pot, brush, roller, and mat knife, a person weighing not 100 pounds can laminate any part of any boat of any size without lifting more than 50 pounds or ever being short of breath. Admittedly, even on small boats, a team of two makes the work more convenient and often more efficient, as do teams of three or more on bigger boats. But no move is too much to make alone, if you are a proper "glass man."

What an individual needs in order to be able to do proper fiberglass work is instruction in the procedures of the trade and enough hands-on experience to convince him that it's best not to break the rules. I shall try to set forth these really very simple procedures as clearly as I can in this chapter. How long it will take you to become proficient in them, I can't say. Some people are persuaded less easily than others, and some are downright wayward. Semantics can also be a problem, so I'll use plain words.

RESINS

Fortunately for the would-be one-off builder, polyester resins are made and sold in vast quantities throughout the world. Thanks to competition, the quality and price of general-purpose boat resins are relatively uniform. To assure yourself of the right quality and price for building a one-off, you have but to buy from the wholesalers who service boatbuilders with drums and larger quantities. If that is not possible, you are better off arranging to buy through a boat company than to take a chance with retailers, no matter how small the boat. "Store-bought" resins are often compounded for repair or other special jobs and may not be suitable for boatbuilding. What's more, the retail, small-quantity price structure is exorbitant due to packaging and handling.

To avoid confusion, I will discuss only two basic laminating resins at this point: resin with wax, and resin with low or no wax. Wax is added to resin to seal the surface of the laminate from contact with the atmosphere. Air inhibits (slows) the curing of resin, and a surface curing in contact with the atmosphere tends to remain soft and tacky for some time. How long can be days or perhaps a month, depending on conditions. But wax floating to the top and sealing the surface causes it to cure within approximately the same period of time as the rest of the laminate. This is important when you want the surface hard and dry for sanding, or when it is finished and done with. Otherwise, the tacky surface gums up sandpaper as fast as you can replace it. If finished, the surface mars easily, and the dirt and soil it picks up like flypaper become a permanent part of it.

Yet, once hard and dry, it is no longer safe to add more layers to the surface of a laminate without sanding it. Sanding is needed to: (1) remove any wax and (2) roughen the surface and possibly expose some of the underlying glass fibers. Unless opened up by sanding, a surface that has cured hard and dry does not bond dependably to new fiberglass.

RULE 1: ALWAYS SAND HARD, DRY FIBERGLASS BEFORE ADDING MORE LAYERS.

Rule 1 implies that if you don't want to sand before adding more layers, you had better put them on before the preceding layers are fully cured. When the resin has wax in it, that period of grace is perhaps 24 hours, but it varies with conditions. One way to tell is to scratch the surface with sandpaper. If it gums up the paper, it will bond with new layers. If it doesn't, you had better sand the entire surface.

Low- or no-wax resins give you a longer time during which you can add more layers safely without sanding. Again, that time varies with different resins and different conditions, but in general it is days, not hours. Further, there is little or no wax on the surface acting as a specific barrier to a good bond between new resin and old. Does this give you ideas about adding putty and paint to a laminate? Good. We'll talk about that in Chapter 10 on finishing. Meanwhile, you need remember only that low- or no-wax resin is the best kind to use when there will be periods longer than, say, 12 to 24 hours between layers. On a little boat, on any job with a big crew, or whenever laminating is expected to proceed continuously with few or no breaks longer than 24 hours, it makes little difference whether there is wax in the resin or not. Also, you must not forget to make sure that the resin contains wax when it is important for the surface to cure promptly. This does not mean, however, that you have to stock up on both kinds of resin to build your one-off. Wax additive is sold separately, and you can mix it into low- or no-wax resin if that's what you are using.

Resin companies list dozens of other resins compounded for specific needs, resins that are flexible, chemical resistant, heat resistant, and fire retardant. There are tooling resins, casting resins, and coating resins. But with the exception of fire-retardant resin, which could be required by law in a commercial boat (or your personal preference), you do not need special resins unless they are specified in conjunction with a particular product. For example, the use of marble-casting resin is recommended with C-Flex to avoid the danger of excessive shrinkage, which would pull it too tight over the form.

FIBERGLASS MATERIALS

The glass fibers used to reinforce resin combine with it to form a "synergetic" material, the physical properties of which are beyond those of either of the components. A lump of cured resin, almost as devoid of structural possibilities as a piece of hard candy, and a handful of soft, flexible glass fibers give little indication of the strong, tough, durable product they can become in combination. Viable boat hulls have been built within a fairly wide range of resin-glass mixtures, all the way from 20 percent to 60 percent glass content by weight. In general, the higher the glass content, the stronger the laminate, that is, up to the point where there is insufficient resin around the fibers to hold them all together.

RULE 2: IN A BOAT LAMINATE, GLASS FIBERS OR RESIN IS NOTHING WITHOUT THE OTHER.

Glass fibers are prepared in two basic ways to combine with resin to make fiberglass, as chopped strands and as continuous strands. For hand layup, chopped strands are made into chopped-strand mat, literally a continuous mat of randomly oriented short strands pressed together and retained in sheet form by a resin-soluble binder. It is sold in various thicknesses, identified by the weight in ounces per square foot. The most commonly available weights are in increments from ¾ ounce to 2 ounces by ¼ ounce or ½ ounce; the most common widths are 38, 50, 60, and 72 inches; and the wholesale units are individual rolls weighing from just under 100 pounds to 200 pounds or pallets of rolls up to a ton or more. Most wholesalers are willing to mix the kinds of fiberglass materials on a pallet and still give you the pallet price break.

Chopped strands are also made from single-strand roving with a chopper at the nozzle of resin spray guns, which spray catalyzed resin and chopped strands onto the part being laminated. However, "choppers" are an expensive production builders' tool not usually justifiable in small custom-building shops, and certainly not in a one-time, one-off builder's shop, except by rental. Further, a prudent owner of one of these intricate machines wouldn't let it out unless a trained operator was hired along with it. Anyway, as far as quality goes, you're better off with the various glass-fiber fabrics laid up by hand, because they make the most uniform laminate.

Chopped strands are also sold in bulk, in lengths that are a fraction of an inch, or ground up into "milled fibers," for use in making strong fillers and putties. These are quite useful in filling cavities or building up the surfaces of fiberglass parts. The coarser the fibers, the more rugged the filler or putty, but the rougher its surface, too. Therefore, your selection of fiber length must be based on an assessment of the strength needed versus the size of the void or the thickness of the application, and whether surface smoothness is important. You want relatively long fibers to fill a hollow keel, but finer-milled fibers for leveling a rough surface, for radiusing a sharp corner prior to laying up more layers, or for bedding a deck joint.

Chopped strands are best at sealing out water, and at adhesion, which is to say at resisting delamination or peeling. Many good boats and parts of boats have been built with nothing but chopped-strand mat. Theirs are the most watertight and cohesive skins, and their durability or resistance to water and weathering are legend. However, all-mat laminates have to be heavier to attain the same strength as laminates containing continuous-strand materials. As a result, a mixture of chopped- and continuous-strand materials is used on almost all boats today. A few boats that need to be extremely light and strong, however, are built mostly or even entirely with continuous-strand materials.

Continuous strands are supplied woven into cloth of different weights and weaves and into a loose weave of flattened, relatively bulky strands called woven roving. In another form, continuous strands are laid out side by side to form a sheet of unidirectional material, loosely joined by rows of stitching and/or to a mat backing with a soluble binder.

Continuous-strand goods are identified by the terms *cloth*, *woven roving*, and *unidirectional roving* or *unidirectional material* and by their weight in ounces per square yard. Note the difference: mat goes by the weight per square *foot*; woven or continuous-strand material goes by the weight per square *yard*. This distinction is always the source of some confusion until you get used to it. To accommodate the use of alternate layers of mat and roving so common today, both woven and unidirectional roving are available bound to a backing layer of mat so that you save considerable labor when you handle, cut, and apply the two layers as one.

Still another form of continuous-strand fiberglass, actually the basic form, is *strand roving*, or just plain *roving*, a single strand made up of many parallel glass fibers lightly stuck together with a binder. Strand roving is supplied in spools packed in cartons and sold by weight. Although it is sold mainly for use in chopper guns, strand roving is useful to the one-off builder to fill sharp corners like those of

A typical fiberglass laminate, represented by a square of the material of each layer. The eight layers of mat and woven roving would be applied in the order left to right in a mold, but right to left on a form. Total thickness would be about 5/16 inch. The schedule reads: mat, roving, mat, roving, mat, roving, mat, mat, from interior to exterior, right to left.

A fiberglass laminate using alternate mat and unidirectional roving, the two layers of the latter being turned at 90° to each other. The mat, roving, mat, roving, mat, mat schedule (always two layers of mat on the exterior) would have a total thickness of about 3/16 to ¼ inch.

coamings and rails, lift strips, and the laps of lapstrakes, usually in a mold. In this use, roving not only acts as a radius to eliminate the bubbles when mat "bridges" the corner, but strengthens and toughens the corner against breakouts.

As implied heretofore, continuous strands make a stiffer, stronger laminate than an equal weight of chopped strands, at least in the direction that its strands run.* And I repeat, fiberglass boatbuilders have found that the best all-around boat laminate is one composed of alternate layers of mat and roving. Woven roving is most often used for this because its woven strands give strength in two directions at 90 degrees to each other. It is also cheaper than unidirectional roving. When the builder has reason to maximize strength in a specific direction, unidirectional roving does this most efficiently. A case in point would be to align

---

*For some interesting charts and tables that compare the physical properties of mat and roving laminates, see Robert J. Scott, Fiberglass Boat Design and Construction *(Tuckahoe, N.Y.: John DeGraff, 1973).*

unidirectional roving athwartships to supplement the purely fore-and-aft strength of C-Flex. In boats where weight is critical, unidirectional reinforcement can beef up highly stressed parts and areas most effectively. Such uses might be to strengthen the connection of a ballast keel to the hull, to form a belt frame or "stirrup" in way of the mast and chainplates, and even to make up the all-important longitudinal fibers of a fiberglass mast itself. But alternating layers of mat and woven roving have been found to have the best multidirectional strength as well as good resistance in general to all the different types of wear and tear that boats endure over a long life.

A large part of the durability of this combination is due to the alternate mat layers and to the two mat layers that are recommended for the outside of the laminate. Mat is the most adhesive of glass-fiber materials. Its short strands create many intimate interconnections between layers. At the same time, these myriad multilayered, multidirectional fibers of mat thoroughly reinforce the resin within each layer against fine cracks and the resulting penetration of water. Also, they do not lead water that follows along them anywhere. By contrast, we have traced mysterious leaks inside a boat to the opened-up ends of roving strands as far away as 10 or 12 feet on the outside of the supposedly solid single skin! Granted that the roving was undoubtedly not wet out with resin properly, the odds against this happening with mat are a thousand times greater.

When a laminate is bent beyond its yield point or shattered by impact, there is a tendency for the layers to shear apart or delaminate. The difference between mat and continuous-strand materials under these circumstances is that continuous strands, due to their enormous tensile strength and poor adhesion to adjacent surfaces, peel away for their full length, often with an astonishingly light pull; but mat tends to break off rather than delaminate fully. This reluctance of mat to delaminate is due partly to its lower tensile strength and partly to its superior adhesion to adjacent surfaces.

What we get, then, by using alternate layers of mat and roving is a combination that fulfills more of the requirements of a good boat laminate. The strengths of each material are listed in the accompanying table:

MAT	WOVEN ROVING*
More watertightness.	High tensile or hoop strength.
More adhesion between layers.	High bending strength.
More resistance to delamination.	Quick buildup of stiffness.
Equal strength, though lower, in all directions.	Higher strength in the two directions of the strands, lower at 45°, or the bias, of the weave.

*Unidirectional roving is similar but "more so." Its strength is higher for the same weight, but very low at 90° to the strands.

This chapter is supposed to be about hand layup, and this procedure is discussed next. However, just as it doesn't do much good to learn how to work wood if you don't know how to select lumber and lay out parts with respect to its grain, neither does good fiberglassing technique amount to much until you know how to select and orient the glass-fiber materials that are the "grain" of fiberglass. When you work out a laminate schedule for any part of your one-off, I hope you will remember the next rule.

RULE 3: MAT FIRST, MAT BETWEEN, AND MAT ON THE OUTSIDE.

"Mat first" is for the best bond to any surface; "mat between" is for the best bond between layers (including, always, mat on both sides of a core); and "mat on the outside" (preferably two layers) is to keep the water out. If you can remember rule 3, your one-off is much less likely to be cited someday in a survey for delamination of one part or another.

RULE 4: ROVING BUILDS STRENGTH AND STIFFNESS; THUS, ALTERNATE MAT AND WOVEN ROVING IS THE BEST ALL-AROUND BOAT LAMINATE.

LAYUP TECHNIQUE

Essentially, to lay up a part, you spread the glass-fiber materials over the form (or mold surface) and saturate them with catalyzed resin. In a little while, the resin hardens and you have a completed part. It sounds easy, and it is, if you are fairly well organized and don't paint yourself into any corners. The basic materials are quite uniform and dependable. And after a quarter of a century of use in essentially their present form, the techniques of applying them are well developed with an eye to avoiding trouble.

Let's start with a checklist based on the preparations an old hand makes for laying any and all fiberglass work:

1. Cut the fiberglass materials ahead in pieces small enough to handle and wet out without being rushed. Cut enough for a continuous laminating session, say, two layers for one side of the boat, so you won't have to leave in the midst of the job to cut more, unless you have plenty of help.

2. Arrange the pieces in order, handy to the job, so they can be picked off without pawing through them with sticky hands.

3. Set out the paper pots, brushes, rollers, scissors, mat knife, wiping rags, and a metal trash container handy to the job.

4. Provide a covered 5-gallon pail containing a gallon of acetone for washing and storing the tools (if they're not already in it).

5. Set out a container big enough to get your hand in, like a 3-pound coffee can with a quart of clean acetone in it for washing hands.

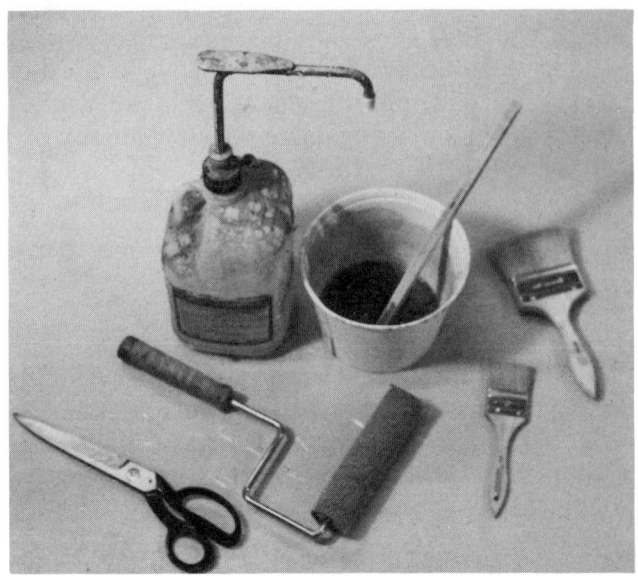

The laminator's hand lay-up tools. Catalyst measuring pump, paper pot and stirrer, brushes, roller, and shears.

6. Put out a modest supply of catalyst in a pint or ½-pint jar or bottle with a cap, and a 1-ounce glass or plastic measurer marked in fractions of an ounce or in cubic centimeters on a safe shelf or table. By safe I mean where it won't get kicked or knocked over onto anybody. Not lower than the knees or higher than the waist seems safest. But if you have sprung for or borrowed a catalyst-metering pump that fits into the top of a gallon jug, this should sit on the floor.

The worst danger of catalyst, when it is 30 percent to 60 percent MEK (methyl ethyl ketone peroxide), is to the eyes. But it does burn the skin and is highly flammable, too. Be sure to have running water or a bottle of pure water and an eyecup nearby.

7. Draw off a quantity of resin suitable for the job or a good part of it from the drum into one or more clean 5-gallon buckets, from which the resin can be handily poured into the paper pots. Set the resin bucket(s) on a disposable surface, like a large piece of pasteboard, that will retain their drip. Then you can conveniently set a paper pot down near the bucket, pour some resin into it, move with it to where the catalyst is, and put in a shot—all without undue worry about spillage.

After you have laid out your glass-material, tool-and-hand-washing, and resin supply stations, you know that everything you need is at hand as you concentrate on laminating. These preparations may seem inconsequential; they certainly are ridiculously simple. But no matter how small the job, they are important if it is to go smoothly.

RULE 5: NEVER START LAMINATING UNTIL YOU LAY OUT ALL MATERIALS, TOOLS, AND EQUIPMENT.

The word *lamination* is used constantly in this book because the actual fabrication of a fiberglass one-off is, precisely, building up layers of material until the appropriate thickness of the particular boat's skin, or skins and core, is achieved. Experienced laminators prefer to do this in stages of two layers at a time. There are a number of reasons why two layers work out best.

If you apply only one layer, especially if it is a first or "cold" layer, it might be reluctant to cure. Resin distributed tenuously through thin glass material may lack a sufficient distribution of catalyst and/or sufficient body or accumulation of exothermic heat (heat given off as resin cures) to promote the spread of the reaction. But although this can happen sometimes, especially in a cold or damp atmosphere, it wastes labor all of the time to move from one end of the job to the other with only one layer. Finally, wetting out the surface again for each layer not only wastes resin, but tends to reduce the proportion of glass to resin, or the strength in relation to the weight and thickness of the laminate.

Of course, more than two layers can be carried along together on a job, and they sometimes are. But here the danger is too rapid a cure, which might cause too much accumulated exothermic heat and too much shrinkage. How many layers can be brought along in the same pass around the part depends partly on ambient conditions. If heat or intense sunlight promotes very rapid cure, as few as 4 to 6 layers could get hot enough to "cook" the resin, which radically reduces or wrecks the strength of the laminate. Aside from that possibility, a thick set of layers curing all at once undergoes powerful shrinkage. This force is exerted against any underlying layers and also against the form or mold. Radical shrinkage distorts the part; it can pull the part away from a mold or compress a form so that the part is a slightly different shape than the lines to which the mold or form was built. The most noticeable effects are dished-in flat areas, flanges that assume a more acute angle, a hollow in hull surfaces just forward of the transom and just abaft the stem, caved-in keel or deadwood sides, and increased tumblehome in the topsides. Noticing such results adds interest to fiberglass "boat watching," for they are indisputable clues to some builders' hot and heavy laminating techniques.

On most boats bigger than a dinghy, you can start at one end and lay up two layers down one side, then down the other. By the time you get back to where you started, the layers will have cured enough for you to start another pair of layers.

RULE 6: LAYING UP TWO LAYERS AT A TIME WORKS OUT BEST ON MOST HULLS AND DECKS UNDER A WIDE RANGE OF CONDITIONS.

If you're wondering when we're ever going to get into the actual laying up of this imaginary one-off, it's right now. Pour 2 quarts of resin into a 2½-quart paper container. Catalyze it by adding ½ ounce or 15 cubic centimeters of 50 percent MEK, or whatever the median amount of the percentage MEK solution you have is recommended for the resin you have. Stir the catalyst thoroughly into the resin, but *not* violently lest you splash it into your eyes. (Should you get any catalyst or catalyzed resin in an eye, flood the eye with water until it is out. Get to a doctor as soon as possible if washing doesn't clear the eye right away.)

RULE 7: IF RUNNING WATER ISN'T CLOSE BY, ALWAYS HAVE A BOTTLE OF PURE WATER AND AN EYECUP HANDY WHILE FIBERGLASSING.

If you are laying up on a surface, such as on a mold, a PVC-covered form, or WLP, wet out that surface with your catalyzed resin where the first piece or two of mat will go. Use a 3½-inch throwaway bristle paintbrush with a bare wooden or solvent-proof plastic handle. There's no need to "paint" the area with an even coat; just get it wet all over as efficiently as possible.

RULE 8: ALWAYS WET OUT A DRY SURFACE WITH RESIN BEFORE APPLYING GLASS-FIBER MATERIALS TO IT.

Take up the first piece of mat and place it as truly as possible over the area it was cut to fit. Pull it around gently until you get it where you want it; then pat and roll it out smooth, forcing it into the wet resin. As soon as it is lying flat in place, start wetting it out from the top down with resin. Apply the resin with the brush, using it more like a two-sided ladle than a brush; that is, dip the brush and spread the resin on one side of it with a short, light stroke, and then spread the resin on its other side with a similar stroke in the opposite direction. Then dip again and repeat. Do *not* brush the resin around on the mat with many successive strokes like a painter. This tends to lift and bunch up the fibers. If you are tempted to spread out a particularly big puddle, bend the brush by pressing it down firmly with its handle almost vertical; then slide it along, pushing the puddle ahead of it like a wave under the bow of a scow. Ladle the resin on in quantities that do not cover every bit of the area but will wet it all when spread evenly. Your roller will do the spreading, and it will do it without lifting or moving the fibers, as long as it is clean and rolling freely. I like the hard, nubbly fabric rollers; other laminators like the grooved aluminum type. The most popular length is 7 inches. The soft, fuzzy paint rollers won't work for rolling down a laminate, although they are preferred for wetting out C-Flex that is suspended in midair on a form yet fastened down. When laminating on a surface, it is, by the way, not forbidden specifically to pour resin from the pot when the surface is not too steep. But if you do that, it should be in puddles small enough to spread out with the roller in your other hand almost immediately. A large puddle standing too long in one spot may float the mat and loosen its binder so much that when you do roll it out, you'll move a wave of fibers out with it.

Still another, and by far the most efficient, way to wet out big jobs is to spray the resin on. This is often done with the spray portion of a portable chopper gun, and production shops have resin piped in under pressure from a resin supply room. But, like chopper guns, this equipment is quite expensive and complicated in its present forms. Moreover, a sprayer requires one man to service and operate it, while it applies resin so fast that several men are kept busy spreading glass ahead of it and rolling out the wet glass behind it. For building a big one-off with a crew of no fewer than three or four persons, a resin spray system might be worth considering. On a small one-off, it would mean more confusion than efficiency, except where it is already in use. I think that the threshold for bringing one in for a single job would be at 2½ to 3 tons total weight of fiberglass to be laid up.

Anyway, after you wet out the first piece of mat, you roll it down. The roller squeezes the wet mat, pressing the resin throughout the fibers and forcing air bubbles beneath the surface either to come out through the top or to move along ahead of the roller to an edge or dry spot where they can escape. Nubbles or grooves on the roller help to remove bubbles by providing indentations that serve as blowholes. Bubbles and as-yet-unsaturated areas both show up as white or crystalline patches in wet glass materials. The name of the game is rolling, rolling to work them out. Unsaturated areas are sometimes stubborn at first, but given a little time for the resin to penetrate them, they disappear. Bubbles move around; sometimes they disappear only to reappear as the glass springs up again off the surface it is bridging. Finally, with conscientious rolling, the glass assumes the consistent, tinted translucence that denotes complete saturation.

About the only time you won't be able to achieve complete saturation is when your batch of resin is catalyzed too heavily and starts to gel before you can work it into the glass material. You can't wet out glass with jelly. If jelly starts to form in the resin pot, that's your warning that it will soon do so on the boat. Throw out such resin immediately, get some fresh resin with about half as much catalyst in it, and finish wetting out the piece quickly before its resin gels and prevents the bubbles from escaping or the dry spots from absorbing more resin. Use less catalyst in your following mixes. This situation reveals several facts about working with resin. The same amount of catalyst can't be used at all times unless ambient temperature, humidity, and actinic light are absolutely controlled. The resin-and-catalyst formulation is identical, and the heat dissipation equal in every use.

At the other extreme is "undercure," resin that never quite cures. Undercure can be a revolting development if it goes undetected until after launching, for the resin washes right out of the glass-fiber materials, leaving you with a limp, crumbling area. I have run across such an area in an occasional production boat. One boat I witnessed mysteriously sank at the mooring and when raised was found to consist of well-laundered mat and roving over a large section of its bottom. However, such an occurrence is rare. Also, you are well protected in hand-layup work: your mixes are divided into small units and your progress is slow, which allows you to observe closely what sort of cure is taking place. In hand layup, undercure is the result of gross undercatalyzing, of not stirring the resin well to mix the catalyst thoroughly or forgetting entirely to catalyze it. In the midst of a laminate, with well-catalyzed layers adjacent to it, the chance is slim that the resin won't cure eventually. If undercure is on the surface, you'll recognize it because it stays soft indefinitely. Then, if overpainting it with a hot mix won't "kick it over," you can always strip it off. It is also true that if left long enough in bright sunlight or high temperatures (although not once it is immersed in water), general-purpose boat resin eventually cures by itself.

RULE 9: NEVER CATALYZE MORE THAN ONE POT PER PERSON APPLYING RESIN AT ONE TIME.

RULE 10: WATCH THE GEL TIME OF YOUR RESIN CONSTANTLY; TRY TO KEEP IT LONGER THAN ½ HOUR AND SHORTER THAN 2 HOURS.

THE SECOND LAYER

When you have put on two or three pieces of the first layer of mat, it is time to go back and bring along the second layer. This layer also ought to be mat if you are working in a mold, but it probably will be woven roving if you are working on a form. Part of the reason, you will remember, for laying up two layers at a time is to cut down the proportion of resin in the laminate, since the second layer shares some of the wetness of the first. For that reason, you should lay up the second layer right on the heels of the first. If by chance your resin is too "hot" and the surface of the first layer goes dry before you get back to start the second, you'll have to remember rule 8 and wet its surface again before putting more glass material on it. Resin coming through from underneath reduces the labor of working it in from the top drastically and minimizes air bubbles.

To keep the joints of the second layer separate from those of the first, the starting piece must be narrower in width than the standard width of the material, assuming that you have been putting the layers on in vertical pieces as wide as the roll on which they come. This is the way you should put them on 90 percent of the time. On small boats and parts of decks where the material happens to fit well in a longitudinal direction, that's the direction in which to put it on.

RULE 11: ON MOST HULLS IT IS MUCH MORE CONVENIENT AND ECONOMICAL TO APPLY GLASS-FIBER MATERIAL IN VERTICAL STRIPS FROM KEEL TO RAIL.

When, because of the size of the boat and/or the number of workers, it is impractical to cover the half-girth in one length, you might cover the keel and bottom of an upside-down form, for instance, as far down as you can comfortably reach standing on a staging. Then, in another pass around the boat, you would cover from there to the rail with the balance of the two layers, perhaps standing on the floor or a low staging. When using two lengths between keel and rail, you should make the pieces of the second layer shorter than the first layer by at least 6 inches to stagger the horizontal joints.

In a form-built one-off I would rather butt all joints of the material than contend with the lumps that overlapping causes at finishing time. Overlaps are stronger, without question. They don't show in a molded boat; and working in a mold, I would overlap every piece a couple of inches, knowing I was building a stronger boat with very little added material. I would do that on the inner skin of a sandwich construction, too.

A frequently used method of improving the smoothness of mat layers at the exterior surface is to comb the edges of the pieces. A good manufactured tool for this is a paintbrush cleaner, which has a single row of needlelike metal tines or teeth. Although sold in paint stores, it is a simple thing to make by pressing a dozen fine brads or nails 1½ to 1¾ inches long, with their heads clipped off, into a row of tight holes spaced ¼ or $5/16$ inch on centers in a wooden handle. Holding the comb parallel to and about an inch in from the edge of the mat, you brush lightly outward to thin or taper it. Blending two such edges makes a softer joint than the lump of overlapped edges or the narrow grooves that you are bound to have when butted edges don't meet all the way along their length. Not that it's perfect, but it's better.

Another way to get a similar tapered edge on mat is to tear or pluck its edge with one hand while holding it with the other. There's a knack to this that is abetted by pressing the mat flat with one hand on a plank or table so that the mat's edge hangs off an inch or two while the thumb and side of the forefinger of the other hand pinch and tear downward. Again, matching torn edges is better than overlapping and usually better than butting edges, which rarely meet perfectly except on dead-flat surfaces. However, torn or combed edges really come into their own on a layer that terminates in the midst of an area, as do the upper edges of layers put on to reinforce the keel and bottom.

RULE 12: BUTTED PIECES MAKE A FAIRER FORM-BUILT ONE-OFF, AND COMBED OR TORN EDGES HELP.

Unfortunately, there is no quick and easy way to accomplish this scarflike joint with woven roving, and butted joints are the only alternative to the very bulky overlap you get with it. What woven roving does have in its favor, when it is not backed with mat, is its ability to bias, which means that you can pull it around on a compound-curved surface until its edge butts all along the edge of the last piece. You can't do this with large pieces of mat, although you can with small presaturated pieces, or strips.

In a thick-skinned boat with many layers of alternate mat and roving, I would not worry about applying mat-backed roving vertically with the butts of the double layers well staggered. But anyone who wants to be that conscientious can always turn one or two of these layers horizontal so that all the vertical butts are crossed by continuous strands. However, in a thin-skinned boat with but a few layers of woven roving, I would use single layers of mat and woven roving, not mat-backed roving, so the joints of the mat are separate from the joints of the roving. As mentioned before, on a little boat or a long, light one, with perhaps only one woven-roving layer in the laminate, I would probably apply all of the mat in vertical pieces and apply the one layer of roving in a longitudinal piece or pieces as long and wide as practicable.

Note that all of these guidelines apply to form-built one-offs, the joints of which are butted to keep the exterior surface as smooth and fair as possible.

RULE 13: WHEN LAMINATING IN A MOLD OR BUILDING UP AN INNER SKIN, VERTICAL PIECES WITH OVERLAPPED EDGES USUALLY MAKE THE STRONGEST BOAT WITH THE LEAST WASTED OR SCRAP MATERIAL.

If you lay out some pieces on the molded boat, you can immediately see whether this rule is valid. And if you think of the overlaps as not only full-strength joins of the material but also a multiplicity of ribs like those in a traditional wooden boat, albeit rather shallow ones, you will see why this orientation of glass materials is popular in molded boats.

LOCAL STRENGTHENING LAYERS

For the obvious reason that boats generally take the most punishment and wear on their bottoms, all but the flimsiest fiberglass boats are built with more thickness there than in the topsides. Indeed, I would feel foolish repeating that the keel, skeg, or whatever area bears on the ground should be particularly strong if I didn't know of so many boats of all sizes that have broken open in this area when they "touched" only once on a ledge or bar. Granted, all of the worst of such calamities seem to happen to production boats built to be extremely competitive in price. Nevertheless, it's still worth reminding a one-off builder of the importance of beefing up this area. Depending on the type of boat and its weight, the total thickness of the fiberglass on its keel should range from twice as thick as that of its topsides (on a small, light boat) to four or five times as thick (on a heavily ballasted auxiliary). On different hull and keel configurations, the extra layers used to build maximum thickness at the bottom of the keel might be tapered off at various heights on the keel itself, carried into the hull's deadrise to strengthen the connection of the keel to the hull, or carried all the way to just above the waterline in order to strengthen the whole bottom. In big boats there are almost always some in each category.

In calling out the laminate schedule of a boat, designers often indicate the extent of these layers on a midship half-section drawing with letters assigned to each portion of the laminate. On a molded boat being built inward from the outermost layers, *A* would indicate those layers that extend from sheer to sheer, *B* those reinforcing layers that extend highest on the hull, *C* the next highest, and so on. The builder normally is expected to apply the layers in the order in which they are listed, although switching or reversing the order of the reinforcing layers does not matter. In the laminate schedule for sandwich construction, the outer-skin layers, the reinforcing layers, the core, and then the inner-skin layers are listed in that order.

On a form-built boat, the layers of which are built up from the inside out, you reverse the order of the laminate schedule. However, a great thickness of reinforcing layers is enough reason for some builders to lay up only the basic or overall layers of a single-skin hull or the outer skin of a sandwich laminate on the form, then to lay up the reinforcing layers on the inside of the turned-over hull. This eliminates the need to make a rather complicated deduction from the section moulds for the tapered thickness of those layers. If many reinforcing layers are added to the outside without deducting their thickness, the keel, at least, can become objectionably thick all over and its after end particularly gross, just where it should be thinned down nicely. Therefore, if you want the easier job of laying up these layers on the outside of the form, you ought to make a deduction for them. Otherwise, you ought to lay them up on the inside where they won't affect the shape. Patches of reinforcement, as in the chainplate area, should not be added to the outside of a form-built boat either without providing a deduction or recess for them in the form. Otherwise, they create unfair lumps in the hull lines.

It should be mentioned that the effect of whole layers added outside the lines of a flat-bottomed or canoe-bodied hull like a sharpie or a shoal-draft centerboarder is usually negligible. Except for deducting from the thickness of a skeg, plank-on-edge keel, or fin keel, it usually can be ignored.

Finally, no matter how many alternate layers of mat and roving are built up on the form-built hull, you should not forget to apply two layers of mat on the outside to seal the laminate against wear, water, and weathering.

LAMINATING IN A MOLD

Laying up the glass-fiber materials in a mold is done in the same manner as on a form, except that it is preceded (usually) by gelcoat, the glass-fiber materials are applied from the outside of the part inward, and there is freedom to overlap the edges of the pieces with abandon.

During the past decade some builders have moved away from gelcoat. Their chief argument is that by the time the boat is ready to be launched, the finish is quite shopworn and the cost of gelcoat repair unacceptably high. The availability of a tough and extremely durable breed of paints, originally developed for aluminum airplanes, has encouraged this approach. Nevertheless, gelcoats, which are high-grade resin with inert fillers and pigments, are compounded to resist the deteriorating effects of water and sunlight, and they do this very well. So far, I know of no paint that lasts as long as a good gelcoat job, although the gap is closing. Neither can a paint job, even a mediocre one, be done as quickly or economically as gelcoating in a mold. Gelcoating on the exterior of a form-built boat is quite another matter, one discussed under finishing (see Chapter 10). But in a mold it is still the quickest, cheapest, and most durable finish. Given a fair, slick, and well-waxed mold, all you do is spray or paint on a coat of gelcoat, and you have your finish. You don't have to brush it out smooth or spray with great precision. Just get it on all over the surface fairly evenly, about 10 to 15 mils thick, and the mold will do the rest. Not that gelcoat finish is a free lunch: in building the mold and polishing its interior, you earn whatever finish it gives the part.

Gelcoat is sold ready to catalyze and use in a wide range of colors. It is also sold

On the following pages:
Laying up Centennial's *deck. A few glimpses, illustrating points covered in this chapter. Details of the construction of* Centennial's *deck mold are shown in photographs in Chapter 2. (Loy photos)*

Top: *Spraying gelcoat onto* Centennial's *deck mold. The inexpensive spray gun uses a frappe container (throwaway paper cup) in which freshly catalyzed batches of gelcoat are mixed and handed to the operator by his tender, the man on the right.* **Bottom:** *Laying strand roving into the corner of the raised deck and topsides, on which gelcoat has cured until gelled. Laying roving in all corners prior to laminating with mat prevents bubbles from forming in the mat. Note the pile of mat and 5-gallon buckets of resin ready for laminating.*

Hand Layup Procedure   161

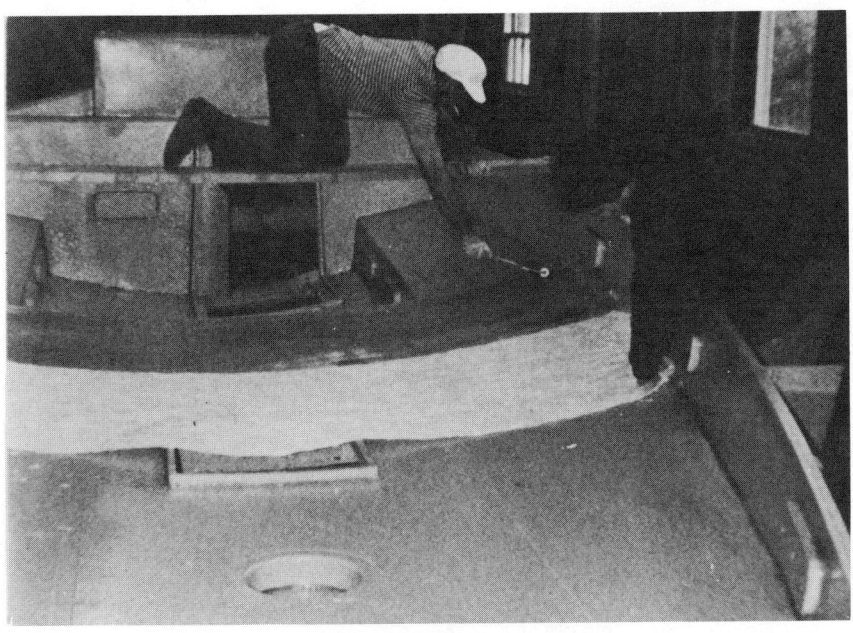

Laying up the outer skin of the deck in the gelcoated mold.

One way to get the resin onto the mat.

Wetting out the mat.

in the neutral or unpigmented state for those who wish to mix their own colors with the dispersion pigments available from the same suppliers.

The most important single lesson to learn about using gelcoat is that, because it is quite viscous, or thick, being loaded with fillers and pigment, catalyst does not spread through it readily.

Therefore we have

RULE 14: ALWAYS STIR THE CATALYST VERY THOROUGHLY INTO GELCOAT.

If this is not done, patches of the gelcoat that are undercured may "alligator," or wrinkle up like alligator skin. Two corollaries of rule 14 are that the gelcoat should be well cured before you lay up any glass-fiber materials over it and generously catalyzed if it is to reach that state within a reasonable time. Because the resin content of gelcoat is rather thinly distributed over the bare surface of the mold, its reaction tends to be retarded in most applications. Also because the resin (usually) doesn't have a wax additive, its surface cure will be inhibited regardless. A slow resin cure is a good thing, because it means that you can "kick" the gelcoat over quickly and still have a gummy surface to which the first layer of glass will bond well. A prompt cure of the gelcoat body is desirable, however, so that you can start covering it right away. Otherwise, it makes a long day to gelcoat a large part as well as cover it with the first layer or two, which may not be possible without a large crew. Covering the gelcoat immediately is not a must; but experienced laminators are nevertheless driven by an urge to lay up some glass over it as soon as possible. First, they fear losing a day, because the first layers should be well cured before more are added; and second, they fear the possibility of physical damage or of foreign matter collecting on it, not to mention the lesser but revolting possibility that the gelcoat might loosen its grip on the waxed surface of the mold and lift up in places, or even fall off a vertical or overhanging surface. Barring these potential problems, gelcoat can stay on a mold for a very long time without losing its ability to hook up with glass-fiber materials laid up on it. I have painted gelcoat on a surface where it stayed sticky for weeks. If you can't cover a gelcoated mold with a layer or two right away, you can guard against damage to it by (1) seeing that it is covered against dust (and against rain by all means), (2) protecting it from physical contacts, (3) turning the mold so that any uncovered portions are not enticed away from it by gravity, (4) deliberately lapping the gelcoat over the edges or stops of the mold, past the limits of the part. You can trim it later; meanwhile, it will hang on better the more corners it turns.

Sometimes this overlap of the gelcoat is enough to keep the laminate from separating at the edge of the mold, too, and a single layer of mat can be extended the same way. However, it is not necessary to do this with more than one layer, and to do so creates an unnecessarily mean trimming job.

When a mold has sharp in corners—such as transom, keel, lift-strip, or deck-flange corners in a hull mold or the coaming and other recesses in a deck mold—it is important to radius these corners after the gelcoat is cured, but before covering it with mat. Otherwise, when you try to tuck the mat into these corners, it will spring out and bridge the corner, leaving a bubble of air between itself and the gelcoat. Once the boat is in use, such bubbles, now along the outside corners on the boat, can be bumped and broken open, leaving an unsightly, jagged edge. A good radiusing fillet for corners, which will make them tough and strong, is strand roving laid lengthwise into them as soon as the gelcoat is ready for covering.

Cut the roving into 2- to 4-foot lengths and drape the lengths over a horizontal pole, or board, spacing them so that you can pick them off one at a time with gooey hands. Dunk each length in a pot of catalyzed resin, wipe off the excess resin by pulling it out through the thumb and finger of one hand held over the pot, then lay it into the corner, stretching it out straight as you do so. You can now prod it into position and smooth it out with the end of your resin brush. This is a job you can do alone, but it goes much faster when one person wets the pieces for a second person who applies them to the mold. Because strand roving is made up of a loose bundle of parallel filaments, not twisted, stroking them with the brush, working away from one end pinned by a finger, forms them into a neat radius.

You can also radius in corners with a hard, polyester putty, wiped smooth with a teaspoon or a little wooden paddle. Although using putty is much better than nothing, it does not impart quite the same ruggedness to a corner that strand roving does. From the beginning, builders of fiberglass boats have been able to avoid the difficulty of making glass-fiber materials take bends by simply rounding all corners generously. However, carried to extremes, this has often given a deck both the bland look and the treacherousness underfoot of a bathtub. In one memorable case, a builder made the fiberglass version of a one-design sailboat pathetically slower than her wooden sisters when he gave her flat transom's immersed corners a 3-inch radius. By the middle 1960s, most designers were drawing clean-cut shapes again, and the better builders were reinforcing the crisp corners on them.

If you wish to avoid shrinkage-related distortion of the molded part, you should allow the first layer, or two layers, of mat to cure well before adding more. This is just as important in a mold as on a form, for the same forces that cause a part to squeeze a form cause it to pull away from a mold. As we said earlier in this chapter, there is no question that the best laminates are those that are built up slowly with not over two layers curing at a time.

One minor problem that occurs in a mold but not on a form is that excess resin tends to pool in the bottom of recesses such as the keel of a hull mold or coamings of a deck mold. A little of this is to be expected and is of no great consequence. However, although a "resin-rich" laminate gains some strength from its added thickness, it is more brittle due to its low glass content; and a puddle that becomes a block of pure resin has no strength at all. There is always the possibility, too, that a deep pool of curing resin in a confined recess will overheat or "cook." Since it is a nuisance to remove resin from deep, narrow places, it is best to work from just above down into them, so the very bottom remains unsaturated until there is less likelihood of added drips and runs into it. Should a puddle of resin collect despite efforts to the contrary, the bulk of it can be sopped up with rags, provided that you get there before it gels. You can take advantage of a modest excess of resin, however, by working in some bottom pieces of the next layers, some extra layers, or some of the filler materials listed in Chapter 11.

Another problem with working in molds is reaching into them. When the out-of-reach area is small, it may be good enough to lash brushes and rollers to long handles. But when there is much work to do, there are two other ways to go: (1) Build a staging that brings you nearer to the elusive surface. (2) Lay up no fewer than two layers on the surfaces that you can reach; then, when they are cured, move in on them and do the uncovered areas. Mylar or waxed pasteboard keeps dirt and spilled materials from building on the area you are traversing.

Don't forget to overlap all pieces about 2 inches (rule 13), and don't forget that if the final layer is mat, it will both seal the laminate and provide a better holding surface than woven roving for tabbing joinerwork.

It is not necessarily good to be in a hurry to remove the part from its mold or to tear the mold away from the part if that is the case. The longer the part can stay in the mold, assuming that the time can be put to good use, the longer it is protected from scratches and dings. Meanwhile, the mold holds the part's shape while you install various items on the interior. On a hull these could be bilge stringers, ribs, the ballast in a sailboat, keel filler, engine beds, bulkheads, any of the joinerwork, or even the deck. In a deck you might have metal reinforcements for a deck-stepped mast, chainplates, or sheet travelers to install; or you might wish to put a finish on the overhead. You are not under pressure to free the mold for the next part, as a production builder usually is.

As far as parting from the mold is concerned, time works in your favor. Not only is the part shrinking away from the mold more and more as it cures, it is also being shaken loose by your tramping about on it. Most often, what can be a frustrating "sticky business" immediately after lamination, with the part clinging stubbornly to the mold, becomes a nonproblem in a few days.

RULE 15: DON'T LET ENTHUSIASM TO RELEASE THE PART FROM ITS MOLD ABORT THE PRACTICAL ADVANTAGES THAT MAY ACCRUE FROM LEAVING IT IN FOR SOME TIME.

10

Finishing Raw Fiberglass

The day you decide to put a finish on a form-built one-off hull is a day of reckoning. Now you must examine your work for bulges and hollows, gauge gentler undulations with battens laid against the surface, outline each with chalk or marker, truncate the highest prominences with sanding, and level all else with applications of putty—over and over—until the surface is utterly fair and smooth. First, you fair; then you smooth. Only after these should you prime and paint.

FAIRING

What is fairness? Ray Hunt called it harmony; L. Francis Herreshoff called it art. Despite a lifetime of concern with it, the best definition I have formulated for fairness is a line or surface without awkward changes in direction. Definable or not, everyone admires fairness and bemoans unfairness.

In one-off fiberglass parts, unfairness of the structure is the result of carelessness in lofting and setting up or in the installation of stringers, linings, and core materials. Unfairness of the laminate is the result of additional layers of glass that are not stepped back enough to make a long taper and of powerful shrinkage that causes areas to cave in. Unfairness is not to be confused with the roughness of the surface of the last layer or two. That's a matter of texture, which needs filling or smoothing. Unfairness is a matter of contour.

Unlike the planking of a wooden boat, a fiberglass shell is too thin, too

The bottom looks a bit like elephant hide here, just after laminating the outer skin. This is Centennial's *hull, the building of which is detailed in photographs in Chapter 7. The photographs in this chapter show stages in the fairing and smoothing of the hull. (Loy photos)*

expensive, and too hard for outboard joining, for planing away great piles of shavings until it is made fair. You can grind down a particularly proud ridge or bump on fiberglass somewhat with coarse abrasive disks on a grinder, and you should. The best approach to fairing fiberglass, however, is by the judicious application of putty. Polyester-resin-based putties can be made up or bought premixed to suit every finishing requirement. Those made by mixing glass fibers into resin have physical properties similar to a fiberglass laminate, but they are more brittle. Long-milled fibers sold for this use make the strongest putty; however, the longer they are, the coarser the putty's texture. A fine putty made with short fibers—they can be milled any length right down to dust—smooths out better, but brittleness increases with smaller particles. Glass-fiber putty is not easy or pleasant to sand, so it is used only to build out a laminate where the strength of the putty is important. It should then be topped off with a putty that sands and polishes readily.

Microballoons, a fine Bakelite flour of tiny "balloons," is mixed with boat resin and used for extensive fairing of fiberglass and wooden hulls. The mixture is a light, tough, tenacious putty suitable for modifying hull shape with applications that might be well over an inch thick in places. Because it combines hardiness with lightness, microballoons is widely used to alter the lines and rating measurements of racing sailboats. If you have created horrendous unfairness in a high-performance boat, microballoons will bail you out. It's an old standby.

There are numerous other fillers for resin with which to make fairing putty. Almost all substances that are inert, and some that are not, have been tried—for example, tiny glass spheres, ground pecan shells, synthetic particles and fibers, asbestos, and other mineral fibers and powders including talc.

Talc has been used as a resin thickener since the beginnings of fiberglass, and quite understandably because it had been so used in the paint industry long before that. It is probably the most popular of all fillers. It is readily available, cheap, inert, and makes a hard, strong putty with good adhesion and a texture fine enough to work in thicknesses from at least ¼ inch down to a few thousandths of an inch. You can use talc putty for smoothing as well as fairing. It takes a good polish, although it is certainly not the softest material to sand. Suppliers to the paint industry and some fiberglass-industry suppliers sell it, like cement, in bags in a demoisturized state, which makes a better putty with resin.

Talc is an ingredient of polyester-based auto-body putties, which are also suitable for use on boats. Auto-parts stores or body-shop suppliers are a reasonably good source of this putty both for the quality of the product and for price. If it stands up in all weather on thin, vibrating steel, it should be all right on a boat. Just make sure that it has a polyester base. At the same time, don't overlook the wholesale suppliers of resins and chemicals to the boatbuilding industry, who often carry both a variety of premixed putties and the raw materials for making them. Further, don't be surprised if the same putty you find in the auto-parts store is actually mixed, packaged, or distributed by these same wholesale suppliers.

You will save money and have greater flexibility to match the physical properties or working consistency of putty to the job at hand if you buy the ingredients and mix your own. This, however, is not worth the trouble when your needs are limited to one small boat, unless you're the type who likes to experiment.

An outline of the steps to take from the time the last layer of the laminate cures through fairing the boat follows:

1. Use a coarse grit on a disk sander to knock off any obvious protrusions above the local plane of the surface—the goose bumps, tufts, or unruly strands that sprang up after you finished flattening them with roller or squeegee for the last time.

2. Wipe off the dust, study the surface for unfairness, and make an encircling mark around any islands projecting above what would be the fair line of the surface. Here's where you'll find a 4- to 6- foot wooden batten handy. If you lay it against the surface, you can tell whether the bump that has caught your eye really extends above the fair line or only seems to do so. It could be sitting in a hollow,

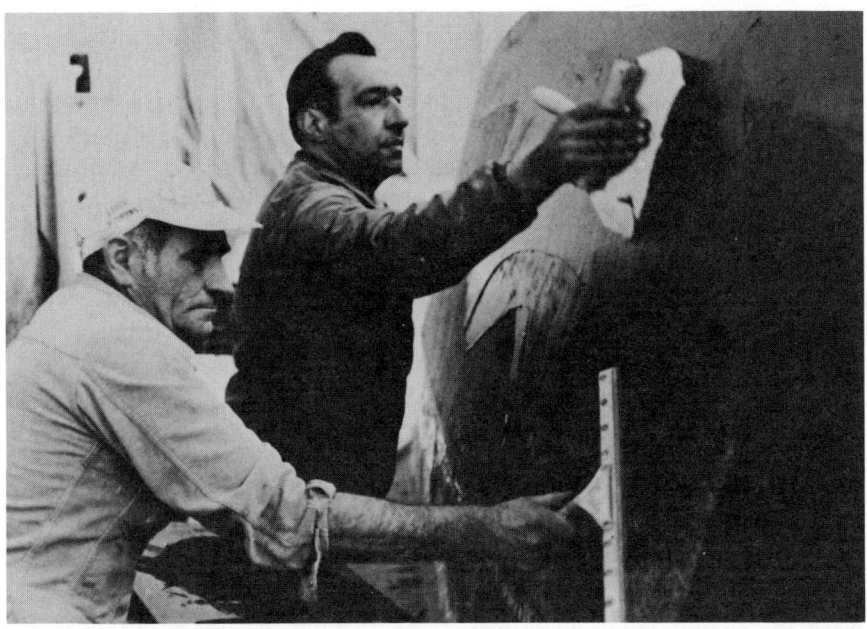

Filling the roughness with filled and pigmented polyester-resin putty.

relative to a larger area, or it could be just the ridge at the edge of a crater. If so, it may need little or no sanding, just a flood tide of putty flush with it, or even covering it, to blend with the whole, faired surface.

Only by studying as large an area as is practicable all at once can you accurately gauge unfairness and know what to do to correct it without wasting a substantial portion of your time and effort. Some people have an innate knack for fairing, can just glance down the boat, take it all in, and say, "Here's a bump. That's a hollow, from here to there. . . ." People who don't know anything about building boats have made such remarks when I was struggling to fair one. It's one of those helpful acts you find it difficult to accept graciously, no matter how right the person is. (It'd be different if that person were seeking employment; he or she would have a job.) If you're one of those people, you might not need a batten; but for most of us, a batten that springs fair against the hull is the sure tool with which to expose unfair bumps and hollows.

3. When you have ground off as much fiberglass from the bumps as needed, or all you dare to remove lest you weaken the laminate too much, then it is time to apply putty with a wide putty knife. It is neither necessary nor desirable to put putty on so thickly that it covers the entire surface. It should fill the hollows only, until they are flush with the high spots. When most of the high spots are beginning to disappear, you had better stop and reassess the surface, for you no longer know where you are and may be just building new unfairness. Checking the surface with a batten between applications of putty is a good plan of action. Keeping the high

areas scraped bare, however, ensures that you are not getting out past the fair line that was based on them in the first place.

4. The best tool for fairing is the longest one you can control with your two hands and arms. The sizes range from 2 to 5 feet, or possibly 6 feet for a tall man, but the contours and size of the surface affect the length, too. A springy metal straightedge, a thin board, or a rubber squeegee all work well when held horizontal and pulled down over the surface of a hull or trunk top that has had a fresh coat of putty smeared on it first with a wide putty knife. You should grasp a straightedge with one hand a little way in from each end and bow it slightly to fit the curvature of the surface. You have to bow the heavier all-rubber squeegees this way, too; but the softer, thinner ones, usually clamped in a metal holder with a pole socket, tend to adapt to the shape. Sometimes, though, the latter squeegees, normally used for washing windows, are too soft for fairing and will not bridge the hollows well enough to do the job. This is not to say you should get rid of one of these in disgust, for it may be just the tool for spreading a thin, creamy putty when smoothing a surface, as opposed to fairing it.

After you have gotten the feel of dragging a straightedge down over a surface, a trick that is greatly facilitated by adjusting the putty to the right consistency, you will be surprised and delighted with the fairness you can create with it. Along with learning to control the straightedge, however, the beginner must learn how to recognize a reasonably fair pass, then to leave well enough alone. The temptation to go back over an area merely to eliminate minor flaws—a track left by a particle in the putty, a slight mussed spot where the tool started or left off—must be resisted. Better to leave these things for the next time around, or for the local sanding and smoothing that follows the broader fairing. To fuss too much wastes not only time but the putty, the gel time of which is ticking steadily away.

5. All resin-based fairing putties shrink when they cure, which is to say a second round may be needed over deep hollows, after some sanding to remove any upstanding flaws left in the first. When all the surface has been brought up to make fair lines, wherever you sight or place a batten, fairing is done and smoothing can begin.

SMOOTHING

Unless laid up in a mold, a fiberglass laminate always needs some smoothing if you want a plain, unblemished finish. And it needs an exhaustive scrubbing when you're going for a highly polished surface. By building truly and laminating neatly, it is possible to avoid fairing but not smoothing, because a laminate is anything but self-leveling. At the same time, fairing does create smoothed-over areas, so wherever you have been fairing, the surface will be, or should be, partially smoothed already.

A sequence of moves paralleling that outlined for fairing is required for smoothing, but this time you are concentrating on eliminating every minute local irregularity rather than general unevenness of contour.

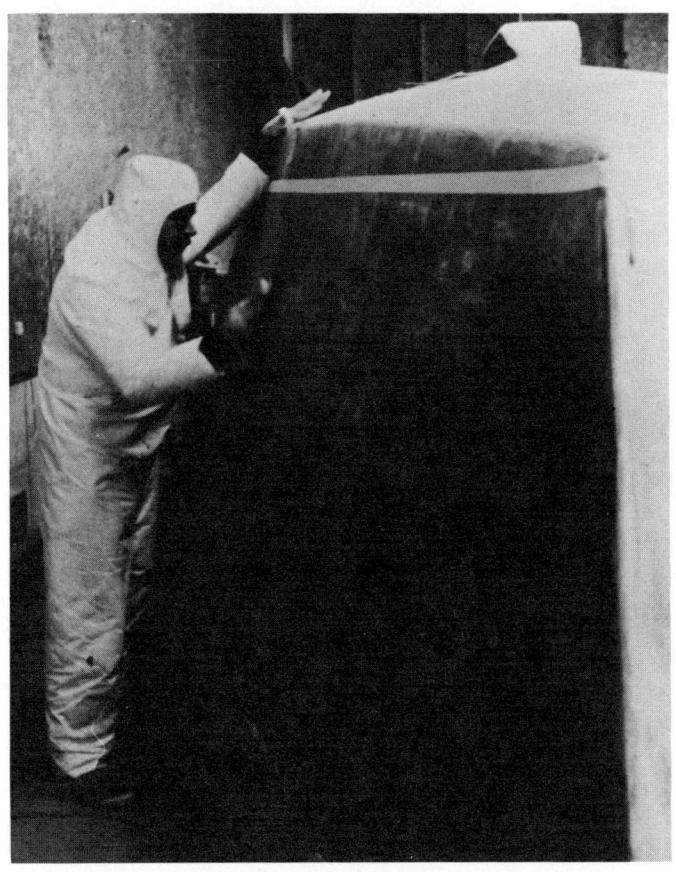

Hand-block sanding is best. Coarse paper on a block cuts down the high spots.

1. Again, the first move is sanding; but it's sanding to flatten the surface, to level or plane down its texture a little, evenly, all over, not more in one spot than in another, lest you create new unfairness. Logically, if the roughness goes deeper in some places than in others, then sanding everywhere to reach the bottom of the roughness will create a very uneven surface unless you sand away large areas around every deep spot. To sand and sand, removing all roughness as well as a good part of the underlying laminate, is a long, dirty job, and a bit silly.

What do you do, then? Use a flat sander, hold it flat, and don't try to eradicate all roughness. Instead, sand only across the top of it, only enough to bring the highest protrusions down to match the average. In other words, when your sander has touched most of the surface in a given area, that is, left its mark generally, skipping over depressions and scuffing off high spots in the process, that's enough—stop.

2. Fill the surface with putty. For this smoothing putty, you can use any fine-grained polyester body putty or surfacing putty. It should be soft and easy to spread, but not so soft that it sags. If you can find one that sands well, so much the better. In any case, apply it neatly to avoid unnecessary sanding. If the surface is not deeply indented, a high-build primer/surfacer might be better to use on it than putty. I'll go into these materials next, but first let's consider the use of putty.

The surface of the hull is looking better.

Catalyze a batch of putty small enough to use up before it starts to gel. Mix it on and dispense it from a board cut out to resemble a Ping-Pong paddle. Using a springy but not too flexible putty knife from 3 to 6 inches wide, as suits the job, take a bite off the puddle of putty and spread it down over the surface, not too thickly. Take another stroke or two at a different angle to the first, firm enough to bare *some* points of the underlying surface as the knife scrapes it smooth. Putty collects on the knife from this scraping action. You remove it by wiping the blade on the edge of the paddle. Only reuse this putty as long as it is in good condition, not partly gelled, dried up with dust, or lumpy with crumbs it has picked up. You should try to keep the putty scraped down enough so that you lose contact with the original surface only where you have covered a definite depression. You're filling potholes, not laying a new surface. Be sure to wipe out any glops or ridges also, as they are more easily eliminated with the knife now than with the sander after they have cured.

3. Once the filling has cured, you can sand again, but only to remove protuberant flaws.

4. Now it's time to reevaluate the surface. Is it smooth enough for priming and painting? If it's in need of another round of putty, it might be time to switch to the alternative to putty mentioned earlier: a high-build primer/surfacer, one of a group of products that might be described as either soft sanding liquid putty, or a very, very thick priming paint. To save confusion, I will call those compounded with a polyester-resin base *surfacers* and those compounded with a paint base *primers*.

When it comes to polishing or fine sanding, a vibrator is of some use. The raised deck is papered over because it is already shiny from the deck mold.

Surfacers are sometimes used right up to the final finish coat, should it be compatible, whereas primers are strictly thickened first coats, like International Paint Company's High-Build Flat White Primer, designed for use with a particular line of paint.

The advantage of the resin-based surfacers is that you can apply gelcoat or gelcoatlike resin-based products over them, and also, with appropriate priming, any of the usual paint systems. The Evercoat Company's Feather Fill is such a product. Over a dozen years ago, the Ferro Company, well known for their gelcoats, came out with a system designed specifically for finishing plugs, direct molds, and one-offs. It consisted of a high-build surfacer with which you could build up a thick, soft sanding coat for the elimination of raw fiberglass texture and a harder product almost like gelcoat with which to finish the surface. New products, all designed to sand better, have been brought out regularly ever since. And I am sure we will see more, as the industry seeks to lessen the chore of smoothing laminates not blessed with the slickness a mold confers.

Meanwhile, long before it was a fiberglass problem, builders smoothed the roughness in wood and metal surfaces with the application of high-build primers compatible with traditional paints. We used some of these on a number of the early one-offs built at my shop. They saved a lot of puttying and sanded very nicely. And, if a lack of reports to the contrary is any indication, they are still at work, hiding the roughness of the laminate from whatever finish paints have since been applied, all except one. This primer—I can't remember what brand it was—alligatored after a year or so, or the paint on it did. But even that condition was repaired fairly easily.

5. You can spray and/or brush high-build surfacers and primers, but however applied, their purpose is to fill and cover roughness as a snowfall fills and covers uneven ground, giving you a thick, soft layer with muted roughness that is easily sanded smooth. The savings in labor are not only in the sanding, but in the application, which, with either method, is much more rapid than puttying.

6. The nearer you get to the end of finishing, the more careful you must be about sanding. A piece of sandpaper wrapped on a block of foam is the safest tool with which to bring a surface to mirrorlike wet-sanded and compounded perfection. Pushing it by hand, you can feel what's happening to the surface, not just see it after it's done. Also, no matter how insensitive or inattentive the operator, it's not cutting fast enough to make deep scars before they're noticed. At the same time, I'm aware that this is a power-tool age, that a vibrator, disk sander, or possibly even a belt sander is what you're more likely to use. That's all right; I became resigned to their use (by anyone not working for me) years ago. They're useful in that order for smoothing and, incidentally, in the reverse of that order for the heavier sanding associated with fairing. If you use them, just remember to take your time, hold the sander flat, and check the surface constantly with eye and hand for *smoothness*. That's what you've been working for, and along about now you should begin to get it, at last.

PAINTING

How to paint, to actually wield brush or spray gun, is hardly within the scope of this book. Like woodworking, foundry work, machinist's, mechanic's, plumber's, and electrician's work, not to mention rigging and sailmaking (some insight into all of which the boatbuilder should possess), painting is a trade in itself, worthy of its own book. As for materials, there are innumerable good marine paints on the market from which to choose. There is also gelcoat. But, wonderful as it is on a molded part, painting or even spraying standard gelcoat on form-built parts is hardly worth the fine sanding, water sanding, and compounding necessary afterward to raise it to the self-leveled, glossy perfection of a properly applied finish coat of paint. True, if you want to work on it long enough, you can take gelcoat beyond the most perfect paint job. It has the fine composition and can be

Moved outside after yet another coat of paint. The brightwood guardrails are papered for painting, and the waterline is taped.

applied thick enough to do that; but I doubt that most one-off builders want to trade the amount of labor involved for a cosmetic perfection that is really only justifiable in tooling, or even the amount needed to equal a good paint job.

Aside from the rich variety of traditional hull and deck paints and the one- and two-part epoxies on the market, we now have a new breed of superslick, tough, and durable coatings, such as U.S. Paint Company's Awlgrip, and International Paint Company's Imron, which are so good that a number of production boatbuilders are molding parts without gelcoat and painting them with these products just prior to completion. It is claimed that this procedure, although initially more expensive than spraying a mold with gelcoat, is less expensive in the end, when you consider the cost of repairing the damage done to gelcoat on the production line. Nor have customers, who seem quick to appreciate the greater ease and lesser cost of touching up or repairing a paint job, voiced any significant objection to the switch away from gelcoat. My many remarks about reprehensible practices of production builders notwithstanding, I know from experience that there is much one-off builders can learn from this branch of the industry, the vast expertise of which is constantly sharpened by competition for the market. Painting rather than gelcoating may be one trick that is worthy of imitation.

11

Keels, Sumps, Rudders, Centerboards, and Tanks

KEELS

With so many older wooden boats still in existence, it wouldn't seem possible that anyone could become a fiberglass boatbuilder without knowing that the wooden versions of, say, 40-foot powerboats or auxiliary sailboats have traditionally had 4- to 6-inch-sided oak keels and deadwood. Yet it appears that a number of today's builders have never thought to compare such scantlings to the thin walls of the fiberglass keels they produce. Not long ago, a brand-new $90,000, 40-foot ketch built by *the* retirement cruising-yacht builder in this country* backed away from a wharf, hit a rock, and opened a hole in the side of her keel that might have promptly swamped her had she not been a mere 200 feet from a Travelift. No way would a wooden keel have suffered comparable damage. A little paint off and possibly a few splinters of wood are the worst you could expect. In repairing the fiberglass keel, we found its wall thickness to be ⅜ inch. When reproached about this, a company spokesman said, "I guess we built that boat's keel a little too thin."

That understatement notwithstanding, the vulnerability of fiberglass keels is not due entirely to a thin laminate or skin. It's due partly to being hollow. If backed up well, a given thickness of fiberglass can withstand many times the impact that would hole it as a hollow structure. Even when a keel has a laminate strong enough

---

*That's not my designation; but the company has a wide, enthusiastic following who seem to believe it.

to withstand the most severe punishment within reason, solid filling can only make it stronger. Nor will a hole in the fiberglass result in a leak as long as the material filling the hollow remains watertight above it. Solid filling can also prevent leaks by covering the inboard ends of bolts that penetrate the hollow keel. For these reasons, I have long been an advocate of solid filling hollow keels—not always of filling them full, but of filling at least their most vulnerable portions.

Innumerable "fillers" or reinforcements can be mixed with resin (casting resin is preferable because large masses of it won't overheat) and poured, shoveled, or smeared into a keel. A few of the many I have used are glass fibers, asbestos fibers, wood sawdust, microballoons, sand, and crushed stone. The first two are very strong; the second two, tough but lightweight; the last two, hard, heavy, and cheap. Because you're going to wonder, I'll confess that I have also poured transit-mixed concrete into hollow keels and, further, have buried steel reinforcing rods and other items in the concrete, or in resin-based fillers. While on the subject of concrete, Travaco Labs, 345 Eastern Avenue, Chelsea, Massachusetts 02150, supplies an epoxy resin that just about doubles the strength of portland-cement mixes. In a large-volume application, some cement or concrete with this product mixed in, if it seems necessary, and a generous amount of steel reinforcement, whether wire, rods, or both, can save considerable money. This filler has many desirable properties as well. However, its weight and bulk rule it out of high-performance boats and those with fine lines.

Obviously, the most vulnerable portion of the traditional full keels on sailboats and single-screw powerboats is their heels. Yet if you go through a storage yard tapping the sides of the keels of fiberglass production models with a hard object, you will usually find that they are hollow right to the metal heel fitting. After innumerable surveys, I know that as I write this the majority of metal sailboat-rudder heel fittings and powerboat skegs have bolts that enter into thin air, or more likely, bilge water and that you will not have to look at many before you see one with water weeping down from it.

Only the bedding with which they're installed keeps most of these bolts from leaking. When it gives out, they leak. Fill the hollow locally to just above the bolts with "keel putty" of resin and chopped-glass fibers, and leaking is almost impossible.

The cost in keel putty and in labor to fill the apex of the heel as shown is modest, because that part of the keel is very narrow. In fact, you get so much leak insurance so cheaply with local filling that you would be well advised to bury any and all exposed bolts on the interior of the hollow keel. Bolts that are too scattered to include in one pour or puddle, you can cover singly with a small mound of filler or putty, which you can keep from cracking up with a patch of fiberglass mat laminate.

For the most enduring seal and for added strength in this portion of the hull, I suggest that you cover all keel putties or filling materials with a laminate of mat, or of alternate mat and roving in big boats, which you then carry up onto the sides of the keel or hull. This adds a welcome rigidity to the structure.

Whether you fill a hollow keel entirely or to some arbitrary level depends upon your assessment of the type and size of it. From the keels I have seen holed by grounding, I gather that the area within a few inches of the bottom of the keel is many times more likely to be damaged than areas higher up. This leads me to believe that partial or shallow solid filling is quite worthwhile and that the first 6 to 8 inches of filling are more useful in resisting damage than all the rest, no matter how deep the keel. Once a boat is washed onto her side in shoal water, she is in a position to be holed at any point all the way up to the turn of the bilge, if not the rail, and no amount of solid keel will necessarily make a difference. Yet at the same time, other uses for parts of the hollow keel might take precedence over solid filling.

SUMPS AND OIL PANS

In theory, fiberglass boats should have dusty, dry bilges. In practice, they almost never do, and a sump where bilge water can collect and stay until pumped out is a very desirable feature. The deeper and narrower the sump, the less likelihood that bilge water will come out and slosh about the interior as the boat heels or rolls. It is therefore a good plan to dam off a pit or well in the filling of a hollow keel to serve as a sump. Small bulkheads of PVC foam are handy for boxing off such an area. The top surface of your keel putty should pitch toward the sump from either end of the boat, and you should provide limber holes through obstructions. Unless you are willing to live with two sumps, it is sometimes necessary to provide an aqueduct past a tank or engine pan, which might be a tunnel left under it or a PVC tube buried in the keel putty.

In some motorboat hulls, you can use the combination of a hollow fiberglass keel and keel putty to alter the migration of bilge water, which tends to run forward when the boat is at rest and then aft as the bow rises and the stern settles underway. If you cannot pitch solid filling from both ends to a sump somewhere between, you might at least be able to create two sumps that will catch enough water to inhibit its traveling back and forth.

Anything you can do to channel bilge water away from collecting under an engine that is low in the bilge will pay off handsomely in rebuilt starters alone. When water rises to the level of the flywheel of many marine engines, you've had it. The starting teeth throw the water around the housing, drowning the starter. This sort of thing can be expected to happen sooner or later to an engine close to bilge water; and, of course, it is most likely to happen to a boat that is already in trouble and sorely needs its engine and/or the electrical power generated by it.

An oil pan under the engine can help to isolate it from splashes of bilge water. But the pan is only as effective in damming water away from the engine as the height of the propeller shaft, which must cross over the aft side of the pan. The need for an oil pan under any engine in any boat, if you are to have clean bilges, is so obvious that I would remind you only not to forget to install one. It's much easier to do in the smooth bilges of a fiberglass boat than in wooden boats, where it must be a separate, complete metal or fiberglass pan built to fit various construction members. With luck, building the "pan" in your one-off may be as simple as damming off the space between fiberglass-covered engine beds. However, you might find it necessary to pipe bilge water through the pan by glassing in a length of PVC tubing or to let the water run underneath by installing a pan bottom that bridges the hollow keel. PVC foam is great stuff for building such items because it is so easy to cut, fit, wedge into place, glue with resin, and cover with fiberglass. It is also resistant to oil, gas, antifreeze, and bilge water, although I certainly wouldn't leave any of it exposed on the interior of the pan. Don't forget to make a sump in the engine pan itself, or at least to make one end lower than the other, so that the last of its contents will settle there. I built one boat with dead-level pans under two big V-8 engines. Needless to say, there was always a residue of something swashing about in those pans, and they were almost impossible to clean. The sump or low end should extend beyond the engine so that you can get a pump or bailer into it to dry it out—which brings up a couple of last points. Bilge sumps should have enough room for the ubiquitous submersible, electric bilge pump and its float switch and/or for the pickup of a sizable manual pump, as well as for arms and hands to reach down and clean out debris and retrieve lost items. The sump is also the logical place for a docking drain, the removable plug at the lowest point in the hull for draining it when the boat is hauled out. A docking drain prevents damage from freezing in cold climates by draining off all bilge water during winter storage. But in any climate it simplifies cleaning and flushing out the bilges whenever the boat is ashore.

EXTERNAL BALLAST KEELS

The ballast keels of sailboats and motorsailers have moved to the inside of the fiberglass hull of most production boats with traditional full keels, although short, deep, narrow fins are still an externally attached lead casting. There is no question that external lead is able to survive the wear and impacts of grounding better than fiberglass, or that iron is the most indestructible of all. However, the costs of bolting on a metal keel and of providing a smooth surface that fairs with the fiberglass hull are greater than the cost of dropping it into a hollow fiberglass keel that is a continuation of the hull laminate, as long as the keel shape is not a difficult one to lay up. Therefore, your choice of which way to build a traditional full keel on your one-off should be guided by how often you expect her to "take the ground" and/or how willing you are to go to some extra labor and expense. Should you decide to have an external metal keel, your first task is to draw it in on the loft floor. This actually amounts to nothing more than outlining the keel on the lines of the boat you have there already. Then, to make a long story short, you build your form or mold for the hull down to that outline and take the pattern or mold for the keel casting off the lines within the outline.

POURING YOUR OWN KEEL

Getting a keel cast at a foundry is the easy way, but even that requires a pattern, the making of which is discussed shortly, or building a direct mold, which is discussed in the next section. If you want to cast your own keel, however, you have to set up a melting pot. The lead for many a keel has been melted down in a cast iron bathtub picked up at a junkyard. Another junkyard find that is likely to be strong enough to hold the tremendous weight of lead you can put in it is one end of a pressure tank. You can have it burned off with a cutting torch and some stout legs welded to it. For heat you can build a wood fire or burn oil in a discarded oil burner. To build a wood fire hot enough, you need a huge supply of small, dry sticks not over 2 inches in diameter or board scraps 2 inches or less in thickness split into narrow pieces. Logs won't produce enough heat in a short time. But if you keep piling on small sticks, you can create a roaring inferno. A loosely piled brick wall helps concentrate the heat on the pot. If you burn oil with its limited heat, this concentration is most important. You should also try to get a burner that burns at least two gallons per hour, or use two smaller burners, if you have over 2,000 pounds to melt. It is hardest to get the melting started when the lead is piled loosely in the pot. When we were faced with large quantities of lead—junk lead especially—we often melted down a good portion of it the day before, knowing that we could liquefy the mass much more quickly on the day of the pouring. With molten lead in the pot, other lead added to it makes complete contact and melts down more readily, too.

Steel legs welded to a pot should be oversized, shielded from the intense heat of the fire by a column of bricks, and sitting on a firm foundation. A pot with thousands of pounds of molten lead in it is *not* something to be jury rigged!

To turn the flow of lead on and off, the simplest solution is to bring ordinary iron pipe out of the pot far enough to put an elbow and a standpipe on it. You turn the standpipe to the vertical position, on its threads, until you want to pour, swing it down to pour, and back up to shut off the flow. Do not bring the pipe too far out from the firebox, and do have a torch handy to heat it when lead "freezes" in it, which is sure to happen not far from the fire. It helps to keep the spout free if it comes off the bottom of the pot well within the fire rather than off the edge of the bottom or off the side of the pot. Do *not* use any brass fittings. The heat will melt them, and whatever lead is in the pot will run out on the ground. That once happened to me, leaving a 40-foot auxiliary's keel 1,000 pounds short. She's one of the few boats around with a 1,000-pound block of lead fitted into the oak keel atop her ballast keel. The only good thing about spilled lead is that you can dig it up and remelt it; and any dirt, stones, or other metals caught up in it float to the top.

Unless your lead pot just about overhangs the mold, you may need something in which to run the lead. Standard-weight iron pipe steals too much heat and plugs up as lead freezes in it; but galvanized-iron down-spout pipe, being thin, is less likely to do that. Give it a good pitch, keep the run short, see that it is well supported on bricks and cement blocks, and keep the seam up.

Pouring a sand-cast lead keel. Note molten lead pouring from down-spout mouth.

Never forget that lead is *hot* and *heavy*. With these facts in mind, you'll agree that the best place for a lead mold is in the ground. There, no matter what happens, the lead can't go far. Nor can it cause a fire or other damage. Never throw anything that contains water, like a piece of lead pipe, into a pot of molten lead lest it explode and shower you with the stuff. You should carefully plan a pouring operation and take every possible precaution. As long as you do, I think you'll find it a fascinating and satisfying undertaking.

DIRECT KEEL MOLDS

Sand-casting is the traditional way to pour one or more lead keels. Today production builders use steel or iron molds to pour identical keels in rapid succession. For a one-off keel, however, building a direct mold might involve less work or expense than either, depending on your personal capabilities, the materials at hand, and other circumstances. A mold to be discarded after one pouring can be built of portland cement and sand, or plaster, or even wood. The wood (oak is suggested because of its high ignition temperature) will char, the plaster will crack, and so might the cement. But as long as you get your keel, who cares? I have always wanted to build a one-off fiberglass direct mold with some sort of fire retardant or at least heat-resistant resin, but never had a good excuse. If you are handy at welding, or can get someone to do it, the best mold to make is one of steel, although it is too expensive for most one-off operations. If the steel is rusty junkyard stuff, it will only prevent any possibility of the lead sticking to it. You should be careful about using very thin steel. Although it may have ample strength for the job, it is likely to buckle when the hot lead heats it unevenly, giving your keel some rumpled or distorted surfaces. It is best to heat up a steel mold all over with a torch if you can, in order to prevent violent expansion of the bottom portion while the top is still cool.

You can form cement or plaster molds by pouring them around a pattern built of wood, or Styrofoam, or why not one-off in fiberglass? At the risk of seeming a worrywart, I'll mention the extreme weight and the pressure the molten lead exerts on the mold once more and advise that any mold you pour above the ground be very strong. What I'm talking about is 5 pounds per square inch, over 700 pounds per square foot, for each foot of height pressing outward as well as downward while the lead is fluid. Back in 1960, we sand-casted an H-28 keel in a "flask," a box of planks on top of the ground similar to a cement form. The planks had been braced to stakes around the outside, but we didn't remember or notice that the braces had been removed. Suddenly the sides of the flask leaned outward, and the lead ran out of a fissure that appeared in the sand at the end of the mold. We yelled at a friend standing there, who sprang back, tripped in the brush, and somersaulted down the hill. As soon as I could afford it, we built a 24-by-5-by-4-foot cement-lined lead pit in a shop floor. But you can simply dig a pit in the ground for one keel.

SAND-CAST KEELS

The pattern for a keel that is sand-cast is traditionally built of wood, often of solid pine, to take the pressure of sand rammed tightly against it in the flask or pit, your pounding on it with a sledgehammer to jar it loose from the sand, and the strain of lifting it out with straps on two eyebolts or pads.

The pattern's dimensions must take into account a shrinkage factor. When you run molten metal into the sand, it shrinks as it cools, and the cold keel is about ⅛ inch smaller for every foot of its measurements than the pattern. Therefore, the dimensions of the pattern should be stretched out ⅛ inch for every foot if you want the keel to fit the boat. Obviously, the shrinkage will be insignificant in the width or height of a narrow or shallow keel, but in a long keel it can easily be an inch or two. This shrinkage factor also applies to building a direct mold.

Having used ⅛ inch to the foot as a shrinkage factor in my shop with accurate results for over 20 years, I was astonished one day to have a young friend call and complain that his first keel didn't shrink that much and had to be cut off to fit the boat. Later, I realized that the keel was poured apparently so slowly that it was

A sand-cast keel for an L. Francis Herreshoff Nereia *ketch. From the look of the pairs of bolts, it would seem that the builder is going to install some floor timber-like members on them after they are offered up through the fiberglass hollow keel. Or maybe he will use solid fill to the threaded height, cap the fill with fiberglass, then use nuts and washers.*

partly cooled by the time the pour ended; yet somehow the mold was kept filled out to the ends. What happened to my friend is a good trick if you can arrange it. Keels that are poured too slowly, however, tend to "layer"; that is, hot lead running out over lead that has chilled too much fails to weld or join with it, and parts of the keel consist ultimately of horizontal slices. To ensure a solid, one-piece keel, you should keep the lead sufficiently hot and fast flowing to prevent hardening of the surfaces farthest from the spout and occasionally paddle the lead toward them with a shovel, until the pour is completed. If you do this, you have shrinkage.

A tricky factor in sand-casting is that a tall keel, like a deep fin, poured standing up has such enormous pressure at the bottom from the weight of the metal that it compresses the sand at the bottom and comes out taller (also possibly a bit wider at the bottom). Therefore, you do not need to account for a shrinkage factor in the height of such keels.

Building a sand-casting pattern takes a fair amount of time and skill, especially the pattern for a shapely round-bottomed keel. Creating such a beautiful thing in wood to make but one keel seems extravagant, unless one enjoys it for its own sake. To save time and money, I have made keel patterns of Styrofoam, which can be shaped very quickly. Also, for keels that are bigger on the bottom than on the top, a Styrofoam pattern has the unique advantage that you can leave it in the sand and allow the molten lead to burn it away. You should not attempt this indoors, however. Styrofoam makes an incredibly foul black smoke when burned. As a matter of fact, you are better off if your entire keel-pouring operation is out-of-doors where you can stay to windward of all fumes and smoke.

You have to use water-based materials to paint and putty the surface of a Styrofoam pattern and to glue pieces of it together, because petroleum products and polyester resin dissolve it. The pattern should consist of one solid piece, and even then you must take care when you pack the sand around it that you don't distort or tear open its surface with careless ramming. A board on top of it with some weights piled on is necessary to keep it from climbing out as the sand squeezes it.

It goes without saying that if you can take the pattern out, you should do so. But if it won't "draw," you may be able to minimize the amount to be burned by cutting out the middle of it with a saw or long knife. If you cannot draw the wooden pattern of a keel, because it is, for instance, longer on the bottom than on the top, you have to fit it with a core, or cores, usually made of wood covered with sheet asbestos. You pack the sand around the pattern and core fitted together, remove the core to get the pattern out, and then replace the core for the pouring. You must cover any such cores, any sand areas overhanging a buried Styrofoam pattern, and the Styrofoam pattern that will be left in place, itself, with boards or metal plates that are loaded with weights or shored down from the overhead. Otherwise, the molten lead will simply float sand, core, or pattern and come right on up to the level of the top of the keel, full length, width, or whatever.

Note that your keelbolts, or rod cores to make holes for them, can be set in boards across the mold. Bolt cores, by the way, can be shellacked and rolled in fine sand, or coated with graphite powder in motor oil to keep them from sticking in the lead. If they're rusty, all the better.

BOLTING KEELS ON

The type of keel usually determines what bolting method will make the installation easiest. When the keel is long and shallow, coring for the bolts saves the most labor. With the keel fitted up under the hull, or the hull fitted onto it, you have only to place a drill in the cored hole, drill up through the fiberglass, and drive each bolt from below. Long through-bolts in a keel of any depth are unnecessarily expensive. As a rule, no bolt needs to project into a lead keel more than about 8 or 10 times its diameter. It also becomes difficult to drill for and drive long bolts from below because of height limitations under the keel. Of course, if you insist on through-bolts in cored holes in a deep keel, you can transfer the location of the holes by boring the holes in a pattern placed against the top of the keel and use the pattern to make holes up through the fiberglass while there is still enough height for a drill under the boat. Then you can drive bolts threaded on both ends from inside

The outside lead keel sand cast for Bright Star *was fitted up to the hollow fiberglass stub keel, whose single skin was about 1 inch thick, and bolted in place with 1-inch stainless-steel threaded rod. The rod was made into self-tapping lags by tapering and grinding cutting slots at the leading ends and using driving nuts on the tops.*

the hull until they project below the keel, put the nuts on the lower ends, drive them back into the countersink, and nut up the upper ends.

However, two less costly ways with deep keels are to cast the bolts into the keel or to drill and tap for the bolts into the keel from inside the hull. Bolts cast into the keel can enter into slightly oversized holes in the hull, predrilled with a pattern taken from the keel *after* the bolts have been cast into it. To make it easy for you to fit the pattern down over the bolts, you should bore extralarge holes in it. Then you can slide a scrap of thin plywood with a hole of more modest clearance down each bolt and fasten it to the pattern. Now, as you lift the pattern off, or try to, knock any bolts straight that are leaning awry and binding against the pattern. Use a wooden mallet or a sledge and a club of hardwood so that you don't damage the threads. When installing a keel this way, you may be forced to enlarge or "ovalize" some of the holes in the fiberglass, but they can be filled with a putty of resin and glass fibers once the keel is fitted up to the boat.

Applying the bolts to a keel from inside the hull is a matter of drilling down into the lead and threading it for the bolts. After drilling the fiberglass of the hull with a clearance hole, and perhaps some distance into the lead if the bolt has a solid shank, you drill a smaller hole and tap it for the bolt. You don't need a drill that is as small as the root diameter of the threads. In fact, you can easily get into trouble and break off the tap if the drill is that small. Even when very sharp, very frequently rotated in reverse to break off the chips, and copiously flooded with cutting oil, a tap tends to squeeze, cold form, and/or "ball up" the lead ahead of it.

Because of this action, you get a full thread in lead with a hole that is smaller than the bolt diameter but not as small as the hole you would bore in more brittle metal.

The malleability of lead makes it possible to tap the hole with the bolt itself, and I have bolted innumerable keels with self-tapping bolts made of stainless-steel threaded rod. This product is very strong and durable, yet cheap and readily available. By tapering the leading end on a grinder, grinding a couple of slots similar to those in a tap in the first few inches, and welding a nut on top (or using a "driving nut," a nut that is closed over on one end), you can make up some very rugged bolts that will wind right down into the correct-sized hole, making their own threads as they go. To find the correct-sized hole for this, you should put a pig of the lead in a vise, bore several holes of barely different sizes, and try one of the bolts in each until it makes a good full thread without binding. To drill the holes, you can use kerosene; and to wind the bolts, motor oil is OK.

No matter how you bolt on a keel, how well filled every bolt hole is, or how well bedded every nut and washer is, it seems a shame not to take advantage of the sealing properties of fiberglass by covering their inboard ends with it as described in the discussion on solid filling earlier in the chapter. However, I wouldn't bury them so deep in short, deep fins and separate skegs that they can't be uncovered for removal and repair. Such appendages have a way of getting damaged sooner or later.

It makes a fairer boat to bed the fit of the keel against the hull, filling up any gaps or pockets between the two surfaces. Putty applied only around the edges of the joint will not stay put long, especially in freezing temperatures. A mastic material such as 3M's Scotch Seal #5200 or #5300, BoatLife, or any number of other bedding and caulking compounds, is best for this use. Bedding is particularly important over an iron keel to inhibit rust on the surface of the join, where it cannot be reached again. On wooden boats we used to use canvas saturated with white lead or red lead. These materials always did a fine job; but now, because of the dangers of ingesting them, they are scarce and expensive. When the keel's top was very rough or big, we used asphalt roofing cement and tar-saturated felt paper at a substantially lower cost than the more sophisticated materials.

So far, I have been talking as though all outside ballast keels were simply bolted through the single, albeit extraheavy, skin of the fiberglass keel or hull bottom. Well, most of them are; but some keels, like the short, deep lead fins so popular today, various short cast-iron keels, some with a bulb at the bottom, and twin keels meant for sitting on the ground at low tide need to be bolted to a stiffer structure. A more effective member, one that can absorb better the extreme leverage that such keels apply at their point of attachment, is the "floor" or "floor timber," long a standard part of wooden-boat construction. Acting as athwartship webs or diaphragms, floors prevent any change in the shape of the skin when the keel tries to bend it. Floors may be of wood or metal in a fiberglass boat as they are in wooden boats, although covered with fiberglass to attach them to the hull laminate. Or they can be all fiberglass, laid up in place over a former or core of PVC foam or any number of other easily shaped and fitted materials.

Note that while the attachment of the keel might be improved by bolting through the flange of a metal floor, it is not necessary to take bolts to the top of the various types of floors shown. In fact, bolts there could cause trouble by admitting water to the interior of the floor, or by compressing an essentially hollow floor. In this case, where fiberglass is stronger in tension than in compression or bending, it is just as good engineering to have the keelbolts pulling on the heavy laminate at the bottom of the structure as on the tops of the floors, as long as they are not too far from the floors' bases.

In the canoe-bodied hulls on which keels of this nature are usually installed, there is often little space under the sole for floors of any depth, particularly in smaller boats where headroom is at a premium. In such boats a stub keel of fiberglass, which is faired into the hull and laminated as part of it, provides space for deep floors without raising the sole. It also provides a deeper sump than the boat ordinarily would have. By the way, don't forget to provide a generous limber hole at the lowest point of every floor!

INTERNAL BALLAST KEELS

If you build a full hollow keel as part of the hull and drop the ballast keel into it, the ballast keel can be a much cruder casting. As a matter of fact, it doesn't *have* to be a casting. Pieces of lead or iron in a variety of shapes and sizes can be packed into the keel and frozen into a solid mass with any of the materials described under keel fillers. In one 32-foot shoal-draft cruising ketch, for example, the long, shallow keel has a single layer of iron reinforcing rods laid along the bottom of the keel with lead pigs tightly packed on top, all filled around with a keel putty of coarse chopped-glass fibers in casting resin. Layers of alternate 1½-ounce mat and 24-ounce roving followed by two of 1½-ounce mat were applied as a cap that lapped well out onto the hull on either side.

In one typical 40-foot ocean cruising sloop, 10,000 pounds of lead cast in three blocks (for easier handling) were lowered into the hollow keel, which was 1½ inches thick at the bottom tapering to ⅞ inch thick at the garboards. The blocks were cast in steel molds with simple shapes made up of flat plates. The spaces between the blocks and the keel were filled with a mixture of resin and "pea stone," pea-sized crushed granite. The aft end of the lead and filler was bulkheaded off to leave space for a fuel tank and a sump aft of that. The forward end was sealed off to leave space for a water tank. The top and ends of the ballast and filler were capped with a 12-layer laminate reaching well out onto the hull. A PVC tube was installed to carry bilge water past the ballast and fuel tank from the water-tank area.

In building our 37-foot fiberglass Meadow Lark ketch, the earlier boats had the casting bolted on; in later boats we lowered the 18-foot-long single piece of ballast weighing over 4,000 pounds into the ¾-inch-thick hollow fiberglass keel, where a puddle of keel putty lay in wait, and sealed over the top with a six-layer laminate.

Another method of getting a more or less solid mass of lead into a hollow keel, one that I have known several builders to use but have not tried myself, is to pile lead pigs in it and pour molten lead over them. The theory is that the pigs take the heat out of the hot lead before it can harm the fiberglass. Although it is said that lead melts at about 624° F and that *cured* fiberglass can resist temperatures up to perhaps 800° F for short periods without igniting or charring, I would want to test the method to satisfy myself that using it would not cause a conflagration or impair the physical properties of the keel laminate. Without a way to monitor the heat of molten lead, I would hasten to pour it as soon as it was fluid, before it had time to soak up too much heat, for I have sometimes gotten lead so hot that the steel pouring spout glowed red. Another problem that looms larger to me as boat size increases is working out a safe and easy way to get so much molten lead up into the boat, while ensuring that nobody slips on the inside of the boat and is burned. Topping off my lack of enthusiasm is the knowledge that with too little heat the pigs will not become a solid mass by any means.

You can be sure of a really solid cast keel if you pour or have it poured in sand or in a direct mold and hoist it aboard. Taking a pattern off the inside of the hull to use for sand-casting, or around which to make a direct mold, is easy and accurate if you pour plaster or portland cement and a light aggregate into the keel hollow. You can line the hollow with Mylar, holding it in place with masking tape, and lighten the mix further with blocks of wood buried in it. You can seal the wood with resin so that it won't swell and crack the casting. You can also lay up a thin skin of fiberglass in the hollow, which with suitable reinforcement can be used either as a male pattern or a female direct mold. Should none of the above patterns appeal to you, you can always make up small wooden moulds, fitted into the keel at intervals. When the tops of these are cut off in a flat plane, and provided with centerline markings, they can be reassembled upside down on the workbench, like the moulds of a form.

However you decide to go about the installation of an internal ballast keel, some important considerations are: the right weight in the right fore-and-aft location, packed as low and as densely as possible; a stout fiberglass keel laminate; and a stout internal covering laminate. The latter laminate should not be skimped, because it is extremely useful to tie the hull together across the top of the keel, to hold the ballast in place if the boat is overturned, to keep bilge water out of the keel from above, and to keep seawater out of the boat if it gets into the keel below.

RUDDERS

In high-speed powerboats, with rather small rudders subjected to a high-pressure flow, it is not worthwhile to try to use fiberglass. Believe it or not, fiberglass is not best for everything. The wash of a high-speed propeller will actually wear it away, if it doesn't bend or break it. Stock bronze rudders are sold in a wide range of shapes and sizes, and some manufacturers customize them within limits. If you can't get the one you want, you can make a pattern and take it to a foundry. Such a pattern is quickly made out of a piece of plywood with a block of pine glued to each side to make the boss, or bosses, the swelled-out portion into which the rudder stock fits. Do not put the hole in the pattern's boss for the rudder stock, because the foundryman cannot cast such a hole as cheaply or as accurately as drilling, and then it must be bored out anyway. It is best to have the hole bored and the stock fitted by a machine shop, unless you are equipped to do it.

Bigger rudders on slower powerboats and sailboats are another matter. As size increases, we soon find that using fiberglass in them is not only quite satisfactory but substantially cheaper than metal and more maintenance free than wood. A combination of all three materials makes an amply strong, durable, inexpensive rudder of the "inboard" types, with stocks that enter the hull. In essence, such a rudder is a wooden blade on a metal stock covered with fiberglass. Cheaper yet is a transom-hung fiberglass-covered blade with pintles or gudgeons mounted on it. How to build this rudder will be apparent from both the description of rudders with a metal stock and the description of hinged rudders for shoal-draft craft that follow.

A spade rudder for either power or sail is built the same, but without a lower bearing; and, depending on its shape, the stock is terminated at some point partway down the blade. The secret of the strength in a rudder of this sort is the metal turning arm within. Flat bars or pieces cut from metal plate, called straps, welded to the stock on each side give the most turning leverage with the least bending strain on the strap and the weld. If you can't get straps welded to the stock, you can use fore-and-aft bolts through holes in the stock. These bolts should be numerous enough and large enough in diameter to resist bending, even though, in tight holes with nuts or washers or L-shaped ends, they are aided by being thrown into tension as the rudder tries to bend. It is not necessary that such bolts or welded-on straps be longer than one-third the blade width, although it certainly won't hurt. You can build out the blade's fore-and-aft width with pieces of natural wood if you want, but a plywood core is more quickly made up and does not have to be drifted together with metal rods as natural wood does.

Note that a plywood core can be made of two pieces glued together, using short nails or screws that are left in place to hold them until the glue sets. This greatly eases the assembly of the rudder when bolts are used, for you can slot the matching face of each piece to make the bolt holes, using a hand power saw or router against a guide. Another advantage of the two-piece plywood core is that you can bevel the end of each piece where it fits against the stock before fastening the two together, avoiding the difficulty of cutting the stock's groove in the edge of a one-piece core.

Flat-bar straps should be welded so that their outside surface is tangent to the stock and let flush into the core material—whether wood, plywood, or foam—if you want a smooth, fair rudder. You can fasten them through the core with rivets or flathead machine screws countersunk into one side and threaded into the other;

190   BOATBUILDING ONE-OFF IN FIBERGLASS

Top: *One approach to a one-off rudder. A plywood core is slotted for rods through the stock.* **Center:** *A central plywood core cut out for straps welded in a plane through the stock centerline.* **Bottom:** *Double straps over a plywood core.*

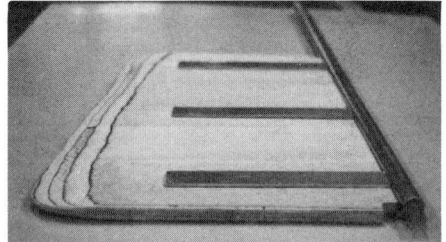

or you can use a number of short flathead wood screws of large wire in each bar. But you should use wood screws only in rudders where you will cover the stock and straps with fiberglass along with the blade so that water is kept out of their lead holes.

The most important feature of the one-off rudder with a wood core is its fiberglass shell. Few builders get this part right, because they do not use a laminate thick enough to make it a truly fiberglass structure that properly seals water out of its interior. Nor do they seem to realize that some mechanical fastenings in the underlayers are a wise investment to keep the glass tight to the flat areas of the blade, come hell or high water. Three layers of mat is the least I would use on the smallest dinghy rudder. They can be of lightweight mat—that's a function of the rudder's size. Only by using a number of layers, however, can you ensure watertightness. As the size and weight of the boat increase, you should use more and heavier layers. Also, you can introduce some woven roving or continuous-strand roving oriented fore and aft on the blade, although you need not turn roving around sharp corners or thin trailing edges.

There are two different approaches to sealing water out of the core. One is to cover and seal the blade before installing it in the metalwork. The other is to cover and seal the whole structure, except the part of the stock that goes into the boat or into a lower bearing, after assembly.

The first method requires that you make the recesses in the core for the straps deep enough for them to fit into after you have fiberglassed the blade. To keep water out of the strap-fastening holes, you fit the stock with its straps on the blade temporarily before covering and drill the blade with locating holes for the fastenings. You then remove the metalwork, bore the holes in the blade out to about three or four times the fastening diameter, and fill them flush with glass-fiber putty. Now, when you fiberglass the blade, fit the stock and straps on again, and rebore the holes for the fastenings, they will pass through solid fiberglass. Whether you cover the metalwork with more fiberglass or just fair around it with putty after final assembly is not structurally important. You will facilitate repairs to damage if you don't. But if you do, you will pretty much eliminate the possibility of corrosion or electrolysis of the covered portion.

Obviously, covering only the blade is not very practicable when you use bolts through the stock in lieu of straps. About the only uncomplicated way to protect this construction from water is to cover and seal the assembled blade including that part of the stock adjacent to it. It is also a perfectly viable way to do a strapped rudder, which will remain as smooth as you make it indefinitely. The most difficult point at which to seal out water when you wrap the whole blade is where you leave off the covering on the stock as it leaves the blade. The stock must get several round turns of mat here, no less than 2 or 3 inches long (the longer the better), to choke off water that might sneak along the stock. The rest of the covering then surrounds and attaches to this sleeve.

A fiberglass sleeve like this tends to shrink tight to anything around which it is wrapped, but you can incorporate added insurance against water penetration by putting a coat of 3M's Scotch Seal, or any similar flexible caulking compound compatible with resin chemically, around the stock under the sleeve. You can either apply the compound and let it cure before you wrap the sleeve over it or wrap a layer or two of mat in it before it cures, then wet it out with resin after it has cured, and add more layers later.

Because there is little room on most rudder stocks beyond the blade for a sleeve, you can notch the blade back to give the sleeve more length. The notch may as well be wide enough to allow you to wrap round turns on the stock without interference and to turn some of the layers covering the blade in there, too. Once you have glassed the blade and adjacent stock well, you can fill the balance of the notch with glass-fiber putty before you apply the last two layers of mat.

The importance of sealing water out of a fiberglass rudder of any kind is naturally greatest in climates where it can freeze and split open the fiberglass. However, the one-off builder is much less likely to have trouble with his hand-wrapped rudder than many production builders are with theirs, which invariably are molded in two pieces. Such rudders aren't bad at all when flooded upon assembly with non-water-absorbent, highly adhesive materials around the metalwork. But many are left hollow to save weight or filled with foam that has voids around it. Thus if the glued-together halves split somewhere along the seam, greater trouble is probably in the offing. The well-wrapped one-off rudder has no seam when you cover the blade before assembly and only one, where the stock exits, when you cover stock and blade both after assembly.

To build a lightweight rudder, you can use PVC foam for the core in almost the same constructions described for wooden cores earlier. The low compression strength of the lighter foams, especially, requires only that you spread the turning force of the straps or centerline drift bolts over a larger area than they need when pressing against wood. There are several ways to insert enough wood and fiberglass layers to spread the turning force of the metal through the foam. In one method, a single sheet of plywood the thickness of the bolts' diameter is simply slotted and positioned in the plane of the bolts. The L-shaped ends on the bolts are to prevent slippage if the whole blade tries to wring or twist around the stock. The spaces around the bolts are puttied with glass-fiber putty, and both sides of the assembly are covered with several layers of mat in the area over the bolts, tapered out to only one layer at the edges of the rudder. Short screws, nails, or pop rivets fasten the glass to the wood mechanically. A layer of foam is then weighted or clamped in wet mat to each side of this centerline assembly, shaped as desired, and the whole rudder covered with a fiberglass skin, including the stock.

In a second method, straps are welded on the centerline of the stock. The straps can be flared or they can be T-shaped or mechanical fastenings can be used to prevent fore-and-aft slippage. Again, fiberglass with mechanical fastenings in the wood is used to make a hard-surfaced pocket for the metal, before the foam is applied.

In a third method, double straps welded tangent to the sides of the stock are fitted over a plywood core.

The stock of a rudder is traditionally bronze or stainless-steel shafting. However, the rage for lightening up everything about the boat, especially toward the ends, combined with extremely deep spade rudders on sailboats, which make a large-diameter stock necessary, has compelled designers and builders to go to stocks made of tubing. Bronze and stainless-steel tubing are the most common. Aluminum has been used, too. With aluminum, however, you have to be careful, for only if tempered does it have the all-important strength in torque and bending. Further, when you weld aluminum, you reduce the temper of the welded area to zero.

Some time ago, I had just about decided that the underbody of a 30-foot production auxiliary I was surveying was in fine shape and that the yard could put her back in the water, when, standing well astern of her, I noticed that the bottom of the deep spade rudder was out of line with the keel by about 6 inches. There wasn't a scratch on the blade. Just how that approximately 3½-inch-diameter heavy-wall aluminum stock got bent that much without other damage was hard to imagine. But a call to the manufacturer elicited this information: "The first stock we used on that model didn't work out. The owner should replace it."

If you use any sort of hollow stock on your rudder, you should be aware that the outside diameter (OD) of what is specified as tubing *is* the dimension by which it is named. Thus, 3-inch tubing is 3 inches OD, and the inside diameter varies with the wall thickness. This is not so with American standard "pipe" sizes. What is called *pipe* is always bigger on the outside than the named size. Thus, 3-inch pipe is approximately 3½ inches OD, for instance, and again the inside diameter varies with the wall thickness. Therefore, no way will pipe fit into machined fittings like stuffing boxes or bearings that are called by the same dimension name. Nor, by the way, will pipe fit into hoses that are named for the inside dimension of the hose if the hose has the same dimension name as the pipe. You'll never get ¾-inch hose over ¾-inch pipe, no matter how much soap and water or grease you use. But hose manufacturers are kind to boatbuilders and plumbers in that they make hose in odd sizes, specified, for instance, as "hose for ¾-inch pipe," which would have to have an inside diameter of about $1^{1}/_{16}$ inches.

At the same time, among the many sizes and wall thicknesses available, certain standard pipes and tubes fit one within the other well enough so that you can make a hollow rudder stock of one and a rudder port, bearing, or stuffing box of the other without machining either part. My point is that you should look into sizes before you build anything and know where you are going to get all of the parts that must fit together so as to avoid difficult or expensive adaptations.

A SHOAL-DRAFT RUDDER

I cannot leave rudders without mentioning the best configuration for steering a shoal-draft boat—in thin water *and* deep—that I have experienced. Francis Herreshoff designed this rudder for the 33-foot Meadow Lark. Besides using this rudder in its original transom-hung form on innumerable boats from 10 to 36 feet, I also adapted it to use on a metal stock through the hull. In both types, it is well suited to one-off fiberglass building with a plywood core, which is the way I have built all of them, except for one size that I put into "half-shell" production molding, since I switched from oak in the late 1960s.

Normally, this rudder reaches as deep as you want, is not pitched out of the water by big seas, allowing the boat to spin off course, and in this position is easy on the helmsman's arm. But then, when you are sailing over bottom on which you could wade ashore, you can pull the blade up no deeper than your skeg and still

A smaller rudder for a shallow-draft boat, as designed by L. Francis Herreshoff for the Meadow Lark. Fiberglass over wood.

have its full area as a powerful sweep. Should it strike bottom, the blade simply swings up; in fact, it usually needs a bit of lead built in to keep it down. When the boat is beached, the blade can be pulled well up out of harm's way. Best of all, it's uncomplicated, simple to build, and has the ruggedness of two hinge plates to keep the blade aligned to the main rudder, which we affectionately dubbed the "lollipop."

On dinghy rudders, I use hinge plates of sheet phosphor bronze or stainless steel $1/16$ inch to $1/8$ inch thick. For big rudders I have a pair of bronze plates cast from a pattern made of plywood. On a 30- to 35-foot boat, a ¼-inch-thick pattern thinned to ⅛ inch along the three sides is about right, cast in manganese bronze. Building up a boss about twice as thick as the plate allows enough metal to thread the pivot-bolt hole in one plate and to countersink the other for a flathead bolt, which you can cotter pin or peen to keep it from working loose—just in case you don't feel up to the lovely gunstock-type bolts Mr. Herreshoff used. On some rudders with cast plates, I have used a pivot bolt threaded on both ends, not unlike the head bolts on an engine. You turn this bolt into one plate's threaded hole, place it in position on the lollipop, and wind the other plate up on it until both plates are a close, sliding fit when clamped tight to the blade. The blade should be no thinner and perhaps just faintly thicker than the lollipop.

You can overbore the pivot hole through a small rudder and fill it with glass-fiber putty (or Marine-Tex) as described for the strap fastenings. On a big rudder I would do the same, but I would either glass in a metal bushing or set metal wear plates in a recess on each side, atop the fiberglass covering. But in the lollipop of an inboard rudder, you can locate one of the pairs of straps so that the hinge-plate pivot bolt passes through them.

A rudder's pintles and gudgeons and/or heel hardware are usually specified or detailed in the boat's plans. You can find many of the items in marine hardware catalogs, although often with the larger sizes you are on your own. To get an idea of physical sizes, you should study other boats or plans of boats similar to the one you are building. It is a pleasant and rewarding experience to make some pine patterns and take them to a foundry. For such fittings, manganese bronze is a good material, and one with which many foundries are familiar. Other alternatives are to have fittings welded up of stainless steel or of iron and have them galvanized.

In an accident, the length and blade area of an inboard rudder can make its stock a powerful can opener, capable of ripping open an ordinary hull laminate. With this in mind, you should heavily reinforce the hull where the stock enters. In too many fiberglass boats, builders have ignored the example of sturdy horn timbers in wooden boats and have done little to beef up the area. I wish that was an overstatement. It is a well-documented fact, however, that one company built scores of fishing boats without extra reinforcement in the hull around the rudder stock. Predictably, some of these rudders broke their rudder ports open. By Murphy's law, any that haven't gotten reinforcement will meet the same fate sooner or later. Personally, I like my hull and rudder port strong enough not to break when the rudder is bent right aft like a duck's other foot, which happened to a 32-foot sailboat and to a 48-foot powerboat that I built. Both were wooden boats; the powerboat had a bronze spade on a solid stock, the sailboat had a fiberglass-covered wooden spade on a solid stock 3 inches in diameter. Although I have lost a record of the details on the powerboat's accident, the boat wasn't flooded. On the sailboat, the rudder port and horn-timber section of the laminated wood keel were not damaged at all. Why not build a fiberglass boat just as stout in that area? It might hit a rock at full speed, too.

Besides a rugged lodging place, a rudder stock needs a bearing at the hull in which to turn. It also needs a high port or tube extending above the waterline or a stuffing box to seal out water. In some sailboats with tiller steering, all of these needs can be met with one simple piece of metal pipe or tubing that is a close enough fit on the stock to serve as a bearing without "knocking" and that extends through the self-bailing cockpit sole or through the afterdeck, where the tiller is fitted. With the tube and the stock within it supported at two well-separated points, this arrangement is inherently very strong. However, I have seen a number of boats from 5 to 10 years old in which such tubes have worked sufficiently loose to weep out of the top of the fiberglass built up around them at the hull. I have also found the tops loose where glassed to the underside of the cockpit, which is not too surprising considering what an awkward spot it is to reach on the average auxiliary and how tenuous the grip of fiberglass is on a smooth metal tube. After a few such encounters, I always insisted on three details when we installed a tube like that. (1) The ends of the metal tube should pass through the laminates of hull and cockpit so that they lean on these physically. (2) The tube should be roughened in some way so that the fiberglass is locked on physically. Threading each end a few inches works well. If that is not practicable, it helps to turn or grind some rings into its surface, welding on slugs of metal, or even just scoring it with a very coarse grinding disk. (3) The entire tube should be wrapped from the bottom of the hull to the top of the sole or deck with two to six layers of 1½-ounce mat, according to the size of the boat.

Sailboats or powerboats with wheel steerers that require quadrants or arms mounted below or close to the waterline will, of course, need a stuffing box at the top of the rudder port. In wooden boats and some fiberglass boats, the functions of bearing and stuffing box are combined in a standard item of cast bronze hardware called a rudder stuffing box/bearing. The square base of this bearing is designed to be bolted to the horn timber of single-screw boats or to backing blocks fitted on the inside of the boat's planking in twin-screw boats.

Note that you have to do some heavy reinforcement in fiberglass to equal the ruggedness of the oak on which the stock ultimately leans. The strongest installation in either material is when a long "horn" or tubular continuation of the bearing below the square base extends through the hull and through an external backing plate, and the bolts as well. Note, too, how much stronger it obviously makes an installation to carry the stock up to a second upper bearing. This sort of treatment is almost necessary if you want to counteract the tremendous leverage that a deep spade rudder (or any other rudder if loose from its lower bearing) would exert on a single stuffing box/bearing mounted just inside the hull.

However, the fact that the cast bronze stuffing box/bearing has been carried over to many fiberglass boats does not necessarily make it the best rudder port for your one-off. It is a simple solution: you buy it and install it. But it is an expensive piece of hardware. Also, it depends on its bolts. Because of its bulk and awkward shape, you can neither stick it to nor wrap it very well with fiberglass. Thus, there is much to recommend the fiberglass rudder ports that more fiberglass-oriented builders have developed. The basis of these ports is the fiberglass tube, which is light, cheap, and capable of being fiberglassed to the hull permanently, and to whatever supports you fabricate around it. A tube of any size and wall thickness is relatively easy to lay up by winding fiberglass material on a mandrel, saturating it as you go. If wrapped of fiberglass cloth, it will be enormously strong; but I like to use two or more turns of mat at the beginning and at the end to minimize the chance of the cloth peeling and to maximize adhesion where it is glassed to the boat. Now, fiberglass is too easily abraded to make a good bearing, so it is best to wrap up a short piece of bearing material in the lower end of the glass tube. This can be as simple as a few inches of metal pipe or tubing itself, or as complex as a tube into which a rubber-lined propeller shaft bearing is pressed and retained with set screws to allow future replacement. Also, Micarta, nylon, and other plastic compositions make a suitable water-lubricated bearing.

At the top end of the fiberglass rudder port, you can use the less-expensive "rubber-neck stuffing box." This is a packing gland on a cast stub of tubing supplied with a short length of heavy rubber hose and clamps, used to connect it to the rudder port. It is easy to build up strengthening members around the fiberglass rudder port, which become, in effect, an integral part of it.

RUDDER STOPS AND STEERERS

Turning a rudder about 35 to 45 degrees past each side of center on most boats causes it to act only as a brake, slowing the boat more than turning it. Whatever limit you set, the health of the rudder depends upon what stops it when it reaches that limit. If, for instance, a rudder mounted on the skeg keel or transom is allowed to go over until its leading edge binds against these parts, or against its own gudgeons and pintles, the enormous leverage of the blade, perhaps between 25 to 1 and 50 to 1, is bound to break up something. Without proper stops, you can often cause serious damage by merely letting go of the helm when backing down.

There are many kinds of stops, and most wheel-steering systems provide an effective place to fit them. When they don't, you have to fit something, like the chain draped from stern to rudder blade on older workboats with drum-driven tiller rope steerers, which are not just a quaint ornament. The rudder-stock-mounted quadrant of a wire-rope steerer needs only a pair of bumpers to limit its swing. In a one-off fiberglass hull, these often take the form of plywood knees glassed to the hull. Screw steerers and geared quadrant catboat steerers usually are self-limited, and powerful enough to mean it, although I have had a heavy rudder break the bronze arms of a screw steerer and have been forced to move up to the next bigger size. Hydraulic steerers are self-limiting at the end of the piston's travel. The only concerns here are that the rudder be free to travel that far, that the tiller arm be keyed well to the stock and massive enough to take the strains, and that the cylinder be bolted well to a stout base. The tiller of a sailboat should be stronger than you might think in order to be a good stop. And if possible it should be able to swing down enough to fetch up against something solid in the cockpit before the rudder hurts. Otherwise, it would be wise to provide some sort of stop blocks against the rudder itself for the day the tiller goes hard over, not catching you in the ribs as it goes, I hope.

To discuss steerers in meaningful depth would only duplicate the excellent installation instructions available with the better brands. However, I will say here that you should provide for any of them stout pads, mounts, or benches, heavily fiberglassed to your hull and/or bolted to lazarette bulkhead or cockpit sole. Speaking of cockpits, if you plan to install a pedestal steerer, you should laminate nothing less than a ¾-inch plywood core under your cockpit sole and brace the cockpit well, not just to support the steerer, but also to counteract the elasticity of fiberglass, which can make your compass do an Indian war dance around in circles when the engine vibrates it. Ruggedness and rigidity are the name of the game in installing a steerer, because if it can move rather than turn the rudder, it will certainly do so, more and more as time goes by.

CENTERBOARDS

Similar in form, living in the same environment, and subjected to more or less comparable strains as the rudder, the centerboard—or daggerboard or leeboards—of a given boat is appropriately built with the same materials and by the same methods. Also appropriately, these materials and methods usually reflect those employed in building the hull. A fiberglass centerboard is a natural choice for the one-off fiberglass boat, as wood is for a wooden boat and steel for a steel boat. As with rudders, I can cite scores of quite successful one-off boards from 2 to 30 square feet in area built by laminating fiberglass over a wooden core.

For the core of a small board, a single piece of natural wood or plywood is OK, but in selecting the piece you should check it for warp. Sometimes you can take out a twist or curl by shaping and tapering more on one side than the other. The sure way to start out with a true core, however, is to glue two thinner pieces together, weighted down on a perfectly flat surface. You should turn the cupped surfaces of the pieces toward each other, because a humped-up center is easier to weight down than are curled-up edges, and their curves tend to cancel out.

While laminating any flat object, you should try to keep the layers of fiberglass on the two sides in balance at all times. Fiberglass allowed to cure completely on one side is likely to warp the board as it shrinks. To avoid this, put two layers on one side; then, as soon as they are firm enough for you to handle without mussing them, turn the board over and put two layers on the other side. If forced to leave only one side covered, you can weight the board down on a flat surface. Use polyethylene between the sticky fiberglass and a piece of plywood placed on top, then pile the weights on the plywood. This prevents dents in the green fiberglass that the weights might otherwise make.

Except in a light boat where you are willing to provide a means of holding a board in the lowered position, a pivoted centerboard or leeboard needs more than enough weight to sink it, because the force of the water against it when the boat is moving ahead tends to push it up. A daggerboard, however, needs little more than enough weight to sink it.

To calculate how much flotation you will have to counteract, you figure the volume and displacement of the board by simple multiplication:

length x width x height = volume; and

volume in cubic feet x 64 pounds (weight of 1 cubic foot of saltwater) = displacement.

To simplify the math, I always express the measurements in feet, using decimals of a foot for inches and fractions of an inch. (For instance, a centerboard 4 feet 6 inches by 2 feet by 1 inch thick = 4.5 feet by 2 feet by 0.083 feet = 0.747 cubic feet. Then 0.747 cubic feet times 64 pounds = 47.808 pounds displacement, or flotation.) So, if a board of these dimensions doesn't weigh more than 48 pounds, it won't sink. How much extra weight you should add to keep the board down against the water flowing by depends upon such variables as the length of the leading edge and the speed of the boat. In practice, at least when sailing, the boat's leeway jams the board against the side of the case so hard that movement up *or* down is inhibited until you come into the wind. Add in the great difference in the percentage of the lateral plane that different centerboards represent and in the speed of different boats, and you have too many variables to predict the exact amount of extra weight needed in a given board. In general, though, I think slower boats can get along with as little as 10 percent added to their displacement weight; but 20 percent makes a more positive-acting board. On a "planing" hull, the board has to be a heavy "drop keel" to stay down, or else a daggerboard, which is not pushed up. Anyway, because extra weight at the keel and below adds stability to a displacement boat, plenty of it is good. What limits extra weight in this instance is your ability to raise and lower the board. Conversely, when weight in any and all parts is unwanted, as on a multihull, your problems are how to build the lightest board strong enough, how to hold it down, and possibly, on a big boat, how to raise it, too.

One important factor that determines the force needed to raise a board is how much of it comes out of the water. Any part lifted clear of the water adds its displacement weight to the "extra weight," whereas the extra weight is all you have to contend with when the board is submerged. Other important factors are the leverage of the pendant, the distance of its point of attachment from the pivot pin on a pivoting board, and the amount of mechanical advantage involved when there is a tackle or winch.

One more fact I might point out is that the extra weight in a pivoted board, usually an insert of lead, is more effective the farther it is from the pivot. There is a good reason, then, for a heavy metal shoe at the point where the board will strike the ground. At my shop we used lead shoes bolted on externally on some boats and a glassed-over lead or iron insert at that corner of the board in others. But you should be careful to wrap an iron insert heavily with fiberglass and to patch it quickly if exposed, or rust will bleed out of it forevermore and eventually explode the fiberglass.

Thus, if your plan does not show how to construct the board the way you want, you should make some calculations before you change the design or design your own to ensure that (1) the board will go down and stay down and (2) the arrangement for raising and lowering it will be adequate. It helps in these calculations to know that lead weighs 709 pounds per cubic foot, and fiberglass weighs 95 pounds per cubic foot, or 1 pound per square foot when ⅛ inch thick. A wooden core weighs 47 pounds per cubic foot if oak, 34 pounds if fir, 35 or more if mahogany, and if plywood you should add the weight of the glue, several pounds per cubic foot, to the weight of the wood.

The pendant of the traditional board lifts it directly up by its top edge. But the preference for deep, narrow boards in recent years makes this impractical without causing the pendant, dangling down underwater to some point on that edge, to drag. That's OK on a small boat where you can attach the pendant to a projection on the top edge of the board. The pendant, then, comes up out of the open-top case and is led horizontally to a point forward of the case, and the hauling part is turned back to the crew. On the smallest boats, the skinny board can have a squared pivot bolt with a lever on it with which to turn it up and down. But on a cruising boat, one of the attractions of the deep, narrow board is hiding its entire case below the cabin sole, even in a canoe-bodied hull with a shallow keel.

The forward end of the board is a semicircle around the pivot pin that is grooved like a quadrant. A pull on the pendant, which is wrapped around this groove from an attachment in the top of the board, rotates the board up into the case. Unfortunately, this requires that the pendant be led forward through a stuffing box, then aft through a turn block, and finally up to the cockpit, or somewhere on deck. By this route, there is little doubt that you need a winch to raise a board of very modest size. True, this type of board is totally submerged and you are only raising the extra weight needed to sink it, but that weight is substantial due to the drag in the system and the pressure of moving through the water on the long, more or less vertical, leading edge. If you decide to install this type of board, your main concerns should be that (1) the groove for the 7-by-19 stainless-steel wire pendant you will probably use is deep; (2) the board is a close enough fit in the trunk so the wire can't become jammed between them; (3) there are stops on the piston to prevent it from being pulled out of the stuffing box, which tends to flood the boat; (4) there is a spring tensioning arrangement in the inboard part to take up slack if the board is bounced up, or at least room in the top of the box for slack cable without jamming everything up in there; (5) there is a winch powerful enough to raise the board; (6) the turn blocks are of ample diameter and very well anchored to the boat. The pull at the forward block is doubled by the 180-degree change in direction, and small-diameter blocks not only add drag to the system but also wear out the wire early on.

It is certainly nice to avoid the intrusion of a centerboard case into the interior arrangement of the boat; and we have the designers' word that deep, narrow (*short*, referring to fore-and-aft length, is the proper term) boards are more efficient, although I have never seen any numbers indicating the magnitude of that efficiency. However, when you see the mechanical complication such boards create, you certainly begin to wonder whether the "improvements" are worth the price on anything but an out-and-out racer.

For pendant hardware in a small centerboard, you can bore the pivot-bolt hole and the bolt holes oversize, fill them with glass-fiber putty, and rebore them. This procedure keeps water out of the wood core. On a big board, you should set some metal pivot-bolt bearing plates and pendant tangs in recesses on each side, over the fiberglass covering, and fit the bolts holding these, too, in fiberglass-lined holes.

A centerboard should be built with plenty of fiberglass, never fewer than 3 layers of mat on the smallest board and about 6 to 8 layers of alternate mat and roving with 2 layers of mat at the end of an 8- to 10-foot board. Also, don't forget to fasten the underlayers of the laminate to the wooden core mechanically. This is not as important near the edges of the board—where the rounding from one side to the other locks on the fiberglass—as it is in the middle of the flat surfaces, where separation could be started by warping or flexing of the board.

Wood is by no means the only core material for a one-off centerboard. PVC foam can be used to build a light board, although, as mentioned before, such a board has to be forced down and held down. Certainly, there would not be much point in building a foam-cored, pivoted board and then adding enough weight to sink it. That would only be a more expensive way to arrive at the same total weight as with a wooden core for a given size of board. But a foam-cored board might have some unique advantages. It could absorb a lot of energy and in a crash grounding crunch or break up rather than damage the case and cause a leak or a sinking.

Extending the premise that laminating fiberglass around some sort of core is the quickest and least expensive way to create a one-off fiberglass board, two quite viable alternatives to a wooden core are aluminum and steel. Both, of course, are frequently used without fiberglass; and, from a functional standpoint, there is little wrong with a metal board. Using the metal as a core inside of fiberglass, however, eliminates problems with corrosion and electrolysis. It also bcomes possible to build up thickness and shape with the fiberglass without adding too much weight or going to the expense of building a hollow metal board.

In planning a board with a metal core, it is useful to know that the weight of steel plate is about 5 pounds per square foot for each ⅛ inch of thickness, of aluminum about 1.8 pounds, and fiberglass, again, about 1 pound. I have included here a

EFFECTS OF STEEL, ALUMINUM, AND OAK CORES ON CENTERBOARD OF SAME SIZE WITH THE SAME THICKNESS OF FIBERGLASS LAMINATE ON EACH

Core	Weight of Core	Weight of ⅛ Inch Fiberglass	Total Weight	Displacement	Extra Weight	Thickness
⅛ inch Steel	120	48	168	48	120	⅜ inch
¼ inch Steel	240	48+	288	64	224	½ inch
⅛ inch Aluminum	43	48	91	48	43	⅜ inch
¼ inch Aluminum	86	48+	134	64	70	½ inch
½ inch Oak	47	49	96	96	0	¾ inch

chart showing the effects of steel and aluminum cores and of an oak core on boards of the same size and with the same ⅛-inch-thick fiberglass laminate. You can see at a glance the wide range of total and extra or submerged weights possible with different cores. For this reason, some calculation is important if you change the construction.

When you build a board with a metal core, you should handle the fiberglass construction details about the same way as with a wood core. Mechanical fastenings are equally essential throughout the flat areas, and you should apply pop rivets or self-tapping screws several inches apart all over both sides after the board has had two layers. You should also bore oversize holes for the pivot bolt and any hardware bolts, fill them, and rebore them to seal water away from the core completely. For a more durable pivot-pin bearing, you can fill the hole with Marine-Tex, bush it with nylon or stainless steel, or provide bearing plates of the same on either side. You could even use bronze, because it is insulated from the steel or aluminum core with fiberglass. However, it is more prudent to avoid mixing incompatible metals wherever possible, and stainless steel gets along best with steel or aluminum. There is a temptation here to let the metal core bear on the pivot bolt, but to expose it at all at any point negates the purpose of covering the metal with fiberglass. In time corrosion will attack that point and give you trouble.

If you want a thicker board without the added weight of a thicker metal core, you can laminate pads of PVC foam onto each side. I would cover the metal core with two layers of 1½-ounce mat, fasten it on mechanically, weight the foam on in a layer of wet mat, shape the foam, and cover it with an outer skin appropriate to the size and weight of the board.

In general, I would not overdo the shaping of traditional pivoted boards lest they develop a flutter or vibration due to an unsteady bearing against the side of the case, although, as long as the part that stays in the case is straight sided, you can do as you will with the rest. Elliptical rounding of the leading edge and a taper at the trailing edge that is not wider than one-fourth to one-third the width of the board should be enough and should leave enough of the board straight sided to bear solidly on the case. It is worth noting that Nathanael Herreshoff did not think it necessary to taper the trailing edges of centerboards at all on many of his boats. Although his rudders often had a taper for their entire width that faired with the keel and deadwood lines, he did not mind leaving the trailing edge rather blunt, or square cornered.

OTHER BOARDS

It should be evident that if your boat calls for tandem boards, two centerboards on the centerline, one abaft the other, you will make even greater savings than with a single board if you build them one-off in fiberglass. Designed to move the center of lateral plane fore and aft for optimum balance under different conditions with different sails set, tandem boards vastly improve performance without the need for constant sail changing. But except when the owner is adamant about minimizing sail changing, designers and builders are inclined to avoid tandem boards due to the cost, which is approximately double that of a single board. Because one-off boards and cases can be built more cheaply in fiberglass than in any other indefinitely durable and trouble-free material (like Monel, bronze, or stainless steel), it is my hope that more tandem boards will be built in the future.

Leeboards are another underutilized boon to thin-water sailers. Here, however, it is certainly not a matter of expense, for you can provide lateral plane more economically with leeboards than any other way. Probably because Americans are unfamiliar with them, they are scarce and considered odd looking in the United States. However, once shipmates with them, any shoal-water cruising man quickly appreciates their many advantages, which include utter simplicity, accessibility, ruggedness, and more efficiency than you might think.

After building perhaps a hundred pairs of leeboards for boats from 8 to 40 feet, I did not expect ever to witness much positive interest in the device. Then one day Ray Hunt startled me by saying, "Allan, I'd like to clean up the flow around a pair of leeboards. They're really great! They just need some study about how to reduce the drag."

Unfortunately, Ray did not live long enough to add that design detail to the myriad of others conceived in his unique problem-solving mind. But perhaps others will, now that it is possible to do things in fiberglass that would have been prohibitively intricate and/or expensive to do in any other material. Anyway, therein lies the advantage of working one-off in fiberglass: not only can you make less-expensive, more trouble-free copies of parts like leeboards, but often you can make the parts themselves better as well.

Most of what is said in this section also applies to building daggerboards. Used for their simplicity, their space-saving configuration, and the efficiency of the dagger shape at high speeds, they make equal sense in the smallest sailboats and in the biggest sailing machines. In "go-fast" monohulls, the daggerboard can be a retractable, ballasted fin keel, whereas in multihulls it can be built so light that it takes a special mechanism to force it down and keep it there. Moving through the water does not force it up, and the daggerboard case can be made enormously strong in big boats by bringing it through the deck. Even more than centerboards and leeboards, a daggerboard is a "piece of cake" to build one-off in fiberglass.

CENTERBOARD CASES

In building a molded fiberglass boat, it is quite possible to set up a male mold for the centerboard case, or "trunk" or "box" as some call it, in the hull mold and build the hull and case as one piece. This is sometimes done in production boats, when the case is simple in shape and when working space in that part of the hull is not too cramped. However, the procedure is rarely worth the trouble in molding a one-off hull and obviously not adaptable to most form-built one-offs. It saves setup and laminating time and makes a much neater job to build a single case off the boat, usually with an integral flange around the bottom. Then you may install the case in the mold or form either before or after laminating the hull. Having it in place and hooking the hull layers directly to it is simpler and quicker; but, again, if the case is a serious obstruction to laying up the hull efficiently, it should be withheld until the hull is completed, or perhaps nearly so. That way, only the small job of glassing the completed case to the completed hull is slow work. When you laminate the hull without the case in place, you should form the centerboard slot through the hull as it is laid up by screwing a waxed stick of wood to the mold or form. Otherwise, you will have to cut out the slot, which is a ridiculous waste in this thickest part of the hull laminate.

Molded centerboard cases are normally laminated around a male mold; and if you want a solid fiberglass case, this is what you'll have to do. However, you should be aware that a deep, parallel-sided object like this can be very difficult to pull off the mold. To avoid a nasty battle you can: (1) make sure that there is good draft at the ends of the case and at least no reverse draft from top to bottom; (2) leave an opening at the top (if it is not an open-top case) through which you can drive out the mold; (3) glass in an air fitting or two so that you can release the part with compressed air; or (4) make up the mold in three layers with the middle layer composed of two wedges as spacer sticks, tacking or gluing the whole thing together lightly so that you can knock it apart.

Now the sides of a centerboard case need stiffness, not unlike the centerboard itself, which tends to pry the case apart as it resists the sideways force of the wind shoving the sailing rig and the whole boat to leeward in the water. To resist this prying, all but the smallest cases require stiffeners or, better, sandwich construction, unless the case is set in solid resin-based fill and ballast or backed up by other hull construction. For stiffening a large, flat surface like a centerboard case, it's hard to beat a plywood core, unless weight is sufficiently critical to make lighter cores worth the extra expense and labor. The safest time for you to add a core to each side of the case is while it is still on the mold. This way, shrinkage of the fiberglass or the warp in the plywood will not distort the case. If there is a curl in the plywood, it should be set on the case concave side down, which will tend to pull or bow the sides of the case apart rather than pinch them together. You should guard at all times against pinching in the middle of the case, which is called hourglassing, because it will surely cause the centerboard to jam.

Of course, you can also wait and add the core to the case after you set up its outer skin in the hull and tab it to the keel. However, if you do that, you should first make sure that the case is well wedged on the inside, in fact, bowed faintly outward if anything, so that the pressure of clamping the wood to it in wet mat can't hourglass it. Because you are covering the case with the inner skin, you get a second chance to tab it to the keel area. This reminds me to mention that if you are going to install a completed case in the boat, you should stop the core a few inches above the flange at the bottom so that you build up a heavy single-skin connection with the keel, not just one connected to the inner skin with the core between it and the outer skin.

You can use much the same construction with cores other than wood. You can use balsa core and, for a very light boat, PVC foam core. If you feel that the board might flex the sides of the case too much with a PVC core, you can build fiberglass stiffening ribs in it or lace it with ribs of wood.

Although a male mold is not difficult to make, I got the notion a few years ago to eliminate that step in building a one-off centerboard case by laminating the case in two pieces, using the sheet-plywood core of each side as the mold and starting material for that side.

1. You lay out and build the centerboard first.
2. Then, drawing around the actual board, you lay out each side of the case on the slab of plywood that will become the wood core of that side. Doing it in this sequence eliminates mistakes, ensuring proper clearance for the board all around and accurate indexing of the all-important pivot-pin hole in the board and in the case (or at least in relation to the case if the pin is fitted through an external ballast keel below the case).
3. Along the top and ends of each side core, you tack or hot-glue a thin border piece of waxed wood to the inside face. The purpose of this temporary piece of wood is to form one half of the top and ends of the case when the inner skin is laid up on the core, turned up against this piece, and trimmed off flush with it. Therefore, the height of the border piece off the core must be exactly half of the width of the assembled case, from the inside of the core on one side to the inside of the core on the other side. But, of course, the opening inside will be less by twice the inner skin's thickness. The border piece overlaps the core by about ¼ inch, and after you lay up the outer skin of each half of the case, you pry out the border pieces, leaving a shallow notch around the outside of the outer skin where the edge of the core projects past it. When the two halves of the case are assembled, the two notches form a recess around the top and ends of the case, which are filled with strips of saturated mat until flush with the core pieces to join the two halves together.
4. Along the bottom of each side core, on the opposite face from the inner skin, you temporarily fasten on another waxed stick flush with the core's edge to form a flange along the bottom of the case when you turn the inner skin layers across the bottom of the core onto it. Its width, or height off the core, will determine the width of the flange. Before you join the halves of the case and cover them with the outer skin, you pry off these flange-forming pieces so that the outer skin can join the flange, adding to its thickness and sealing off the core.
5. When you have laid up the inner skin, but just before you join the two halves, you should place the centerboard in one half and then the other to locate the pivot-pin hole and the pendant bee hole. You then bore the pivot-pin hole and any hardware bolt holes oversize and fill them with fiberglass.
6. Again, you place the centerboard in one side and bore the correct-size pivot-

pin hole through that side. Next, you assemble the second side with the first side and the centerboard and run the drill back through them. If you do this atop a pair of sawhorses, where you can drill down into the first half and up through the second half, you can avoid lifting heavy parts around unnecessarily.

7. Now, when you assemble and join the halves, everything will be prefitted to perfection, and all holes through the core will be glass lined. But do yourself one more kindness before final assembly: Give the interior of each side a couple of coats of antifouling paint.

This procedure reduces radically the labor of attacking board and case as separate projects, minimizes the chance of error, and wastes almost no material. I have followed its general outline as often as possible for some years. However, if I know there is a possibility of building another such board and case, especially when the parts are extraheavy, I do allow myself the luxury of a ¼-inch plywood pattern of the centerboard, on which I make sketches of the construction details and mark the all-important pivot center and point of pendant attachment. Starting with this much, I can whip up another board and case very quickly. Meanwhile, not being a young bull anymore, I'm often willing to settle for flipping the pattern around to save moves with a heavy set of parts.

I almost forgot (but don't you!) that there should be mechanical fastenings into a wooden core through the first couple of layers of both inner and outer skins of a centerboard case. I should also remind you once more to take care when building your one-off centerboard case to seal the water out of any core reinforcements it has. Only with PVC foam have you got half a chance of getting away with it if the water should get in.

A daggerboard case is not essentially different from a case for pivoted boards—just a taller, narrower box—and can be built in much the same way. But if it is very tall, perhaps housing a many-thousand-pound drop keel, it needs some strong end logs and stiffeners worked in to resist bending as well as being torn out of the boat if the board strikes ground. Although I have built a daggerboard case in the bow of a 48-foot high-speed lobsterboat, for better steering control and tight turning, and one in the 60-foot Newick-designed trimaran *Gulf Streamer*, I never have had the doubtful pleasure of worrying about the strength of the case for a heavy drop keel; so I won't try to tell you how to build one.

Clearance has long been the big problem with centerboard cases. The traditional wooden boards and cases warp and hourglass pretty badly at times, which makes a lot of clearance between board and case a necessity. A proper fiberglass set of these parts should be able to get along with a lot less clearance. This is good, because the older boards knock about annoyingly in the case at times. Theoretically, ⅛ inch for dinghy boards, ¼ inch for boards in boats up to 30 feet, and ⅜ to ½ inch as boards get bigger should be enough; but these measurements depend on how true and straight you build the boards in the first place, too. Therefore, prudence might dictate starting with a little more clearance and building up a board if it is too rattling loose. That's a lot easier and better for the board than grinding any off.

CENTERBOARD HARDWARE

With centerboard hardware, as with everything about a boat, you should always consider the simplest rigs first. The minimum requirements are a plain bolt for a pivot pin with a leather washer at each side of the case if it's inside the boat, or a piece of metal rod or shafting in a hole through the keel with a bronze retaining plate over each end if it's outside the boat, and a rope, or tackle if needed, with which to raise and lower away. For a light board that floats, a length of galvanized steel, bronze, or stainless-steel rod hooked to the top edge will do to push it down, and a light lanyard or shock cord will hold it down, yet give way if the board is bounced by striking bottom. Beyond these are many proprietary items that can be bought, and many you can put together yourself: square-shouldered pivot pins with hand levers on them for dinghies, and differential, worm gear, and halyard-type winches for handling larger boards. Naturally, as the board gets heavier, you need to think about bushings or metal bearing plates at the pivot pin and tangs to take pendant strains.

Perhaps because one of my first jobs in a boatyard was painting bottoms—*after* lugging planks and rollers, dragging winch wires to cradles and snatch blocks, jacking and blocking and more jacking and blocking, and, yes, digging pits under centerboards—there is one piece of centerboard hardware that will always be a favorite with me. The old "patent hanger" is a most practical device for shipping and unshipping a large traditional pivoted centerboard while the boat is in the water.

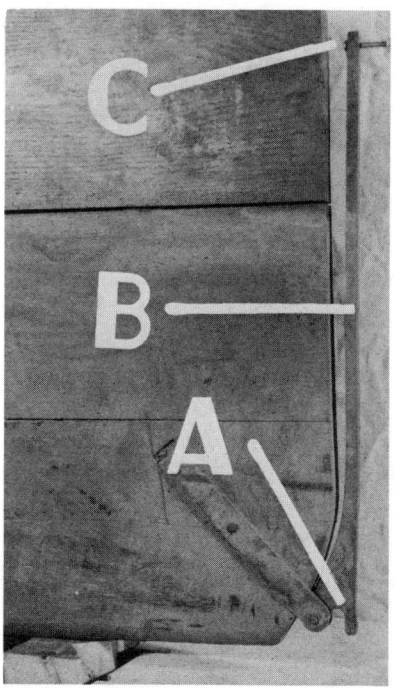

The patent hanger for centerboards: "A" is a notch or fork that fits on the "pin" through the keel or trunk. "B" is an arm that comes within reach of the top of the trunk. "C" is the bolt that locks the hanger and board in place until you want to remove them, an operation that can be done with the boat in the water.

The centerboard actually pivots on a rivet through this long-handled fitting, usually a bronze casting; and a slot in the fitting just forward of the rivet fits on what would be the normal pivot pin through the case or keel. The long "handle" of the fitting runs up the forward inside end of the case to the top, where you can reach a bolt that secures it to the case and prevents the slot from being bounced up, which would unship the fitting and board from the pin fast in the boat. By removing this one bolt at the top of the handle, then, and making a line fast to the handle, you can lift the patent hanger with the board on it off the boat's pin, freeing the board to be lowered out of the boat by the line on the handle and the centerboard pendant. You fish for these lines from under the boat with a boathook and take the centerboard ashore. To rehang the board, you drop the lines down through the centerboard case, fish them up, and fasten them to the board. You then launch the board and haul it up in place. We did this for years in storage yards with never a problem except once, when I forgot a boat had a hanger, hauled her, and put her in the shed. It's not quite the godsend it was a half-century ago, but even with Travelifts, haulouts still cost enough to pay for this fitting very quickly and may be fraught with additional expenses or inconvenience. Maybe it's just that you can't teach an old dog new tricks. I saw my first patent hanger in a derelict catboat in 1934, bought the boat to get it, and installed my last pair in a tandem-centerboard ketch in 1974. But if you try it, I think you'll like it.

ONE-OFF TANKS

When you have brought a one-off fiberglass boat to the point of needing tanks, you won't have a bit of trouble building them one-off with the same basic techniques. But before discussing how you can do that, I must confess that such tanks are not the least expensive. They cost less than any tanks built in nonferrous metals or stainless steel, although they are hardly as cheap as standard-size-and-shape steel tanks for fuel or water and polyethylene tanks for water.

I guess I've installed a hundred or more standard steel tanks and a few dozen of the polyethylene type, and I see more and more tanks of both materials in production boats every year. Polyethylene makes a tasteless, easily cleaned freshwater tank; and, of course, it is not subject to corrosion or attack by most common substances. I have no idea what its life expectancy is. Tucked away in a boat, it might last a long time. But it hardly matters when one to replace it is very cheap.

The best bargain among the standard steel tanks is the galvanized cylindrical type widely used for water tanks ashore, but fitted for boat use by the same manufacturers. They are fairly heavy-gauge steel, well galvanized, and built to stand the pressure of water systems. Being mass produced, they are very competitively priced; but for the same reason, the manufacturers are not wild about special orders. If you ask them to leave the tanks ungalvanized so that you can use them for diesel fuel, you might run into delays and an extra charge "for pulling them out of the production line." Nevertheless, we used to put up with the hassle, learned to order early, and thereby won some excellent little tanks for diesel fuel that matched the ones for gasoline and water. I call them *little* tanks because, having no baffles, there are limits to the size you should use in a boat, even of a very strong tank like these. Anyway, when the ungalvanized tanks came in, you may be sure that the first thing we did was to cover the outside with fiberglass. The glass men got so that they didn't even ask.

There are some solutions, then, to the cost problem with tanks. If standard sizes and shapes will fit and capacity requirements are modest, use polyethylene or galvanized steel for water, galvanized steel for gasoline, or plain steel fiberglassed on the outside with two or three layers of 1-ounce or 1½-ounce mat for diesel.

Leaping from the plain and practical to the sublime, I find it a high point in a survey when my flashlight discloses the greenish glint of Monel. Like a dovetail joint, true wood paneling, or a floor on every frame, a Monel tank is one of the precious stones that make up a real piece of marine jewelry. If you don't know the age of the boat, staring at its Monel tanks won't give you a clue. They look just the same after 5 years or 50. However, only the most expensive boats get Monel tanks anymore, for their current price is fantastic.

Stainless steel is great stuff, but it, too, is expensive to the point that the temptation is to use it too thin. Engine vibration and flexing when the liquid is surging inside can work to harden thin stainless; then it cracks along a weld or around a fitting. For that reason I have come to trust standard production stainless tanks or those that tank-making companies manufacture more than those a general welder has made, unless he has an excellent record.

I was an early booster of aluminum tanks, and from my experience I've found that the material gets along just fine with fresh water, gasoline, or diesel fuel. At first we used to get a lot of flak from insurance companies about aluminum tanks, but their attitude has improved during the past decade. However, that is not to say that salt water and electrolysis still can't make a mess of aluminum, given the right conditions. Consequently, I prefer to use fiberglass to isolate the outside of the aluminum in my tanks from a potentially hostile environment, as you'll soon see.

These then are the circumstances that surround the one-off builder's choice of tankage, as I see them. If nothing else, they are my rationale for building one-off all-fiberglass and metal-lined-fiberglass tanks. In late years I have become convinced that, for a one-off or custom tank, you can't beat fiberglass in the two configurations I am (finally) about to outline.

ALL-FIBERGLASS TANKS

I'll begin with their faults. Fiberglass tanks have been known to impart a taste to water if not well cured, to create static electricity when gasoline or fuel oil sloshes about in them, and to flake off or generate particles that will clog filters and cause engine failures. As far as I know, that's the full list of complaints, unless you also want to include the fact that a well-built tank is moderately expensive. However, I take exception to any complaint about cost, and I think you will, too, when you have priced any other tank proven to have indefinite longevity. For all we know, fiberglass tanks may last as long as or longer than Monel. In over 30 years, I haven't seen a properly built fiberglass tank that showed any signs of wearing out.

Let me respond to the other three counts. You can steam or bake the taste out of a tank, as long as you got a high percentage of complete cure in the first place. You can drain away static electricity by grounding metal that extends inside the tank, your metal supply or "pickup" tube, the deck fill plate, and fill piping to the boat's electrical ground. You can preclude flaking, whether of glass fibers or resin, with a good job of gelcoating and lamination. These are all problems that we can eliminate, not acts of God beyond our control. Therefore, I count it no more damning than to say that metals can fail where welded or soldered, or even where overbent or allowed to vibrate too much, and also that they can rust or corrode. However, if you don't believe that tackling these problems is quite that easy, or don't trust your laminating expertise, you can skip this section and take up the next section, which describes the metal-lined fiberglass tank that I developed specifically to minimize the possibility of such problems arising, as well as to facilitate speedy construction.

It is natural to build a tank on a male mold if only because you want a reasonably slick gelcoat job on the inside to prevent sloshing liquids from eroding particles out of the laminate. This means building all of its sides but one, because you have to leave one side open for removing the mold, even as you do with a female mold. Normally, the side left open is the top, which is usually the biggest, flattest side, easily made up on a flat surface. This also puts the joint of the cover piece around the top edge, where leaking would be minimized, if there were any. However, this is just the way it turns out and is not a hard-and-fast rule. Nor is a male mold a categorical imperative. You can use a female mold all right. You'll just get a less slick interior, and you'll have to use wax additive in the gelcoat to prevent air inhibition of its surface cure. The last thing you want inside a tank is gummy, undercured surfaces.

After all I have said about building molds in this book, I don't think I need to rehash the basics here. You may want to incorporate a flange around the top edge of the molded part of the tank, depending partly on whether you want to have a bolted-on, removable cover. A flange and screws or rivets help when you are just going to put the cover on top and seal it on, too. Without mechanical help to hold the sides and cover in position, the shrinkage of the tabbing or sealing layers can push the sides of the tank inward and the cover downward unless you build up the laminate slowly. If the tank is a water tank and will be in a place where you can get at it to remove the cover, there is much to be gained by installing it with bolts or screws and a gasket. I wouldn't want a mechnical seal on the entire top of a fuel tank to worry about. But should a water tank become contaminated, it can be wonderful to be able to get in and scrub every inch well enough to make the water safe to drink and/or tasteless again. However, if you decide to have a removable cover, don't take the short-cut of some production builders and screw on merely a piece of plywood smeared with gelcoat. I have found the bottom of such covers not only flaking off into the water, but harboring a very unappetizing black mold. Remember the rule: Never fewer than three layers of mat on a wooden surface like this, and some mechanical fastenings throughout the middle of the panel through the first layer. (I know I sound like a broken record, but here we are, 20 years after it was proven not to work, with builders still trying to get away with few or no glass fibers, just resin or gelcoat on wood.)

Before we go too far into the subject of one-off tank building, I must remind you that there are the *Rules and Regulations for Recreational Boats*, promulgated and enforced by the Coast Guard. As of 1982, these regulations referred only to gasoline tanks in recreational boats, but that could change. There is also a much more comprehensive body of regulations dealing with tankage in boats carrying passengers for hire, including Coast Guard inspections while the boat is being built. Therefore, I would advise you to familiarize yourself with the current regulations before you build, install, or hook up a fuel tank. Obtain a copy of the regulations and the latest "update" bulletins from your Coast Guard district office.

The subject of baffles and how to install them in one-off tanks reminds me to give you this advice, because I am baffled myself to find that they are not mentioned in the recreational-boat regulations. "Slosh testing," however, is mentioned, in which tanks are rocked to see if the sloshing of the contents will cause them to leak. That's fair, because a strong tank can be bigger without baffles before sloshing would cause it to fail. Nevertheless, baffles cut down sloshing and cut back the outrageous amount of material that would be needed to make big tanks strong enough to resist the battering-ram effect of the contents in rough conditions. A good general rule is that there should be no space between walls of a tank and/or baffles greater than 30 inches. But do keep an eye out for regulations; more and more of them are a less attractive feature of our times.

You can fiberglass baffles to the sides and bottom of a one-off tank before you put the cover on, and a baffle can have a flange along its top edge to which you fasten the cover with self-tapping screws or pop rivets, glassed over on top, of course. An alternative method of securing baffles, which I prefer, is to put a strip of wood or metal on a male mold, or two parallel strips in a female mold, to form a groove into which you can slide the baffle. The cover can be treated the same way. If the baffle is made about ⅛ inch thick in a tank less than 18 inches in width and height, or ¼ inch thick and up in bigger tanks, it should not break up or get out of a groove that is about ⅜ inch deep. You can stiffen a baffle by fitting strips of wood with a half-round or truncated prism section on the surface where you lay it up. You can core the baffle, too, with PVC foam, plywood, or metal.

Baffles must have ample holes in them that will allow both the liquid and the air in the tank to flow freely when the tank is being filled. A generous triangle cut off each corner, perhaps 2 inches along each tank side, is a good place for some of the holes. This eliminates dirt-catching corners in the tank and, equally important, much fussy glass work and fitting of the groove formers and baffles there. Along with the truncated baffle corners, there ought to be several more holes in the baffle 2 or 3 inches in diameter to allow quick leveling of the many gallons per minute at which tanks are sometimes filled. The penalty for insufficient holes in baffles is "blow back" of the liquid out the fill plate, which is dangerous with gasoline and at least messy with other liquids. The danger of such spills, by the way, is also ample reason to carry the full ½-inch pipe size of the vent fitting on the tank all the way to the vent and to install the vent high and well outboard, either in the topsides or over a weather deck, besides the obvious reason that you don't want the tank's contents spilled out during heeling or rolling.

The basic pipelines to and from tanks are a fill, a supply, a vent, and, for many diesel engines, a fuel return line. Deck fill plates, fill pipe, and tank fill fittings are 1½ inches standard IPS (iron pipe size) on small- and medium-sized tanks, and 2 inches IPS on big tanks. To provide flexibility in the fill line and take up movement of the deck, the rigid pipe should always be interrupted by a piece of hose for that size of pipe. This may be a very short length or a long run, depending on where it has to run and whether you prefer using mostly pipe or mostly hose. But remember to say "hose for 1½-inch pipe (or for 2-inch pipe)," meaning hose that fits over that size of pipe. Otherwise, you'll come home with the wrong size.

The standard size for supply-line, vent, and return-line fittings on small- and medium-sized tanks, up to perhaps 150 to 200 gallons, is always ½-inch IPS, regardless of the fact that the supply line to a small engine is often much smaller than that and reduced right at the tank. On big tanks, bigger fittings are used as required. On metal tanks the standard fitting on all openings is a female-threaded, welded- or soldered-on boss or half-coupling into which pipe fittings can be threaded. Since the early days of fiberglass-tank building, bosses of thick laminate have been built up and tapped for pipe fittings, or sometimes actually laid up around a waxed pipe fitting to create threads. But although this is still done for commercial tanks, it has been abandoned in boat tanks in favor of glassing on a length of IPS-sized fiberglass tubing or pipe to which a hose for that size of pipe can be directly connected, at least for all connections except the supply line of a tank for fuel. As fiberglass "welded" to fiberglass, this arrangement is more surely liquid tight. It is also cheaper to clamp a hose straight onto the line than to make up the line with pipe fittings. Fiberglass nipples can be made up with a flange on one end, to be hot-glued on the mold surface for the tank cover or installed through a hole in the cover after lamination. The flange isn't necessary, but it's bound to add strength and tightness to the attachment. Note that you can improve the tightness of the hose's fit on the nipple by wrapping several rings of strand roving around it, then covering them with a layer or two of cloth or mat. This builds ridges in the surface, which, when the hose clamps press the rubber to the fiberglass (you should always use two clamps at each end of a hose), form a tight seal and prevent slipping.

A tank manifold: a steel plate with welding spuds that are threaded for a 1½-inch IPS fill and ½-inch IPS supply, return, and vent lines. The plate will be bolted over a hole in the top of the tank.

A supply line requires a pickup, a tube reaching down inside the tank close to the bottom, and there should be a shutoff valve in the line as close as practicable to its exit from the tank. For these two reasons, it is easier to stay with metal pipe fittings until after the valve. The simplest thing seems to be to glass a close ½-inch pipe nipple into the tank with a nut on the bottom and a coupling on top. You screw a street elbow with the pickup tube soldered into its male end into the coupling and pipe the valve and supply line from its female end. By the way, it is best, and a regulation for gasoline tanks, to put all "openings" or connections in the top of the tank. Only a water tank should have a connection running off the bottom or side. A connection in the top minimizes the chances of the tank's draining into a boat when a pipe springs a leak.

Another way to make connections to a fiberglass tank is via a flange, for a single connection, or a manifold, which is made up of a plate with several connections welded to it. The flange or manifold is gasketed and bolted through the top of the tank with machine screws into a backing plate on the underside of the top. Again, the best fitting for making the connection seems to be a half-coupling welded to the plate, for this allows taking apart any one line without disturbing the others. But in a situation where height over the top of the tank is limited and all lines must leave horizontally, I have used elbows for all but the supply line welded to the manifold plate. Being much smaller, the supply line made into a half-coupling as described before will be no higher than the fill, and it is important that you be able to pull that pickup tube to clear or repair it quickly. The advantages of a manifold bolted to the top of a tank are some very solid connections and an inspection or clean-out plate all in one fitting.

What should the laminate schedule of a fiberglass tank be? It is hard to give any but basic guidelines, because the amount of support it has and its shape affect the amount of physical strength it needs as well as its size. I have been assuming, by the way, that if you are going to build a tank, you might as well shape it so that it fits efficiently into the space allotted to it. You want the most capacity for the amount of space taken up and minimal interference with the interior arrangement. A tank must be well secured, for its contents become restless and can make it hop around like a Mexican jumping bean in rough weather. Thus, you must prevent it from moving in all directions. Supporting a tank is different from securing it, although some "tank racks" do both. Support, on the one hand, implies a bed underneath, stanchions alongside, and blocking overhead, all of which help to keep the tank from bulging or "oilcanning" as the liquid is tossed this way and that. You secure a tank, on the other hand, with one or two metal or nylon straps, cinching it tight to a bed or to a pair of chocks, which might be fitted to any side of it, including overhead. Naturally, a tank secured with local restraints and otherwise unsupported must be stronger. Shape also affects the need for strength. Large, flat surfaces are weaker than those with curves or angles in them, because the materials are much stronger in tension than in bending. For this reason, a cylindrical tank with convex ends is the strongest (and most practical) shape.

Getting back to the laminate, five layers make a good basic schedule. Starting on the inside of the tank, you might use:

1. Gelcoat
2. Three layers of 1½-ounce mat
3. One layer of 18-ounce or 24-ounce woven roving
4. One layer of 1½-ounce mat.

You should overlap all of the pieces and build up extra mat around piping connections as needed. Set the cover piece in wet mat or glass-fiber putty and then tab with the same schedule of layers as listed, starting with a 3-inch-wide piece and making each piece wider up to 8 inches for the last piece.

Using three layers of mat before you apply any roving is important, for mat makes the most liquid-proof laminate. The roving provides the "hoop" strength to prevent excessive flexing and/or eventual splitting open. The mat on the outside ensures better attachment of anything glassed to the tank, seals the roving (which, by the way, should be kept back a bit from any openings) from liquid migration along its strands, and adds more stiffness by adding thickness.

To resist liquid penetration alone, a tank doesn't have to have any more glass than this, no matter what its size. What a tank needs as it gets bigger is more strength and rigidity. You can increase both indefinitely by adding more and more alternate layers of mat and roving, but beyond seven to nine layers it becomes much less expensive to reinforce the exterior with sandwich construction. Balsa core, the PVC foams, and sheet plywood are all less expensive than additional layers of fiberglass piled on to build up strength in a big tank.

As you might expect, the mention of plywood brings up another way of starting a one-off fiberglass tank and, along with it, my standard lament about people who put a little fiberglass on wood. There is no doubt that you can build a tank as strong and durable as any other by starting with a plywood mold, male or female, left in place as a core—that is, fiberglassed on both sides. Tanks of all kinds, some of them enormous in size, are built that way every day. However, many of them are awful. Sooner or later in rough going, the violent sloshing of their contents causes them to dribble like a frightened puppy. Almost always their problems are due to too little fiberglass.

I'll not soon forget the leaking tank of one new 60-foot fishing boat that I was asked to diagnose. When I crawled into the engine space, there, flanking the great, gleaming V-8 "Jimmy," were two huge plywood boxes, the grain of the wood showing through as though they were waxed, not fiberglassed. Sure enough, there was a clocklike drip off the corner of one. Luckily, once the oil was drained clear of it, the leak was stopped with a "hot patch" of saturated mat. But the unbelievable answer to my circumspect questions was that these tanks were built of ¾-inch plywood screwed to triangular fillets cut from 2-inch stock and fiberglassed with two layers of fiberglass cloth inside and out. I didn't have the heart to say all that I thought about these tanks in the owner's expensive new craft. What a way to carry several hundred gallons of fuel oil around in a boat!

Nevertheless, you can build a good tank with almost exactly the same method of construction. You just have to use about six times as much fiberglass by weight, use mat and some roving instead of cloth, mechanically fasten the laminate to the wood, seal off the openings with fiberglass to keep the liquid out of the core, coat the inside with gelcoat, and seal the cover on with a heavy tabbing. The resulting wood-core reinforced fiberglass tank will be about 2 inches bigger in each dimension than a steel tank of the same capacity; but unless you are a welder, it will cost less, weigh less, and last longer.

THE METAL-LINED FIBERGLASS TANK

As a one-off-tank material, properly laminated fiberglass is almost ideal. Then again, the few problems likely to occur with a fiberglass tank are not problems of metal tanks. Considering these facts, I got the notion back in the 1960s to try combining the two. For once with a new idea, everything worked out fine right from the first tank. The only changes I've made in over a dozen years of building them have been to simplify and devise handier methods.

The idea is to build a form or male mold of sheet metal that remains in place as a liner after you lay up a fiberglass tank around it. No attempt is made to make the liner liquid-tight. The fiberglass lamination does that. Our early liners were faithfully covered all over with epoxy before the tank was laminated on them with polyester resin. Soon, some of the older glass men took exception to the practice: "Why do we worry about gluing the glass to the liner? If it isn't stuck at all, where can the liner go?"

"The liner's too stiff to ever get loose."

"So what if the fuel or water could get between the liner and the fiberglass? What difference would it make?"

Not finding words to justify my vague sense of caution, I allowed that they were probably right. We canned the epoxy glue. As far as I know, it made no difference, for no trouble has been reported to date with the scores of such tanks that are in use in boats up to 55 feet. However, up to a little over a decade is hardly proof positive.

Given a few more decades of experience with it, I might tell you it's absolutely the best way I know of to build a one-off fiberglass tank.

Some metals that might be used for liners are: steel for diesel, lubricating, and hydraulic oils; galvanized steel for gasoline and water; and aluminum and stainless steel for all of these. Tinned copper and Monel, expecially Monel, would no doubt make excellent liners for liquids appropriate to them. But except for some old wornout tanks of these metals, around which I built fiberglass tanks, I haven't been able to try tinned copper or Monel as a liner because of the expense.

Aluminum satisfies more of the requirements for a good fiberglass-tank liner than any other metal, at present. It is readily available, relatively low in cost, soft, and easily worked. It can be used in thicknesses that make the most rigid liners for their weight and seems to be compatible with all of the liquids commonly stored in boat tanks.

After aluminum, stainless steel probably has the best range of assets as a liner. It gets along with just about any boating liquid and is less subject to corrosion than the best aluminum. However, stainless steel costs more and is much more difficult to work, even in the thin gauges that its great strength and stiffness allow.

I half expect to be criticized for suggesting the use of plain steel as a liner in a fiberglass diesel or other oil tank. Some people will probably say that it can only cause eventual trouble to have steel in there, trouble that an all-fiberglass tank could not cause. I can only point out that as the cheapest of all liners, it maximizes the economy of building a tank around one, that it is readily available and fairly easy to work, and that it has a very long life expectancy when the atmosphere and moisture are sealed away from its exterior. Aside from using it as a form for building the tank, a steel liner has two other advantages. If you remember, it eliminates the possibility of resin or fiberglass particles being washed out of the laminate in any significant quantities, and it is a built-in static-electricity collector.

But if there might be criticism of plain steel linings in oil tanks, there could be a greater flap about using galvanized steel as a liner in gasoline tanks. Critics might think this practice is in opposition to the Coast Guard's *Rules and Regulations for Recreational Boats*, which state: "A fuel tank encased in . . . fiber reinforced plastic must not be constructed from a ferrous alloy." (The quote refers to "all boats that have gasoline engines" only.)

In truth, however, we are discussing a fiberglass tank, not a tank encased in fiberglass. Our liner is in no way a "fuel tank," not intended to contain the gasoline in the first place. Nevertheless, the cost of aluminum is so little more than the cost of galvanized steel that I doubt it is worthwhile to risk running afoul of an official who doesn't know the difference between a tank and a liner. Therefore, even though I have used galvanized liners for gasoline and know they work OK, I wouldn't bother to use one unless or until it was Coast Guard approved. Anyway, there's nothing wrong with using such a liner in a water tank.

Putting a metal tank together is tinsmiths' work. Building a metal liner is more like building a pasteboard box with paper fasteners.

When it comes to cutting out the metal pieces, aluminum is kind to the boatbuilder, for it can be cut with almost any woodworking power tool, using hardened steel or carbide-tipped blades. Even a portable power jigsaw will do it. When it comes to tougher, meaner metals—especially stainless steel, the meanest of all to work—metal-cutting bandsaw and jigsaw blades may work. But I have often resorted to abrasive cutting wheels and carbide-tipped blades on a hand circular saw or to speeding up the bandsaw and "friction cutting" the metals, actually burning through them.

These are not the traditional sheet-metal cutting tools, which are usually based on a shearing action. You can, indeed, cut a tank liner out of sheet metals with good-quality hand metal shears. The longer the handles, the heavier the gauge they will cut. There are hand electric-power "nibblers," too, which take most of the ache out of cutting the stuff by hand.

Suppliers of sheet metals often have a cutting service. If your supplier does, you can make patterns of the tank parts and have them cut out of the sheets you're buying. The supplier might not be able to make all of the cuts if he has but a big power shear that makes only straight "cut-off" cuts. Even so, you can have him shear the various pieces to size. It can be well worth the cutting charge to have the basic long cuts made in a fraction of a second for you. You may farm out the work further if you find a sheet-metal shop that will both cut out the pieces of the material and fold them up for you on their "break." However, you must explain carefully what you want. Sheet-metal-shop employees are in the habit of turning flanges out at the ends of tanks so that they can be soldered or welded, and it will be difficult to laminate your fiberglass tank around such ends.

Note that you should fit the end pieces of the liner into the body of the tank with their flanges facing in, leaving a relatively bald corner. You fasten the long panels (top, sides, and bottom), which may be one or more pieces wrapped around the ends, to the ends' flanges with stainless-steel sheet-metal or self-tapping screws or pop rivets. You make and fasten the baffles the same way, but if necessary they should be of heavier stock, as they must stand alone. If it is not possible to obtain the small amount of metal needed for baffles in a heavier gauge without buying too large a quantity and you have enough thin stock left over from the long panels and ends, you can make up double-thick baffles, actually two of them riveted together back to back with flanges looking both ways.

In laying out the long sides of the liner, it makes assembly a little easier if the joint or joints, which can be a plain overlap of about an inch, are at or near a corner. Here, the short flange has the stiffness imparted by the adjacent bend to buck up the edge of the panel you fasten to it.

The essential patterns for a tank shaped to fit against the side of the boat or, if in the bilge, against both sides, are a template of each end and one of the top surface of the tank. These can consist of an open frame of pieces of ¼-inch wood, plywood, or hardboard, or a single piece of sheet stock cut to shape. Tanks are normally installed with their tops in a level plane and their ends vertical. That's why it's easy to use only these three patterns. When you set up the pattern for each end normal (at 90 degrees) to the pattern for the top, you have three sides of the

On the following pages:
Building a metal-lined fiberglass tank.

Starting a metal liner for a fiberglass tank, shaped to fit against the hull. An end pattern lies on the table; the two end pieces are set up; and the baffle is being scribed, using a straightedge that rests on the end pieces and is slotted over the baffle.

Bending the metal for the liner.

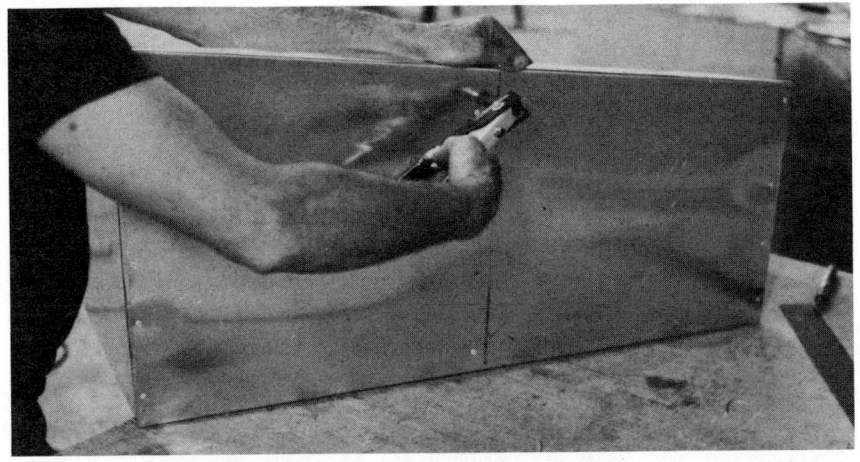

Pop-riveting the metal liner (at the baffle).

Partially assembled metal liner. Note baffle corners cut off for flow-by of air and liquid.

Assembled tank liner with pipe nipple connections held in place by ring/nuts sawn from pipe couplings.

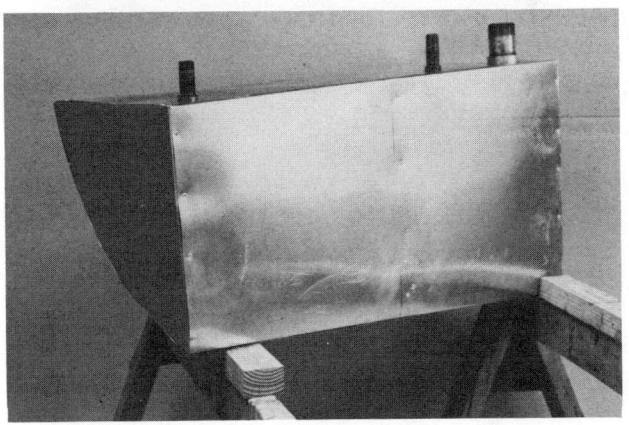

Covering the leaky edge of the tank liner with a strip of mat before putting on any large pieces of the laminate makes the work easier.

Laminating the metal-lined tank. Tearing the edge that has to bend over the rounded end, where the mat wants to fold over on itself.

Rolling down the mat.

tank; and the missing sides are surfaces delineated by straight lines connecting the two end pieces.

Now, the side of the boat undoubtedly has some curve fore and aft, usually outward, between the two ends of the tank. But because even the thinnest sheet material can't bend in two directions, this curve is ignored in tank making in favor of the vertical curve. Thus, the side of the tank is shaped to fit the fuller sweep of the boat's section. Since both the metal-lined and molded all-fiberglass one-off tanks are started off with sheet materials, we might as well take the same approach. Sure, you could wax up that section of the boat's interior, put up the ends and inboard side of a female mold, and mold an all-fiberglass tank that fitted perfectly in place. Maybe I'm just lazy, but the bit of capacity gained or the advantage of a better fit hardly seems worth the trouble to me. I must also say that if the idea of building tanks integral with the hull is beginning to intrigue you, past experience with integral tanks in fiberglass boats has not been good. Generally, they are considered a no-no for reasons I'll go into later.

Note that you have a choice whether to make the bottom and/or side of the tank against the hull a continuous curve or a series of flat surfaces subtending that curve. The series of flats is better adapted to building a metal liner, because the flange on the end pieces wants to bend in a straight line, and you would have to nip the flange into many short sections to get it to form a curve. When building a plywood or hardboard mold for an all-fiberglass tank, you can have it either way,

Pieces of roving help stiffen the flat panels, but, especially on small tanks, need not be taken around the corners, which get built up with extra mat doubled around them.

Lamination of the bottom, sides, and ends is completed, but the top has been left until last. Now it can be done all at once, lapping the laminate well down onto the sides and ends and fussing with the connections as needed.

although it takes rather thin mold material to make the bend of the curved side.

The easiest way to get the pattern of a baffle in a shaped tank with one end bigger than the other is to set up an oversized pattern at the baffle location on the overturned pattern of the top of the tank, which has the end patterns set up on it. The baffle's shape can then be found with a notched straightedge, or one with gauge blocks on it, resting on the two end patterns.

To make bends or angles in long pieces of sheet metal not having a break, you can clamp them between two heavy sticks of wood, such as 4 x 4s, or under one stick at the edge of a bench, start the bend by hand if possible, and then firm up the angle with a block of oak struck with a heavy hammer. There's nothing to be gained by beating these corners until they are sharp; better a little softness or slight round, which makes laminating fiberglass over them easier. During this operation, you should try not to dish in the flat surfaces. Any concavity will be accentuated by the shrinkage of the laminate, which could give the tank a disturbing caved-in look.

Presaturating small pieces of mat for wrapping around tank connections. Wet out and tapped into place with a not-too-wet brush, these form a less bunched and puddled buildup, one with a higher glass content.

Metal-lined fiberglass tank, completed.

Far better looking and stronger, too, is the tank with convex sides. If you want, you can give a tank a full, healthy look by substituting a slight crown for the straight lines on the edges of your patterns for the ends. If you decide to try that, the best way to make up your end and baffle pieces is to clamp them right to the patterns, bend the flanges down over the patterns, and beat them to the shape of the crown. This requires thicker patterns, however, than the ¼-inch stock mentioned. Note that if you bend all of the flanges over the pattern, you will add the thickness of the metal of the flange on each side of the piece. The piece will be that much bigger than the pattern all around. This means that the tank's perimeter will grow longer by four times the thickness of the metal. That's not much, but it's enough to make the corners of long panels made to fit the patterns misfits on the actual parts. To avoid this, you can wait to make up the long sides and bend them to fit after the end parts are made (which is a prudent idea in any case); or, if you have already bent up the long sides, you can subtract the thickness of the metal from the patterns before you turn the flanges on the ends and baffles.

The connections to a metal-lined fiberglass tank ought to be the same fittings you would use on an all-fiberglass tank, installed in the same ways. Any fiberglass tubes you use for hose are best made with flanges, which can be riveted or screwed to the liner before laminating the tank. But you can also hot-glue a plain length of the tube to the liner, or tab it on with fiberglass after the first two layers of the laminate are in place. You can clamp a close or short pipe nipple with a coupling on top to a hole in the liner with two thin nuts on its lower end. Alternatively, you can bolt individual pipe flanges with gaskets through the completed tank's laminate to a backing plate threaded for these bolts, or you can install a manifold plate with all or some of the connections in the same way. If the backing plate for this type of connection is riveted to the lining, then again to the laminate, it will stay in place while being drilled and tapped for the machine screws. It also won't drop into the tank when the flange or manifold is removed for any reason.

You should use a waxed wooden plug to stop the laminate at the opening and build up a boss in the laminate in the region of the fitting. It should be mentioned here that when a large flow of fuel is returned to the tank from engines that use it to cool the injection system, the supply- and return-line connections should be well separated from each other on the tank to prevent recirculation of the same oil before it can cool down. When there are two or more tanks, valves are sometimes arranged to draw the oil from one tank and return it to another.

Needless to say, you should fit all the tank openings or connections before the liner is assembled, while you can still reach the underside of the top panel with hands and tools. When you have made up the connections, you can screw or rivet the long pieces that make up the top, sides, and bottom to the baffles and end pieces. This is easiest to do by starting with one edge of a long panel or at a corner of the tank. Fasten each end piece and baffle near this corner, then continue with the adjacent fastenings—one in each end or baffle at a time—across that panel and on around the tank in the same direction until the piece is wrapped on. You can use either tapping screws or pop rivets to fasten the liner parts together. Make no attempt to pull the overlaps up liquid tight; they should just be well fastened and neat enough so that laminating over them will not be difficult. The corners at the ends will be softer if you let the end pieces project a little so that the bends of their flanges form the tank's end corners and the sharp edges of the ends of the long pieces are back a bit from the corner.

Not only can baffles calm the surge of a tank's contents, but they can support its walls as well, which gives us another good reason to anchor them well. Often just fastening them to the liner is enough, if it is fairly stiff metal, but fastening them to the tank itself is strongest. To accomplish this, you apply a row of fastenings through at least two layers of the laminate into the baffle flanges. To avoid disrupting the laminating process while you stop to get out tools and fastenings, or if you forget to install these fastenings at all, you can do this as a separate operation as soon as the liner is assembled. Put a 6-inch band of saturated mat followed by a 4-inch band of saturated roving around the tank, centered on each baffle. When cured, fasten through it into the baffle flanges. Then you can laminate the tank without interruption, and the baffles will be fastened to it. My instinct, by the way, would be to have the fastenings passing through one additional layer of fiberglass for each 50 gallons of capacity. (You'd be surprised how much boatbuilding has been done by instinct. That's probably why, traditionally, boatbuilding went by the name of the builder, not some amorphous company name: owners wanted to know whose instincts they were trusting.)

In laying up the fiberglass tank, you get the most strength and tightness for the number of layers or total amount of fiberglass used by overlapping all pieces about 2 inches. You create a slight ridge at every overlap, but the effect on the appearance of the tank is of no significance, and every overlap clinches the integrity of the layer as an "envelope," while adding a stiffening "rib" of double thickness. Of course, the overlaps in each layer should be kept away from the overlaps in other layers.

INTEGRAL TANKS

Tanks built into the hull of a fiberglass boat are economical of space and material. It certainly looks good, on paper at least, to bulkhead off and cap a section of the hollow keel and/or bilges to create a tank that yields a maximum amount of liquid capacity with a minimum amount of construction using a minimum amount of space from the interior arrangement. The suitability of fiberglass as a tank material and the well-known longevity of similar tanks employed in metal vessels seem to promise success. In practice, though, integral tanks in fiberglass boats have at best an indifferent record of staying out of trouble. This is not just my opinion either. At risk of seeming to endorse government-enforced consumerism, I quote the Coast Guard "manufacturers' requirements for recreational boats." Gasoline tanks "must not be integral with any boat structure." That sounds as though someone else doesn't trust them either.

Thinking back over my own limited experience with integral tanks, I am surprised to remember more of them that leaked than didn't. True, some had not leaked until they were 10 or 12 years old. But at least one leaked before the boat left the dealer's yard. Then it filled the fuel filters with debris so faithfully that the owner hardly got out of the harbor for 6 years without a breakdown; and in the long run it cost the dealer $20,000. I haven't heard whether a handful of integral tanks built at my shop have leaked or not, but some of the tanks I have run into since then were enough to make me wonder. Anyway, I'll review some of the complaints about integral tanks; then you can decide for yourself whether you want to try to construct one.

1. One cause of trouble with an integral tank is the flexibility of fiberglass. The constant flexing of the hull laminate works on "hard spots" where flexing is restrained, like those where an integral tank is fiberglassed to it. After a great number of bending cycles, the hull sometimes breaks away from the tabbing, or, if either is thin skinned, a crack appears in the hull or tank parallel to the joint.

2. It is difficult to see what you are doing when fiberglassing the end bulkheads of a tank in a deep, hollow keel. Often the attachment or seal of the tank to the hull in that area is less than perfect. Getting in there to do a repair after the interior joinerwork has been built over the tank is still more difficult. If the boat has been in use, your troubles are compounded further by the necessity of steam cleaning both the interior of the tank (if it has had anything but water in it) and the bilge, which might now be coated with dirt and engine oil as well as salt water.

3. An accident that damages the hull area covered by the tank damages the tank, too, of course; then there's double trouble. If the hull is holed, seawater will join the contents, and vice versa. There's no need to go into the consequences of that.

When it comes to repairing damage within the perimeter of the tank, the hull repairs must be done from the outside of the hull, unless a hole is cut in the tank. Similarly, any walls of the tank that are included in the damage require a one-sided repair or a hole in the tank.

4. Integral tanks that become contaminated are much harder to clean out than a removable tank. This is especially true now that (almost) everybody is frowning on drain plugs or valves in tank bottoms, and Coast Guard regulations forbid them in gasoline tanks.

Considering the potential problems with them, it's understandable that there are fewer integral tanks built into fiberglass boats lately than 15 or 20 years ago. Even the ubiquitous integral V-berth water tank on small production auxiliaries seems to be losing favor to polyethylene and aluminum removables. However, this could be simply because the polyethylene tank, at least, has become cheaper than the labor of building the two watertight bulkheads and top of the integral version.

Nevertheless, there are situations where an integral tank is well worth considering. If I were you and had a section of the hollow keel, space under some berths, or space in the engine room suitable for an integral tank, I would carefully weigh the advantages and disadvantages of building it in against those of building a shaped removable tank to fit the same space. Then, as long as you are willing to gamble with what might happen to an integral tank in order to enjoy its greater capacity and lower cost, why not build one? It's still legal—except for gasoline tanks.

It may seem premature to talk about tanks in this chapter, but a tank is an awkward thing at best and often installed in an awkward place to reach. Usually, the sooner it can be put to bed the better.

12

Installing Bulkheads, Engine Beds, and Other Parts

BULKHEADS

Historically, boatbuilders have underutilized bulkheads as structural members, treating them only as partitions in the arrangement. This was just fine whenever other members strengthened the hull and deck enough to make the shape-retaining function of bulkheads redundant. In wooden boats, before plywood became reliable and plentiful, a strong bulkhead was more complicated and expensive to construct than such members as hanging knees, harpins, web frames, and "strong" deckbeams. With these members in place, boats could have huge sections of their interiors wide open without a significant loss of strength, and many did. Moreover, most of the bulkheads they did have were plain boards, tongue-and-groove or half-lapped staving, or wood paneling, none of which has good bracing strength. When a really stout bulkhead was desired, it was double planked, often diagonally.

Flexible though fiberglass boats are, they, too, can be made independent of bulkheads. The hull and deck can be reinforced with longitudinal stringers, ribs, or knees; or they can be made so stiff, as with sandwich construction, that they hardly need strong, well-attached bulkheads to help them hold their shape. Production builders' bulkheads are often only lightly secured partitions, especially those associated with a molded fiberglass interior liner. Often the bulkheads are simply slipped into grooves in such liners or screwed to flats at the ends of berths and lockers. Thus, the work that the bulkheads might do is assumed in some measure by the liner and some special reinforcements in the laminate. Much of the time this arrangement seems to work OK. However, after years of surveying production fiberglass sailboats with mast and rigging installations dependent on a bulkhead or two, with the chainplates bolted directly to the bulkheads, and/or the mast stepped atop one of them, I can't let all builders off that easily. Time and again, bulkheads used to anchor shrouds are found to be adrift in a few years because they were tabbed too lightly to hull and deck. And bulkheads bearing deck-stepped masts are bowed under the pressure, split apart up vertical corners, or—a first sign of trouble—displaced enough to prevent a door from entering its jamb. These experiences have shown that a structural bulkhead had better be well reinforced and securely fastened in place.

Today, bulkheads are built almost exclusively of plywood, which, when constructed with rot-resistant varieties of wood, waterproof glue, and a minimum of internal voids, is uniquely suited for use as large, flat panels in a boat. The tensile strength of plywood edgewise, as a knee or web, is enormous. It is good in compression, too, if it is restrained from buckling. Add on the economy of labor in constructing a bulkhead of single pieces as large as 4 feet by 12 feet, and plywood becomes all but irresistible.

I say *all but* because I still prefer to be shipmates with natural wood paneling or even humble staving, as I think most people would if they could afford them. Of course, this yen for a "natural" interior is not lost on the suppliers of plywood. It is available with a veneer of almost any variety of wood you could want; and if that is too expensive, it comes with a plastic surface printed with photographically perfect, imitation wood grain and a tape of the same with which to bind its edges.

When you select plywood for bulkheads in your one-off, you should be careful about several details:

1. Make sure it is "exterior" glued. The same glue is used in the exterior grade that is used in "marine" plywood. Marine plywood is supposed to be free of voids in the inner layers, which would weaken it and form pockets where rot might start. It is much more expensive and less readily available than exterior plywood; so although marine grade is preferred for use on the outside of a boat, it is not generally considered essential for use in the interior.

2. Make sure the core is not a rot-susceptible wood. Only the other day I was aboard a stock wooden powerboat built in 1960. Her bulkheads were cored with a soft, light-colored mahogany. Wherever these bulkheads originally touched the hull, and some places where they didn't, their tattered, rotten edges now clear it by 1 to 3 inches, and they are held up literally by the berths and lockers that are fastened to them.

Douglas fir, the most common core used in the U.S., is reasonably rot resistant, it is stiff and strong for its weight, and as a surface veneer it bonds well with fiberglass or any glued-on material.

3. Select a surface that is suitable for the intended use. Fir, good as it is for the core or as a bonding surface, is just about the worst possible surface to paint or varnish. No matter how you prime or seal it, its hard and soft grains always come

back to haunt you sooner or later. A rotary-cut Philippine mahogany face, by comparison, is an excellent surface for painting. It is readily available in all of the standard thicknesses and modest in cost. It has an even, stable texture, sands easily, and is just porous enough to hold paint, glues, and resins well. When finished bright, rotary-cut mahogany (peeled off a spinning log) is bland and uninteresting, however. A more attractive grain for a natural finish is obtained when the log is sliced through, not peeled. As mentioned earlier, this sort of natural-wood-grain veneer is available as a plywood face in many other woods as well as in mahogany and teak, although, looking through yachts of the past few decades, you'd hardly think so.

4. Use an appropriate thickness for the job. Here again I can't list any "average" scantlings. If the designer does not call out the thickness you should use, it is best to study similar boats with similar construction. For instance, it might be all right to use ⅜-inch bulkheads in a very light, PVC-cored 30-foot multihull. But it might not be wise to use less than ½ inch in a similarly constructed 25-foot high-speed launch, or less than ¾ inch in a 30-foot auxiliary sloop with a deck-stepped mast atop the bulkhead, the upper chainplates bolted to it, and a heavy ballast keel under it. The following conditions affect the optimum thickness of a bulkhead:

1. The size of the bulkhead, especially of its largest unsupported panel.
2. How well it will be stiffened by joinerwork, berths, lockers, or other bulkheads meeting it, particularly along its edge at any opening.
3. How much use you want to make of it to stiffen the hull, and what extra loads will be placed on it, like engine beds terminating against it, or the cockpit, or the cabin trunk. Is it a "crash bulkhead" to keep out flooding after a collision? Obviously, many "main" bulkheads at the after end of a cabin trunk and forward end of a cockpit, with the engine just aft of them, must bear the strains imposed by all three. At the same time, on some boats there's little main bulkhead left after it is cut away for a companionway, two quarter berths, and an engine-access opening. You may have to build in two stout stiffeners or stanchions, one on either side of the companionway, to shore up the deck. But you also have the option of reinforcing the deck there with some sort of strong beam, as we did on wooden boats. This could take the form of a fiberglass beam with a hat-shaped section formed over foam, or one partly strengthened with wood or metal encapsulated within.

You might well ask whether the difficulty of fastening joinerwork to thin plywood and the flimsy feel of it in use are worth the weight saved by using this material. If the boat is an ultralight high-performance craft, they might be; but you can build a bulkhead that is as light or lighter, much stiffer, and quieter, too, with a PVC-foam core. By this I don't mean that you have to settle for a fiberglass-surfaced bulkhead, although you could. Working on a flat table with weights or vacuum bagging, you can sandwich the foam between two thin sheets of plywood. There is, by the way, a high-grade plywood known as aircraft plywood, available as thin as $1/16$ inch, which you might find useful in building bulkheads, and other parts, too, in an ultralight boat.

A big boat—say, 50 or 60 feet and up, weighing 20 to 30 tons or more—might need thicker bulkheads than are readily obtainable in sheet plywood. There are many advantages to laminating such bulkheads with two layers of standard thickness, or even three. You can also strengthen bulkheads with vertical or horizontal stiffeners. You can install these on a single layer on the opposite side from the accommodations, such as on the engine-room side or toward the ends of the boat, or use them between two layers to make a hollow bulkhead.

Unless a bulkhead is very heavy, well stiffened, or securely fastened all around, and has no large, unsupported areas, I prefer to keep it balanced, that is, to use the same thickness and the same material on each side of center. That way, I know that the bulkhead will not have a strong tendency to warp or curl due to dissimilar rates of shrinkage and swelling on its opposite sides. If you look at the edges of plywood sheets, you will notice that the arrangement of the layers is symmetrical from the center to each surface, both in respect to the thickness of the layers and the direction of the grain. The same variety of wood is also usually used in opposing layers, even to scrap pieces of the facing wood on the back surface of sheets that are "good one side." With unbalanced layers, sheets of plywood not forcibly restrained would curl up like giant potato chips, and so might an unbalanced bulkhead.

Installing a bulkhead in a one-off hull built with most construction methods is a matter of tabbing it to the inner skin. If it is a plywood bulkhead—and few are not nowadays—a little extra labor and material invested in a sturdy tabbing can put its edgewise strength to work providing tremendous reinforcement and shape retention to the shell. Regardless of whether or not the bulkhead in question is positioned to carry some particular load, it seems foolish to let slip the opportunity to enlist its support of the hull at so little cost. No boat can ever be too strong.

I also happen to think no boat can be too stiff. When a patriarch of the local yachting fraternity came to see a cold-molded boat I was building in the early 1960s, his comment was, "I don't think she'll be very fast. She's too stiff. A boat has to be flexible. . . ."

Said boat has been a winner ever since, but I can't tell you how much that pearl of yachting mythology annoyed me. I often wonder what my elder friend, who has since joined the eternal yacht club, thought about those fiberglass racers with oilcanning bows that have bounced bunks straight off the wall in a head sea. A boat that does that should be flexible enough for anyone.

It is my contention that all bulkheads or partial bulkheads with inherent strength should be stoutly fastened to the shell of a boat, not just to hold themselves up, but to contribute whatever reinforcement they can. Tabbing with strips of fiberglass is the most direct and simple method of attachment and, for that reason, the most common. Tapes from 4 to 10 inches in width, depending on the proportions of the boat and its parts, are laminated into the angle that the bulkhead forms with the hull, preferably on both sides of it.

A plain angle is the one you see on most boats. Its resistance to being pulled away from the shell is hundreds of pounds per running foot per pair of alternate

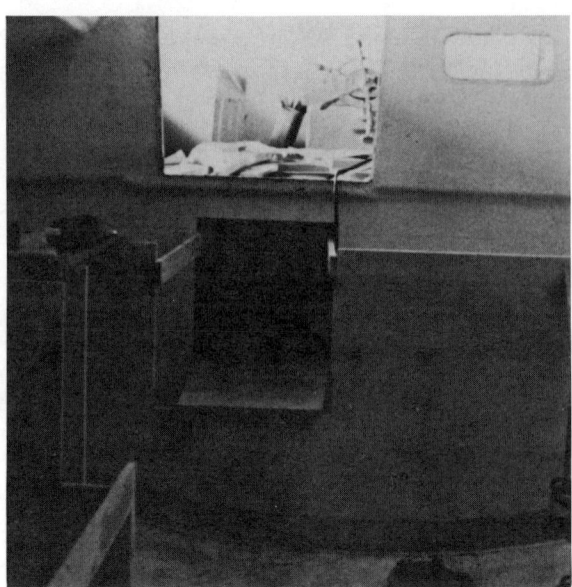

Setting up Centennial's *joinerwork bulkheads and fronts. Note the strip left bare along the bottom of the bulkhead for fiberglass tabbing.* (Loy photo)

layers of 1½-ounce mat and 18- or 24-ounce roving, up to perhaps 5,000 pounds per foot with a total of 8 or 10 layers. Unlike working with metals, it is not practical to make up a chart giving the strength of a fiberglass lamination like this within a narrow range. There are too many variables involved in laying it up by hand. However, I know from pulling hulls and decks out of molds and lifting parts around with laminates of this nature that they have the magnitude of strength so indicated. Throughout the industry, 5,000- or 6,000-pound parts are lifted with slings through strap eyes built by laying up 8 or 10 total layers of alternate mat and roving over 6-inch lengths of pipe or tubing against the inner skin. Often in the process of breaking a part away from the mold, the mold is picked up along with the part until it is a few inches off the floor and held there until it drops off. Because a production mold weighs two or three times as much as a part and the two are suspended by three or four such straps, you can develop considerable respect for the strength of fiberglass tabbing.

How you relate such information to the needs of a given bulkhead in a given hull is another matter. The best approach is to study and compare the tabbing in a number of older fiberglass boats. Meanwhile, several factors will influence the effectiveness of your tabbing:

1. The bond of fiberglass to fiberglass is stronger than that of fiberglass to wood. When the tabbing is not fastened to the wood mechanically, 90 percent of the failures I have seen are separation of that leg of the angle from the wood. Therefore, *all* tabbing should be locked to the wood mechanically. Staples, ring nails, screws, or bolts are appropriate fastenings for this job. You can drill a number of holes right through the wood and fill them with fiberglass putty also, as described in Chapter 7 on wood left in place. When the tabbing is bonded to these

fiberglass plugs, they become large-diameter rivets. They are most useful on thin bulkheads where bolts are the only other really strong fastening.

2. Preparation of the surface is important for a good bond with the fiberglass shell. If the inner skin is freshly laid up, the bond will be excellent. Any other condition calls for an acetone wipe or sanding, depending on how hard and slick or coated with foreign materials the surface is.

3. The angle will be stronger and more resilient if it is laminated over a fillet. You can build a curved transition in the angle with fiberglass putty or a flatter fillet by tacking or hot-gluing PVC-foam strips with a triangular section into it. Tests, and time, have shown that easy corners are more durable than sharp ones.

4. Except in hulls with sandwich construction, a bulkhead should not be fitted tight against the shell. If it is, it may "print" through, or make a hard spot that shows on the exterior of the boat. The best arrangement is to fit a strip of PVC foam between the bulkhead and the shell. Such a strip can be wider than the thickness of the bulkhead so as to include the fillets, which can be formed by angle cuts on its edges.

Admittedly, a strip of tabbing around the borders of a bulkhead is not particularly beautiful. Nevertheless, it is an honest, functional arrangement that, if neatly done, I rather like to look at; because, like the ribs of a wooden boat, it reminds me of the structure I've got around me. But in deference to those who could care less about viewing construction, you can rabbet the border of the bulkhead so that the tabbing is not noticed when painted over. You can also cover it with trim.

A different approach to fastening bulkheads, but one that entails more work, is to lay up a hat-shaped rib, then fasten the bulkhead to it. The rib is laid up over a former of PVC foam hot-glued to the shell and can be any sided or molded dimension, as we used to say (meaning width or height). The advantage is purely cosmetic, for you can bring one side of a single bulkhead, or both sides of a hollow bulkhead, close enough to the hull to hide the rib and/or to blend with wood or other sheathing on the inside of the hull. Covering all traces of the fiberglass construction is not by any means a frivolous achievement to anyone who enjoys the warmth and charm of an interior finished in wood.

A hat-shaped fiberglass rib is in itself a structural member. In fact, you can put all the ribs you want in a hull or under a deck as beams. Or you can build just a few hefty ones wherever you think the boat needs them. If you would like to construct bulkheads of staving or natural-wood paneling, you can use hat-shaped fiberglass ribs and deckbeams as a base to which to fasten them and, at the same time, as hull stiffening that the bulkheads don't supply.

In all but the smallest hulls, there are bulkheads running fore and aft as well as those that run athwartships. In most boats these bulkheads are treated as joinerwork, not structural members. However, if they are plywood they can contribute useful support. They are especially helpful in powerboats with very wide cabin trunks or flush decks and in sailboats where they divide quarter berths from the engine space and support the cockpit and where they pass under the mast

Centennial's joinerwork bulkheads and fronts, looking forward. In this WLP hull with Airex-cored deck, bulkheads were tabbed to the inner skin but cleats were screwed through it. (Loy photo)

partners or under a deck-stepped mast. A fore-and-aft bulkhead can also serve as a stiffener to keep a heavily loaded athwartship bulkhead from buckling where the two meet at right angles to form a corner. Perhaps the ultimate case of this is when the corner is under a deck-stepped mast. A corner is by nature strong, but if you are going to make the best of it, you need a stout corner post to which you fasten both bulkheads well—*not* a light batten or trim piece with a row of small fastenings in it.

For high-performance boats, I have sometimes built a fiberglass-ribbed version of the PVC-foam bulkhead. Using planks of foam as wide as the rib (or stiffener) spacing desired, you build a stiffener on the edge of each plank as you place it on the already laminated skin of one side of the bulkhead. To get a smooth surface, you rabbet the planks for the stiffeners' flanges. These rabbets and the bevel cuts on the edges of the planks are quickly made on a table saw or radial saw. The angle of the bevel is not critical, except that the steeper the edge, the stronger the stiffener. However, the more it slopes, the easier it is to lay up the stiffener. Mat is best to use for the stiffeners, because it is easily formed and adheres best to the skins. The bulkhead's thickness, the spacing of the stiffeners, the amount of material in the skins and in the stiffeners, and the density of the foam used are all variable. Adjusting these variables, you can design a bulkhead with whatever weight, strength, or stiffness you feel is appropriate.

I developed this construction for sharpie-type hulls and for decks, for years using 2-pound-density polyurethane foam before trying it with PVC foam. It was a good test for the fiberglass components, because polyurethane foam has almost no strength. But today a whole range of foams from purely polyurethane through the cross-linked polyurethane-PVC to purely PVC are available in various densities, with which to construct sandwiches. Only on an unusual boat might you feel the need to construct a bulkhead this way. Nevertheless, the ribs do add a lot of stiffness for little weight, the foam has useful insulating qualities, and with no wood you need not worry about rot in a dank location.

I should not leave bulkheads without reminding you of the traditional double-diagonal construction used for strong wooden bulkheads before the time of dependable plywood. With the waterproof glues available today, you can make such a bulkhead watertight without cloth between the layers or caulking its seams. You can also assemble it more rapidly with today's power tools. What is the difference between a bulkhead built this way and one of plywood? If you glue up many thin veneers, there is very little. But if you use the traditional boards—a minimum number of layers of thicker sawn wood—it is much stiffer and more puncture resistant for its weight. It also functions better as a crash bulkhead or as a true watertight bulkhead, installed to prevent water in a flooded compartment from entering another. It can have any variety of appropriate woods on either surface as boards, not veneer; therefore, you can build it to blend with a wood interior, such as that of a WLP construction. If well sealed to the hull and provided with stout mechanical fastenings in its leg of the tabbing, this bulkhead is probably the best you can build for the weight (although I have built bulkheads of almost the same physical properties and weight with ribbed PVC foam). However, because plywood is fitted so much more quickly, it is a rare boat in which you find a traditional double-diagonal bulkhead.

ENGINE BEDS

In almost all one-off fiberglass constructions, the area under and around the engine is left as a single skin, at least until the engine bed has been installed and fiberglassed to it. The main reasons for this are space and strength. Most designers and builders do not wish to bed an engine on a sandwich, fearing that the weight, thrust, and vibration will loosen the bed from the inner skin or cause it to settle into a core that has low compressive strength. But in auxiliary sailboats, and to a lesser degree in powerboats, the extra inch or two of hull thickness sometimes makes a critical difference in shaft angle, how far aft you can install an engine, what size engine you can fit, or whether there is room for a substantial bed.

In a one-off, you fabricate the bed most easily by building it in place with fiberglass over a wood core. You cut the wood core pieces from a plank, fit them to the hull, and hot glue or tab them in place with patches of wet mat. It is wise to set the core on a strip of pasteboard or thin PVC foam and to fillet the corners at the hull as described for setting bulkheads. You then build a heavy fiberglass laminate up over the core, carrying each layer farther out into the hull until there is a flange 4 to 6 inches wide around beds for smaller engines and 8 to 12 inches around big, heavy engines. The laminate might be ½ inch thick for a brutish diesel, but it should not be less than ⅛ inch for the smallest one- and two-cylinder put-puts. The wood you use for the core should not be softer than fir. You can build the core up of plywood if it is to have metal rails to which you bolt the engine mounts. But natural wood holds lags or hanger bolts through engine mounts better, and oak, the traditional wood for beds, holds them best. Yellow pine also makes excellent beds. Whatever wood you use should be dry and completely encapsulated with no less than ⅛ inch of fiberglass, at least three layers of which are mat. If thoroughly sealed from air and moisture, the core will not rot.

For engines up to about 2,000 pounds, 1½-to-2-inch-thick stock makes a good core. These thicknesses are easy to obtain also. Nominal 2-inch stock, which is actually dressed to 1½ inches, is used in framing buildings, whereas the full 2-inch thickness is a common size in rough-sawn lumber. For really big, heavy diesels, you'd want to go up to 2½ or 3 inches of core thickness. But the thickness of the core and of the laminate over it and the width of the flange on the hull are not the only considerations. Beds should be as long as is practicable so as to distribute the weight of the engine over a large area of the hull. In a high-speed one-off powerboat, it is still a good idea to attach engine beds to deep stringers that run the length of the boat's bottom until they die out against its rise at the bow. The stringers not only carry the engine, but reinforce the bottom against pounding at high speed. When the length of beds is limited by the accommodations and/or boat shape, you may be able to "hang" one end of them on a bulkhead, incorporate some transverse members similar to floor timbers, or at least fit some knees between the outboard sides of the beds and the bottom. Any of these help create a grid that distributes the engine's pressures over the bottom.

Sometimes space for engine beds is all but nonexistent in an auxiliary with wineglass sections that nearly touch the engine mounts and the engine's base. There may be room only for a small wedge-shaped block glassed to the hull under each mount. In this case, and in any case where you can't extend the beds over an area big enough, you should increase the hull's laminate thickness locally until you have an engine pad. A nice feature of fiberglass construction is the way you can build up the strength of an area by simply adding on layers. As I write this, my mind goes back to Platt Monfort's Str-r-etch Mesh. Would a layer of it within the pad under an engine, or perhaps a 1 x 3 strip running down the hull like a rib under each engine-mount block, stiffen the area better than a plain buildup of the laminate? If I had a hefty engine to "shoehorn" into a fine stern, I might make a sample section with Str-r-etch Mesh in it and one without, and compare them. Then I could find out just what using the wire in the area might do for it.

You should align engine beds so that they are centered on the shaft centerline in the plan view and profile them in the side view to accept the engine mounts when the engine coupling's axis coincides with the shaft centerline. Before you install the beds, there are other considerations as well:

1. You should always leave space between the top of the beds and the bottom of the engine mounts (unless the mounts are adjustable in height). A reasonable allowance is ½ inch. It is very easy to shim up an engine, but chopping into the beds to lower it is hard labor.

2. You should study the engine for parts that you need to be able to reach, remove occasionally, or service and cut away the beds (within reason) to allow access to these parts.

3. If you drop a wrench under the engine, will you be able to fish it out?

4. Don't forget the engine pan. Whether loose or integral with the beds and hull, this is an important item if you want to keep your bilges free of the inevitable drips from an engine.

But how do you get started with engine beds in the first place? The job involves the shaft log, stuffing box, and stern bearing or strut intimately, so let's proceed to these items.

SHAFT LOGS, STUFFING BOXES, STERN BEARINGS, AND STRUTS

Because boat parts are apt to acquire different names in different localities, some definitions may be useful. The hole through which propeller shafts of inboard powerboats exit the hull is called the shaft log, also the stern tube or shaft alley. Aft of the shaft log, but just forward of the propeller, there has to be a bearing to support the shaft, which, when it is in the aft end of the shaft log, in a sternpost or skeg, is called the stern bearing. But in twin-screw and off-center installations, where the shaft goes through the skin of the hull, there has to be a metal strut to hold the bearing just forward of the propeller; and if the shaft has to travel a long way in midwater to the strut, an intermediate bearing may have to restrain it from whipping. This bearing may be another shorter strut, but usually only a housing or barrel supports the bearing on a pad or base. Finally, a seal must keep water from following along the shaft into the hull. This usually takes the form of a stuffing box, a hollow cylinder riding the shaft that is packed with rings of flax impregnated with wax or grease. By screwing the cylinder onto a blunt-ended pipe or base, which is made fast to the shaft log, the flax is squeezed against the shaft and is lubricated and/or cooled by water entering through the base.

Sometimes, the stern bearing and stuffing box are combined in a single fitting—the flax-packed stern bearing. Installed on the outside of the boat, on the sternpost or skeg, a flax-packed stern bearing solves the problem created by long, narrow, hollow keels, such as those Novis or down-east powerboats have. In such keels, it is almost impossible to reach an inside stuffing box unless it is at the forward end of a 10- to 15-foot shaft log. Since this stern bearing is all things in one fitting, the base of which is made fast and watertight to the outer face of the sternpost, it is considerably cheaper. However, by far the most popular arrangement nowadays is a rubber-lined stern bearing on the outside of the boat and a separate flax-packed stuffing box on the inside. When installed inboard, the stuffing box can be serviced without hauling the boat out of the water or visiting it underwater with a pair of wrenches in hand. I must say, however, that I have seen many stuffing boxes on the inside that are so inaccessible that I'd almost rather work on one that is underwater.

Anyway, the propeller shaft has to pass through these parts, clearing the walls of the shaft log and lining up perfectly in the bearing. It used to have to line up perfectly with the inside stuffing box also, the base of which was solidly fastened to the hull and/or shaft log. However, in current practice, the inside stuffing box is provided with a "rubber neck" (a length of hose, actually) that bends into alignment with the shaft, eliminating the need to adjust a rigid base.

At the other end of the shaft is the engine, with its reverse gear. The axis of the drive shaft and coupling of this gear has to coincide rather precisely with the axis of the propeller shaft. Thus, the centerline of the shaft, as drawn in the plan and as set up in the boat, must be a dead-straight line from the engine right through the propeller, with all of the aforementioned parts centered on it.

In wooden-boat construction, we used to stretch a wire representing the shaft centerline through a pilot hole in the wood. The forward and aft ends of the wire were fixed at "target" points carefully laid out from the plan. We set up guides for a boring bar centered on the wire and bored out the shaft log to size. We then used the wire, restrung through the shaft log, to lay out the engine beds, sometimes by measurement, but at other times with the visual aid of a side-view profile pattern of the engine with the location of the engine mounts marked on it. We also aligned the aft bearing, whether in the form of a strut or of a casting bolted to the sternpost, with the wire, as well as the stuffing box and any intermediate bearings. After all the parts were fitted, we took a measurement for the shaft's length, made it up, and installed it. With a little final shimming of engine and bearings, all was ready for launching. After several days or a week afloat, we checked the alignment again, for a wooden boat was quite likely to have changed shape during that time.

This relatively involved process to obtain an accurately bored shaft log, which was sometimes a hole several feet long through solid timber, was more or less mandatory. Occasionally, builders, with careful lofting and setup, prebored the shaft log, but most of them liked to "play it safe" and bore it on the job.

Although you can follow a similar procedure to install the propulsion gear in one-off fiberglass boats, it is really a waste of time. There isn't a long shaft log that needs to be aimed through the thin shell of a fiberglass boat precisely. If you make a mistake in locating the hole you cut, it doesn't really matter in fiberglass: it's so easy to glass it over again. Therefore, the least time-consuming approach is to reverse the order of the steps of traditional procedures, that is, to start with the engine propped up in the boat with a shaft coupled up to it and heading out through a rough hole in the boat to a target that represents the center of the propeller. The shaft can be a temporary shaft borrowed from a propeller shop. Or you can use the actual shaft you will be installing, but left a little long, to be safe. (If you're worrying about how to find out where that rough hole for the shaft should be cut, don't. I discuss it later in this chapter.)

With the engine and shaft rigged up where you want them to be, you can now measure for the engine beds quite accurately. You can even make up their cores and try them in place before lifting the engine out of the way and building the beds. If there is to be a strut or struts at the aft end of the shaft, and perhaps an intermediate bearing, this is also the time to measure for these parts and make them up.

What about the shaft log, the stuffing box, and, if this boat's propeller is behind a sternpost, the stern bearing? It's best to do nothing until the engine is sitting on its completed beds and the shaft is either sitting in its bearing in the strut or back in the target, which holds it in alignment with the engine, when there is no strut. Once the engine and shaft are in final alignment from engine to propeller, you can slide any parts between—the shaft log, a stern bearing, or an intermediate bearing—up the shaft into position, center them on it, and fasten them in place.

Shaft Logs

In a fiberglass boat, the best shaft log is a fiberglass tube. It is impossible to make the traditional metal stern tubes, cast-bronze stern bearings, bronze stuffing-box bases, or flax-packed stuffing box/bearings as much an integral part of the boat or as watertight to the hull as a fiberglass shaft log. Even if it were possible, they add nothing and cost much more, so there is no point in using them. There is always a rubber-necked stuffing box clamped to the fiberglass tube on its inboard end. Note also that it is not necessary to use a cast-bronze stern bearing, but only the rubber-bearing insert in its bronze shell. You lay the bearing up in or press it into the fiberglass shaft log, just as into a bronze casting, and retain it there with set screws the same way, too. For holding the set screws better, you lay up a strip of bronze in the shaft-log laminate and bore and tap the set-screw holes through it. To replace the bearing, you release the set screws and pull the bearing.

Every fiberglass boatshop needs a slow-turning lathelike machine on which to wind tubes and to leave them turning as on a rotisserie until the resin gels. Without such luxury, you can wind tubes perfectly well by hand, as long as you set up a mandrel, on which to wind them, on a horizontal axis, even if it is only a piece of dowel with a nail in each end. It's just a bit less convenient.

The inside diameter of a fiberglass shaft log should not be less than 25 percent greater than the diameter of the shaft. More clearance than that does no harm; and unless restricted by the walls of a hollow keel, I'd be generous. Less clearance doesn't give much room for a shift in the alignment of the shaft. But the length of the shaft log also affects how much change in the shaft's angle it will take to make the shaft bear against the wall of the tube. A long shaft log needs more clearance than a short one.

Also, 25 percent of the shaft diameter seems to me a good measurement for the wall thickness of a fiberglass shaft log. The usual construction is a solid winding of fiberglass cloth, which makes an extremely rugged tube. I have always built them with cloth, but I like to start off and end up with a few layers of mat. I use mat on the inside because a badly misaligned shaft can burn away the resin, peel cloth out of the tube, and wind it up on itself until it stops the engine. I'd find that hard to believe if I hadn't cut the cloth off one shaft myself. Having no continuous strands, mat can't peel like cloth does. My reason for using some mat on the outside of a shaft log is to provide a better bond when the tube is glassed into the boat. Mat laid up at the same time as the cloth beneath it will have the best possible "primary" bond to it. Then, when the tube is tabbed in place in the hull, that unavoidable "secondary" bond will be better with mat than with cloth. Although I have not heard of another case of a shaft destroying a shaft log before or since (and thousands, if not millions, of all-cloth shaft logs are in service), I have seen a goodly number of cloth-surfaced shaft logs and rudder ports that have loosened up where tabbed to the hull. Then there's Murphy's Law.

The outside diameter of the inboard end of the shaft log has to be adjusted so that the hose of the rubber-necked stuffing box fits snugly over it. This end should bury in the hose far enough to make room for two hose clamps with ¼ to ½ inch of the buried section to spare on all sides of them. When building up the outside diameter of a tube for hose, you can wrap on a few thin rings consisting of a turn or two of narrow cloth tape to improve the grip of the hose on the tube. Or, if you are turning the tube down to fit the hose, you can get a similar effect by cutting in a few shallow grooves.

When there is to be a rubber stern bearing in the after end of the shaft log, you have to adjust the inside dimensions of the tube at that end to accept it. The simplest way to do that, of course, is to attach the bearing itself to the mandrel on which you are winding the tube. However, you should give the bearing an exceptionally heavy coat of wax, or it will be very difficult to pull out of the tube when the day comes that you have to replace it.

A different approach is to bore out the end of the tube in a lathe to a "press" fit for the bearing. I should mention that rubber bearings, which are molded into their brass sleeves, are available in more than one outside dimension for a given shaft size; that is, the rubber and brass shell may be thick or thin walled. The thinner-walled sizes are, I presume, for light duty, and the thicker ones for heavy duty.

In any case, partway through the laminate you should remember to lay on the strip of brass or bronze through which to bore and tap for the set screws. This can be a piece of flat stock or a strip sawn lengthwise from a piece of pipe, which, if it has the appropriate diameter, will have a curve to match the tube. I would leave its edges square, stick it on with hot-melt glue or 5-minute epoxy, fillet the edges with fiberglass putty, and continue winding the tube. You should install two set screws some distance along the length of the bearing. If the bearing is buried too much in the sternpost for that, you can install them on opposite sides of the tube.

Another requirement with rubber stern bearings is a hole in each side of the sternpost leading into the shaft log just forward of the bearing. The purpose of the holes is to feed water into the bearing and up to the stuffing box. Except in deep, low-speed installations, the flow of water past the end tends to drag water out of the stern tube. When the stuffing box runs dry, it overheats, and a rubber stern bearing wears out quickly without a good supply of water to lubricate it. Few surfaces are more slippery than wet rubber, but few grip and wear more than dry rubber against a turning shaft (which is why you should never run your propeller shaft ashore without playing a hose on the bearing). Small scoops formed on the sternpost over the water holes, facing forward, help catch and direct water into the tube faster than it is dragged out. These can be made similar to those in the bases of cast-bronze rubber-lined stern bearings.

High-speed boats are the most likely to dry out their shaft logs, and fast twin-screw boats with open-ended shaft tubes can starve the stuffing box for water as much as, or more than, boats with a single screw and stern bearing. The surest way to keep inside stuffing boxes cool at high speed is to split off some of the raw engine-cooling water, where it is about to go into the exhaust, and pipe it into the shaft log or stuffing-box casing as close abaft the packing as is feasible.

Let us go back to the actual installation of the shaft log. If you remember, we had the engine installed on its bed and the shaft fitted through the strut (with its bearing), if there is one, or to a target that takes the shaft's weight and holds it in alignment, if not. You now slide the shaft log up the shaft and into position in the rough hole in the hull. Make sure the shaft is aligned, center both ends of the shaft log on the shaft, and then fiberglass the log to the hull. If it is a centerline shaft log with a stern bearing in it, the aft end will center itself naturally, but a ring of four or five small wooden wedges driven into the open end of a shaft log helps keep it equidistant all around until the fiberglassing fixes it there.

Despite the oblique angle at which it passes through the hull, it is relatively easy to fasten an off-center shaft log with fiberglass tabbing. At least the shell's surface is more or less flat and quite accessible from inside the boat and out. It is definitely not so easy to fasten a log with fiberglass within the walls of a hollow keel, where you may not be able to reach between the walls and the log to get at its underside. If the log isn't too long, you may be able to remove the shaft after tabbing the tube in place with a few pieces of saturated mat, then reach under it from the forward end as you build up the massive laminate all around that this crucial, hard-working part deserves. When the situation is too tight to permit proper access for fiberglass tabbing, it is best to fit a PVC-foam dam into the hollow keel around the shaft log, not closer than 5 or 6 inches to its inboard end, and solid fill the area with "keel putty."

Note that when you solid fill this section of some hollow keels, you also fill the region where a skeg or rudder-heel fitting will be bolted on. Since I have discussed in Chapter 11 the potential problems headed off by solid filling hollow keels generally and filling over bolted-on heel fittings particularly, I must resist the temptation to belabor the subject. Nevertheless, achieving a satisfactory shaft-log installation within a narrow hollow keel involves closely related problems that are best solved with solid filling.

In my opinion, these problems helped touch off the slide into bankruptcy of a large producer of fiberglass commercial fishing boats. The shaft logs in these boats consisted of a cast-bronze rubber-lined stern bearing with a four-bolt base, into the forward end of which a bronze stern tube was threaded. The forward end of the tube was threaded into a bronze stuffing box. The whole shaft log was fitted through a hole in the fiberglass sternpost and fastened there with four bolts through the stern-bearing base. Sound familiar? It will if you're an old-timer, because it's just about what might have been installed in a high-grade wooden boat any time in the past 50 years. There was, by the test of time, little wrong with the shaft-log assembly itself. However, its installation in the hollow fiberglass keels of these fishing boats had some crucial differences from that in wooden boats.

1. The shaft log was bolted through the relatively thin fiberglass laminate, not into solid oak.

2. No metal backing plate was used to spread the strains out over the fiberglass.

3. When the propeller shaft was in place, there was no way to get at the nuts on the two lower bolts, because the shaft log and shaft filled up the space between the walls of the keel to within an inch or so on each side. This meant that there was no way to get at the skeg bolts penetrating the bottom of the keel (also not provided with a backing plate and not fiberglassed or filled over).

4. Except for where it was bolted to the aft face of the fiberglass sternpost, the entire assembly hung in midair in the hollow keel. Thus, it was unable to lean on, and its leaks were not confined to, a hole within a massive wooden timber. Given an accident to the large propeller and shaft turned by a powerful diesel—and what fishing boat has not gotten a tow wire or other gear in its wheel at one time or another?—the potential for a copious leak in the hollow keel was many times greater and the leak much less manageable than in a wooden boat.

That this installation was a disaster waiting to happen should have been obvious. That there were floodings, sinkings, and many lay days ashore for repairs to these boats due to their shaft-log installation is a matter of record. In my opinion, 90 percent of the problems would not have occurred, or would have been less serious, had the shaft log been a fiberglass tube surrounded by solid filling. With only the rubber bearing itself, not the cast base, and with a rubber-necked stuffing box clamped to a fiberglass tube rather than threaded to a bronze tube, the assembly and its installation would probably have been less expensive, too. But regardless of initial cost, the fiberglass log would have been less expensive in the long run.

Struts

As stated earlier, when the engine is positioned in the boat and a shaft coupled to it is headed out through a rough hole in the hull to where the propeller will be, you can measure up for the strut, obtain it, and install it. The position of the engine and the position of the propeller, I should remind you, are the two most important concerns when installing the propulsion system. A propeller needs solid, undisturbed water flowing into and out of it if it is to do its job efficiently. The axioms around boatyards are that the tips of the propeller blades should clear the hull and skeg by at least 1 inch for small propellers and 2 inches for larger propellers; the hub should clear the aft end of a rubber-lined bearing by at least one shaft diameter, but not more than two; and sternposts and rudder stocks should be kept at a good distance and faired as much as possible to allow a clean flow of water into the blades. For these reasons and others, I like to see the engine and shaft actually set up in place. Although usually you can't put the engine on the shaft yet, you can hold the propeller up beside the shaft, if it helps you decide whether it has the right clearances. Meanwhile, everyone who has lived with engines in boats knows the importance of locating the engine with enough clearance on all sides to maintain and repair it in place: to change oil and replace hoses and belts; to remove and reinstall starters, alternators, pumps, filters; even to remove a head or gear box; or at least to get to the coupling bolts and the engine mounts. You should be satisfied, then, with the location of engine and propeller before you install a strut or engine beds or a shaft log.

Once you have set the engine in place, you can also find out for sure where to cut the rough opening for shafts that go through the hull (and not through a sternpost or aperture), through which to poke the shaft (or to string a wire if you're clinging to tradition). It does look a little confusing at first, but if taken step by step, it's simple:

1. With the engine positioned approximately in place and a target set up that represents the center of the shaft at the center of the propeller, draw the shaft line in the plan view (looking down on it) on the inside of the hull. You establish the engine end of this line by plumbing down from the center of the coupling. The propeller end of the line is established by measuring up its location on the outside along the surface of the hull. You measure fore and aft parallel to the centerline from the transom to a point plumb above the center of the propeller and athwartships from the center of the hull to that same point. Then, you transfer these measurements to the inside of the hull. (Be sure to deduct the thickness of the transom.) When you have marked the centers of the propeller and coupling on the inside, you can connect them with a line established by plumbing down from a wire or straightedge running between them. (You should always level up a hull both fore and aft and athwartships before you try to install anything on the interior. A level and/or a plumb bob are thus invaluable aids to every step in finishing off a boat. You will notice that all plans today are drawn with the waterline plane level.)

2. Shift the engine until it is as closely centered as possible on the line drawn on the inside of the hull. At least make sure that the coupling is exactly centered over the line. You should also try to tilt the engine at the approximate angle (downhill aft) that you estimate the shaft will take. To help you do this, you can measure the "shaft angle," the number of degrees off the horizontal, from the plan. Note that having the engine too level means that you can jack up its forward end, whereas

starting with it tilted too much might make its base hit the hull when you try to lower its forward end.

3. Now take measurements along the hull to the spot plumb below the coupling, on the inside, from the centerline of the hull and the transom.

4. Using the measurements taken in number 3, measure along the hull on the outside and locate the spot below the coupling there. (Remember to add the thickness of the transom to that measurement, just as you deducted it from the earlier measurement to the propeller when transferring it from outside to inside.)

5. Measure the height of the coupling above the hull, and add the thickness of the hull to it to get the "height of coupling above the outside of hull," HO.

6. Set up a straightedge that runs through a point HO below the center of the propeller and ends up on the spot on the hull's outside directly below the coupling.

7. Slide a block that is HO high up the straightedge, holding it plumb. The point at which it hits the hull is the center of the hole you should cut in the hull. Blocks half a shaft diameter taller or shorter than HO will outline the top and bottom of the shaft.

I worked out this procedure for my mechanics to avoid the confusion created when owner after owner opted for a different engine than the one drawn in the plans, or for different engines in the same semiproduction hull. The mechanics got so that they would lay out the installation in less time than it took me to find words to describe what they did, but that's not surprising.

Once you head the shaft coupled to the engine out the rough hole, you can measure and obtain the strut. A number of marine hardware manufacturers make up struts, whether V or single, to order. Their catalogs tell you how to measure the "drop" and angle so that they can adjust their pattern to fit your boat. Given the shaft size, they will ship the strut with the rubber-lined bearing in place.

You can also make your own pattern and take it to a foundry, then to a machine shop. The foundry will cast the strut so that it has a rough, undersized hole for the bearing. The machine shop will bore out the hole, press the bearing into it, and install the set screws to hold it in place. Whether you have them bore and countersink the holes in the base or do this yourself is up to you. If possible, it is a good idea to show the strut pattern to the foundryman when you have it carved, but before you finish it, to find out whether it can make a good casting. He can also instantly see whether you are making a pattern that will "draw" out of the sand, which is necessary if you want a simple, inexpensive casting. He will not want a hole in the pattern where the bearing is to be fitted, but, rather, a short dowel projecting from each end of the barrel that is the size of the hole as cast. A "standard" dowel ⅝ inch in diameter is also acceptable to some foundries, no matter what size hole is called for. The dowel makes a print in the sand into which the foundryman fits a core that forms the hole in the casting when the metal is poured around it. Manganese bronze is a good, strong alloy for struts, and one that most foundries can handle.

A third way to obtain a strut is to make it, or have it made up, as a weldment. You can get an extremely strong strut with stainless-steel parts heliarc-welded together, and a bronze strut can be fabricated this way, too. About the only disadvantage of welded struts is that they are usually a bit slab sided, or less sleek looking. It is just too difficult to work metal plate down to the same lovely shape you can carve into a casting's wooden pattern.

The "pad," "palm," or base of a strut should have a bearing surface on fiberglass about the same as on wood; for the fiberglass, although less compressible, is likely to be more flexible. It is important to lay up a patch of reinforcement on the inside of the hull where you will bolt on a strut. I might use a patch 6 inches bigger than the pad all around for a strut carrying up to a 1-inch shaft and not less than another 6 inches all around for each additional inch of shaft diameter. I would taper the patch off toward the edges, but increase the total thickness of fiberglass in the hull at the pad by about 25 to 50 percent. Any sandwich-hull-laminate core softer than wood must, of course, be replaced with harder stuff where a strut is bolted on. Above all, a strut should have a generous backing block. Oak or mahogany is all right, but I like metal best, a nice stiff slab of bronze or stainless steel a few inches bigger than the pad all around. You can use plain steel, but it should have oversized holes so that you can seal it against rusting, and you should cover it with fiberglass for the same reason. Then you need some large washers to span the oversized holes.

All this reinforcement will more than help the strut do its job; but you ought to look beyond normal duty to possible accidents, such as when the propeller strikes an object it can't cut. The ideal installation is designed to ensure that the underwater gear, if bent out of shape or even "wiped out," will not break a piece out of the hull. It is bad enough to replace parts, but it's a calamity if the hull is also flooded.

Intermediate Bearings

Long propeller shafts need more support than they get from the engine coupling forward and a single bearing aft, or else they develop a whip or vibration. At what length a shaft develops this annoying and destructive action depends on its size, the speed at which it is turning, and numerous other factors. The best place from which to get advice about the need for an intermediate bearing is the makers or suppliers of shafting, but you can also check to see whether one is required on boats with similar engine installations. Offhand as this may sound, if in doubt, you can launch the boat without the intermediate bearing, see whether the shaft runs smoothly or not, and install one only if vibration develops. This will not harm anything as long as the boat is not run with the shaft vibrating any longer than it takes to identify the problem, and the boat can be run indefinitely at any speed below that at which vibration is noticeable.

In general, when the engine is near the middle of the boat, an intermediate bearing is usually necessary. In a centerline installation with a full keel and a stern bearing, the intermediate bearing is located inside the hull. With a cutaway keel, it is more likely to be on the outside. It is almost always outside when the shaft is installed off center. For a bearing mounted inside the boat, you can use a standard pillow-block bearing, whether "self-lubricated" or equipped with a grease fitting. You can bolt it to a floor-timber-like member that can actually be a piece of channel or angle iron. You should keep the top surface of this support for the bearing low and use shims to adjust the bearing's height, just in case you ever need to lower it. It will save time if you do not install the bearing until after the engine and aft bearing are installed and aligned. By the way, the best and simplest test for this type of bearing is how hard it is to turn the shaft in it with your hand. If the shaft turns easily after the bearing is bolted tightly in place, the alignment is excellent. Conversely, you may be sure that the harder it becomes to turn the shaft, the worse the bearing's alignment.

The majority of twin-screw and off-center single-screw installations in boats over 30 feet with the engine near the middle of the boat usually have intermediate bearings on the outside of the hull. If the engine or engines are installed way forward, two intermediates, one inside and one outside, may be necessary.

An outside intermediate bearing is usually a bronze casting built just like a strut and obtainable in the same ways. It is sometimes actually a shorter strut forward of the main strut, but more often the barrel for the bearing sits more or less directly on the base or pad for bolting to the hull. I have even built intermediate bearings with a base that extended from each side of the barrel like a pair of wings. The bearing must divide the overall length of the shaft so that neither span is long enough to vibrate, which determines the drop or distance from the surface against the hull to the shaft. However, there is often considerable latitude equal to the difference between the critical length of the shaft (the length at which it begins to vibrate) and the overall length.

Although it is not as important to beef up the hull where you bolt on an outside intermediate bearing as it is where you attach a strut, you should at least make sure that the hull is not so limber in way of the bearing that it will simply take to vibrating along with the shaft and bearing. In any event, a backing plate should be used.

MAST STEPS, CHAINPLATES, AND THEIR REINFORCEMENTS

Other parts that should be installed, or at least provided for, before there is too much joinerwork in the way are those associated with a mast. In past, simpler times, they consisted of only the mast partner in the deck structure, a step in the bilge, and chainplates at the rail. Today, small- or medium-sized boats often have deck-stepped masts, reflecting the preference of production builders who relish the lower cost and the absence of the mast from the middle of the accommodations. Even more frequently, chainplates are installed well inboard, thanks to those who copy racing boats and wish to clear the decks for overlapping headsails.

Design is not the subject of this book, so I spare you any discourse or opinions on the advantages or disadvantages of these two features. However, if your boat is to have them, she will need substantial reinforcement of the deck to counter the downward pressure of the mast and/or the upward pull of the shrouds. In 1982 I surveyed two fiberglass boats, each of which had a beam, built under the deck to support the mast, that had broken under the strain. One of the beams was fiberglass; the other was wooden. Another boat had a buckled bulkhead from the same cause. I saw one set of loosened bulkheads to which chainplates were bolted and one pair of cabin trunk sides that were cracked where chainplates were bolted on. They represent a heavy percentage of the few fiberglass boats surveyed with such rigs. It isn't all coincidence either. Some such failures are present in each year's crop of surveys.

However, I have yet to see structural failures in some fiberglass production models that have steel reinforcements laid up within the laminates of decks with masts stepped on or shrouds anchored to them. Some of the boats in which bulkheads take the strains of the rig look just the same as the day they were built, after a decade of hard sailing, too. I haven't seen trouble on many boats in which substantial knees, posts, and beams have been provided below decks either. These successful installations more than justify the belief that masts can be stepped on deck and shrouds can be moved inboard without structural failure. The logical conclusion is that there are some boatbuilders who respect the strains imposed by masts and shrouds, and some who grossly underestimate them.

Deck-Stepped Masts

The following are some reinforcements that help a deck survive the stress of carrying a mast:

1. A post. Nothing is more supportive and simple than a post, a piece of pipe or tubing, directly under the mast. It can be relatively small in diameter because it is short and its ends can be well secured, both of which conditions minimize the tendency to buckle. A post does not clear the space for accommodations entirely, but it can be much less bulky than a mast and still do the job. There should be substantial flanges on the top and bottom of the post, well fastened to deck and hull. Fiberglassing the bottom flange to the keel and bolting the top one to the deck right through the mast step above it (which has to be bolted anyway) are obviously the easiest ways to secure them.

2. A beam or beams. To carry a deck-stepped mast unaided across the full width of a boat, or even across a cabin trunk, beams of fiberglass or wood or a combination of the two may have to be much deeper than headroom allows. The two beams I found broken recently were single beams not over 2 inches deep,

under fiberglass-sandwich decks. That's asking too much, unless you want to use a number of such beams and a mast step that is itself a girder long enough fore and aft to span a number of them. This was frequently done on wooden boats, especially by British builders who didn't seem to mind the looks of fairly bulky galvanized iron steps 3 or 4 feet long. It was practical, because the deckbeams were already there; but, leaving nothing to chance, they usually reinforced the beams with some rather intricate galvanized knees or arches extending well down onto the topsides, too, in larger boats. Only when the span is shortened to about the width of a doorway is there much hope of supporting a mast with a reasonable depth of wood or fiberglass. Otherwise, it is a job best given to steel in one form or another.

To keep the depth of a steel beam or beams minimal in fiberglass boats, I have installed a channel section with its wide face against the underside of the deck. When bulkheads are involved, you might find that a steel angle bar bolted to one side of the bulkhead, or two bolted one on each side, can be used and perhaps covered with trim. I have always wanted to try some rectangular-section steel beams, too, for such a section seems quite appropriate in this use. Whatever steel is built in under a fiberglass deck should be well fiberglassed to it and well encapsulated, if it is not galvanized, to seal it against oxidation.

3. Bulkheads. A bulkhead directly under a deck-stepped mast is an ideal support for it as long as the bulkhead is well stiffened with a vertical stiffener or stiffeners that prevent buckling under compression. As mentioned in the section on bulkheads, it is a happy coincidence when fore-and-aft and athwartship bulkheads meet under the mast step with a stout corner post to join them. It should be obvious that to be effective in this duty a bulkhead must also be heavily tabbed to the hull and deck.

4. Knees. When there are no bulkheads, or even partial bulkheads near the deck-stepped mast, it might be important to install some hanging knees against topsides and side deck, and/or against trunk sides and top if the mast is stepped on the trunk top. Despite supporting beams or a post, the shape of the boat in section has a tendency to distort. When a boat is hard pressed under sail, the interaction of mast, shrouds, and ballast is like squeezing the boat in a giant hand.

The neatest method of countering distortion, which some production builders use, is to fiberglass steel right into or onto the underside of the laminate. It is relatively inexpensive and very effective to cut, bend, and/or weld up some steel plate, bar, or shallow stock to fit sections in way of the mast and to fiberglass them in. Such imbedded steel allows the fiberglass layers under and over them to connect with each other at close intervals. Large, shaped plates should have frequent holes or slots in them, through which they are well captured by frequent buttons or rivets of fiberglass. This sort of steel reinforcement might, by a stretch of imagination and a contradiction in terms, be called flat hanging knees. Some hanging knees with a more traditional shape and molded dimensions will do a better job, however, if there's headroom for them. You can lay them up in fiberglass in place over a steel, wood, or foam core. Or they can be of bronze, stainless, or laminated wood left exposed and tabbed to the fiberglass laminate of the boat. In this case, mechanical fastenings through the tabbing into the knee are a must!

In a deck that has sandwich construction, as most of them do, you should replace any core softer than wood in way of the mast with wood, fiberglass, and/or steel as mentioned. In fact, whether a mast is stepped on or through the deck, I like to lay up a flat, laminated wooden beam 12 to 18 inches wide right across the deck as a replacement for the core. This beam is made up of two to four thin layers of wood or plywood with wet mat between them.

Inboard Chainplates

Moving chainplates inboard on your one-off creates the problem of getting a solid attachment for them. When they are at the rail, fastened to the topsides, they pull mostly upward in line with the hull's laminate, although there is an inward component of their pull edgewise against the deck. Putting the laminate of the hull in tension is fine. Fiberglass is very strong in tension. However, attaching them anywhere inboard of the rail imposes a bending force on the deck structure, which is not good, because fiberglass bends very readily. There are three common methods of anchoring inboard chainplates so that they won't distort the deck:

1. Bolt the chainplate to a bulkhead. You will find that innumerable production builders are using bulkheads to transmit the pull of inboard chainplates to the hull. It becomes obvious when you look at a few of their boats that they have designed the proportions of the rig and the layout of the interior so that one to three bulkheads fall in line with the chainplates. Ordinarily, there is a bulkhead with its top edge under a deck-stepped mast or close to being in line with a mast stepped through the deck. To a bulkhead in this location, the chainplates of the upper shrouds are bolted, with, at worst, a spacing block or wedge to maintain alignment with the centerline of the mast.

Sometimes a lower shroud is also led in line with the mast to share a double chainplate with the upper shroud. More frequently, the lower shroud tends aft. There, likely as not, is another strategically located bulkhead to take the bolts of its chainplate.

The ultimate in convenience to which I have found this shroud-on-bulkhead method carried is on some boats rigged with double lower shrouds and an upper, where each of the three shrouds on a side is led to its own bulkhead. The forward and aft tending lowers lead to chainplates on the forward and aft bulkheads of a head and a hanging locker opposite. Meanwhile, one upper's chainplate is on a bulkhead that divides a locker within the head, while the other's chainplate is on a bulkhead dividing the hanging locker.

When you think about it, what better anchor could a shroud have than a bulkhead? If you add that to what it can do to counter the strains imposed by a mast, a bulkhead is a very useful thing.

2. Bolt the chainplate to a hanging knee. A knee transmits the tension of the shroud to the hull in much the same way that a bulkhead does, but, of course, more locally. If the interior arrangement allows it, you can extend the lower part of the knee down the hull to distribute the pull over a larger area. Naturally, the more area involved the better, not only to disperse the stress, but also to stiffen the area as a rib or a bulkhead would.

3. Use some metal. Once again, when it comes to carrying the biggest load with the least obtrusive member, you can't beat metal. In this particular use, I feel more comfortable if the metal to which the chainplates are attached is bronze, stainless steel, or at least galvanized steel. Invariably, chainplates wiggle loose in the deck and lead the water that runs down the shrouds below decks. I have seen too many pieces of plain steel in this situation erupting with rust, whether buried in fiberglass or not. However, I'm willing to admit that careful insulation of any bolt holes through the steel with a product like Marine-Tex, an epoxy putty, might stave off the evil day indefinitely. Meanwhile, you can even leave bronze, stainless, or galvanized steel exposed without fear of more than light staining of the interior from water that sneaks in.

You can make up metal to reinforce an area for chainplates so that it follows the contours of the boat vertically, as described for reinforcement in way of deck-stepped masts. You can also make it up to run horizontally fore and aft, if you feel that it is more suitable to the construction and arrangement of the hull and deck. Suppose the chainplates are but a short distance inboard of the rail and your hull and deck in this area already quite massive and stiff. For such a situation, an angle or a channel of metal running fore and aft under the side deck will spread the load in that direction. If its length is generous, it can be used to pick up the chainplate of more than one shroud; and its stiffness will resist inward, as well as upward, distortion of the deck, as harpins do in wooden boats. When chainplates are on or close to the side of the cabin trunk, a metal angle made up to match the angle of deck to trunk side will spread the strain along that corner. Such a member is not difficult to encase in the laminate or cover with trim. I'm sure an angle would have prevented the breaks I found in the trunk sides of the boat mentioned earlier. On that particular boat, which is 27 feet, a 1-to-2-foot length of 1-by-2-inch-stainless angle $3/32$-inch to $1/8$-inch thick, catching the lower bolt of the chainplate would, in my opinion, have been enough to carry the aft-tending lowers attached there.

To me, it would be fascinating to know what effect laying up a material like Str-r-etch Mesh in the laminate would have to inhibit bending in way of inboard shrouds, or shrouds at the rail for that matter. As I say, it's not in tension but in *bending* that the fiberglass needs reinforcement most.

Before leaving the subject, I should mention that many builders, and therefore perhaps designers, make the mistake of using huge bolts to secure chainplates. It is, I suppose, a good direction in which to err, but although a chainplate should be massive enough so that it will never break, what it needs for adequate attachment to the boat is great length and many bolts to diffuse its tug on the materials to which it is bolted. When a shroud is attached to the chainplate with a $5/8$-inch bolt, for instance, what kind of engineering is it that calls for four or five $5/8$-inch bolts through a wooden bulkhead? Two such bolts would plow a slot right up through the bulkhead, tabbing, deck, and all before anything happened to them. If not, the one bolt above decks would break before they did. A longer tail on the chainplate, a backing plate on the other side of the bulkhead, and a half-dozen or more ⅜- or ½-inch bolts down the length of them would be a much better arrangement. I would just make a case for greater length and more bolts without mentioning size were it not a fact that the price jumps enormously after ½ inch.

Through-the-Deck Masts

The traditional reinforcements for masts stepped through the deck are mast partners, sometimes hanging knees, and, less often, harpins. In fiberglass boats, the partner is rarely like the wooden boat's heavy block of oak around the mast bolted "through and through" two deckbeams. This is still the best arrangement for any construction in which there are beams, but a more moderate approach is usually taken in all-fiberglass or sandwich construction. In a sandwich, replacing the core with a wide laminated wood beam usually suffices. If there is not a molded-in mast collar, the wood should be kept back from the mast hole and the space between the inner and outer skins filled with solid fiberglass to seal the core against water penetration. Given a solid-fiberglass deck laminate, it might be wise to build up such a beam under the deck, perhaps filling the space between two stiffeners.

When there are no bulkheads nearby to keep the deck from moving up and down, a small-diameter post of pipe or tubing alongside the forward or aft face of the mast might be needed to act as both support post and tie rod, just as these have long been used in wooden boats. My reason for suggesting the one member is that it is less complicated than the older two items, yet quite easily fabricated of stout stainless steel with the heliarc welding so commonplace today. If sturdy flanges are welded top and bottom, they can be bolted or fiberglassed to the boat— whichever is most appropriate in a particular construction. Without this feature, it may be impossible to keep wedges in the mast partner, and the deck may work up and down alarmingly.

When a shape-retaining bulkhead near the mast is lacking, another possible requirement might be some hanging knees. Although the mast is pressing down on the keel area now, and not on the deck, the shrouds are still pulling inward, trying to buckle the deck laminate. With the shrouds at the sheer, the topsides want to bend inward, and the deck, being crowned, wants to bend upward, forcing the corner of deck to hull to straighten out. Meanwhile, when the mast is stepped through the cabin-trunk top, the side deck tries to fold in the trunk sides, sometimes forcing the inboard edge of the side deck to bend noticeably downward in time. Once more, a well-secured bulkhead is the obvious preventive for almost any or all such contortions. Without that restraint, some knees or kneelike reinforcements might be in order.

Through-the-Deck Mast Steps

A mast step has two essential functions: to provide a base to absorb the downward pressure of the mast and to prevent horizontal movement of its heel. Traditionally, the step was a hardwood timber, which distributed the pressure, and a hole in it for a tongue projecting from the mast was enough to hold the heel captive. But in the last few decades, builders have used metal mast steps increasingly, even in wooden boats, to resist the enormous thrust of masts carrying large headsails with bowstring luffs, kept taut with backstay tensioners. The step has now become a spider of metal floors topped by a heavy metal plate with a metal box for the heel of the mast bolted to it. This change is much for the better, as attested by the still-numerous repairs to broken wooden steps and/or floor timbers necessary on boats without metal reinforcements.

In view of this history, you may rest assured that a metal mast step for your fiberglass one-off is not just the current fashion, but quite appropriate in any boat; the more taut the rig, the more so. Even in a full WLP construction, a wooden step under a "modern" rig could be a regrettable anachronism. How extensive a metal step should be is another design detail that the builder hopes the designer has spelled out. In little boats, a simple box to contain the heel of the mast or a metal plug over which the heel of the mast fits is the usual arrangement. Either may have a flange around the base to spread the load and to facilitate fiberglassing it to the hull. As the mast gets bigger, you can fiberglass a separate base plate to the hull and machine screw the box or step to it. This is better, especially if you care about being able to move the mast forward or aft a bit to adjust the rig.

I might interject here that steps for deck-stepped masts are often similar in construction, although they are also likely to be double steps, one hinged inside the other, to allow the mast to be swung down without disengaging the heel. These have been dubbed "tabernacles," being somewhat like the tall steps with two bolts, one above the other, that, when the bottom one is pulled, allow the mast to be swung down and carried horizontally on deck. Although I built a number of the latter steps for the Meadow Lark ketches we used to build, they are more popular in England and Europe than in the United States.

In larger boats and in racing boats with light hulls, high ballast ratios, and tightly strung rigs, the step for a through-the-deck mast may require some floors that spread its thrust out into the hull. If well covered all over with fiberglass, there is little reason to worry about making up a plain steel weldment and glassing it to the hull.

Unless the boat is very large, it may not be necessary to build the entire "spider" of reinforcement in way of the mast with metal. A set of fiberglass floors can reinforce the hull; then the metal mast plate and step can be fitted atop these floors, as long as there are one or more solid pillars or some steel legs directly under the step to transmit compression to the solid fiberglass of the keel area. This very necessary solidity under compression can be achieved by filling the fiberglass floors and/or an area between them with cast, filled resin.

THE CABIN SOLE

It is good to get the cabin sole down as early as possible in a one-off fiberglass boat. Until it is in place, interior work is severely hampered by the tendency of everything, and everybody, to slide down to the keel. Although fiberglass soles are durable and maintenance free, I have yet to hear someone say they are charming or pleasant. An indication of how they strike people is that they almost always get covered with carpeting. The trouble with carpeting is that it is the hardest surface of all to keep clean on a boat, miserable under bare or stockinged feet when wet, and takes its own sweet time to dry out. However, if a fiberglass sole appeals to you, there are, as always, several ways to build it. Taking a pattern of the area, you can lay it up on a table, in sections if necessary, complete with a nonskid, gelcoated surface, rabbets to receive hatches, and a PVC core. To make up that pattern, you need some sole beams, temporary or permanent, to support the pattern material while you fit it. But the easier and less expensive way to build a fiberglass sole is to fabricate it in place with a plywood base or core topped with a pigmented, rolled mat finish, as you might any deck. I would call the plywood a base when you cover only the top and call it a core when you cover both sides with fiberglass. I hope you don't forget to fasten the fiberglass to the plywood mechanically. Although it is slightly more expensive, the fiberglass purist can use fairly high-density, rigid PVC foam for the core and build fiberglass stiffeners on the bottom if he doesn't want wooden sole beams. But he can also wrap up "sticks" of foam in mat and roving and fit them like beams and then lay his PVC sheets with their bottom surface fiberglassed on these beams in wet mat.

Fortunately for those who prefer wood underfoot, a wooden sole is easy to build. The cost of materials depends upon the variety of wood used. The cheapest possible sole material is plain native softwood boards, such as pine, cedar, fir, or yellow pine. The most expensive is an exotic wood, which can be expensive to install as well if you use two or more varieties in strips of contrasting shades or in an intricate pattern, perhaps over a plywood sublayer. The mahoganies, oak, and teak are all used in cabin soles, too.

Cabin-Sole Beams

The most efficient support for a narrow cabin sole deep in the hull is a set of athwartship wooden sole beams. They have the shortest span; therefore, they can be of moderate size and need few if any intermediate supports. Oak, mahogany, fir, and yellow pine are the most commonly used woods for sole beams. To fit a set of sole beams so that the ends rest on the deadrise of the hull, you must first establish the height of the top of the beams and run a string or wire down the center of the compartment at that height. Place a beam that is longer than needed over its fore-and-aft location and level it. Set your pencil dividers, or compass, to the height of the top of the beam above the string; then scribe the side at each end for the cut, holding the dividers vertical. You can get the horizontal bevel with a parallel-sided block lying against the hull or with an adjustable bevel; or you can scribe both of the sides and get the bevel by connecting the two. Assuming that the beams come to rest firmly on the deadrise of the hull, as they do in most boats, all that remains to be done after fitting them is to tab them in place.

Beams that end against the topsides where it is too steep to get a good bearing should be provided with a stringer, or "riser," along the hull on which to rest. You could fiberglass each beam to the topsides, but it would probably be more work. You can build a fiberglass stringer by hot-gluing polyurethane foam, PVC foam, or softwood (laminated if there is much bend) against the side of the hull and covering it with an appropriate number of glass layers. Another way is to build a fiberglass angle by bringing the laminate down the hull and out on the top face of what now becomes a removable form. When you have built up enough fiberglass to hold the beam ends, you can tear out the foam or wood. You can either fasten the beam ends mechanically with through-bolts or screws or tab them on each side out onto the side of the hull and the top of the stringer.

It is customary not to cut off beams and framing around hatches, or "pickups," in a wooden sole unless there are items installed or stowed under it that won't fit between them. Leaving the beams intact allows hatches to be of generous proportions, in any combination of locations, without significantly weakening the sole. For the past few decades, it has annoyed everyone, except perhaps the builders, that larger and larger areas of the bilge are sealed over with fiberglass liner/soles, making them completely inaccessible. Perhaps this is because the bilge of the currently popular canoe-bodied hulls with fin keels is too shoal for any other use than collecting a little water. No doubt, it is also to save the cost of more access than the scattered small hatches so often found. That's fine, as long as nothing goes wrong. What bothers me—and I hope you think about it before you build a sole that denies access to any part of the bilge—is that a person in a boat taking on water fast is barred from seeking out the source and possibly stemming the flow. Somehow, if a part of a boat can't be reached on the interior, that's where the rock or the drifting log is going to punch the hole. But having to cut out sections of the sole to make repairs is an expensive business, often more so in current boats than the repair itself!

DECKHOUSE AND FULL-WIDTH-COCKPIT SOLES

Although athwartship beams are best for narrow soles, it often makes more sense to use longitudinal beams in compartments or cockpits where the sole is wide, where hatches would interrupt the majority of athwartship beams, where sheet materials and fiberglass make the orientation of beams inconsequential, and especially where there are closely spaced bulkheads to support longitudinals. In other words, when athwartship beams would be as long or longer than fore-and-aft members and would probably require the support of some of these members anyway, then using longitudinals would be more efficient.

A sturdy, relatively inexpensive weather deck can be built up over longitudinal stringers by laminating sheet plywood over them and covering it with fiberglass. The plywood lamination can consist of two or three ¼-inch layers in a small boat or as many as four to six ½-inch layers in a 50- to 60-foot commercial fishing boat. The fiberglass surface can be three to four layers of 1-ounce mat on the small boat, or six to eight layers of 1½-ounce mat on the big one. The plywood should be glued as well as fastened mechanically, and the fiberglass should be fastened mechanically as well as glued. You knew I'd say that, didn't you? Well, you ought to see some of the boats I've seen, only 5 or 6 years old, in which these things weren't done. Other important details are carrying the fiberglass down into the rabbet where flush hatches or deck plates are fitted and carrying it up, over, and down inside any raised wooden hatch coamings, unless these are massive hardwood well bolted and bedded.

The soles of enclosed pilothouses and deckhouses will probably be flat, unless they happen to be a continuation of a weather deck. The absence of crown enables the builder to use fewer, thicker layers of plywood, or only one. Being under cover, the surface used becomes a matter of utility and aesthetics rather than of weather tightness.

It is not at all necessary to use plywood for either sheltered or exposed soles. For centuries, both were built of natural-wood decking, the durability of which is excellent. But in weather decks, covering this material properly with fiberglass will extend its life indefinitely. (Cheer up, that may be the last time in this book that I emphasize covering wood properly with fiberglass.) Then there's sheet PVC foam. With it, you can create a sole with superior sound- and heat-insulating qualities and lighter weight as well.

The simplest way I know to build a PVC-cored sole in place is to put down a layer of fairly thin plywood or Masonite first, lay up the inner skin on it, weight the foam down in wet mat, and then lay up the outer skin. However, it is also possible to cover one side of the PVC sheets first, fasten them in place on the beams in wet mat, and then cover the whole top surface.

Who knows what new materials scientists will develop with which boatbuilders will fabricate a sole of superlative quality. To me, it seems that walking and working surfaces are falling behind the rest of the boat. But that's only on weather decks where teak is not appropriate. I'm perfectly happy with what materials are available for enclosed decks in any kind of boat.

13

Finishing Details

JOINERWORK

In the midst of assembling my thoughts for this section, it struck me that perhaps my old-time name for the subject, *joinerwork*, has been dropped from current boatbuilding jargon. In a mild panic, I leafed through boating books and magazines for almost an hour, until the word turned up in a recent issue of *Yachting*.

Why be concerned about whether the word is used much anymore? As long as readers understand that joinerwork denotes the cabinetwork and other woodwork that make up a boat's accommodations, what difference does it make if most writers now use such terms as *furniture, arrangement, interior finish, layout,* and even *on the inside?*

Frankly, my concern for the word is mixed fondness and nostalgia, the feeling with which a person inquires after the well-being of an old friend. As long as the word lives, it is a link to the boatbuilding of past years. It recalls the throb of a mill, the buzz of a carpenter shop, the swish of a hand plane, the smell of different woods when cut and of glues, stains, oils, and varnish; as well as the warm, charming, restful presence of natural wood in hundreds of boats.

To be realistic, the word is losing ground. But that is to be expected, for it describes less and less aptly what builders are installing in the majority of boats today, which are, of course, production boats. No way is a fiberglass liner joinerwork, although it might be argued that the name applies to the teak woodwork and trim with which liners are embellished. Then again, there's so much teak that isn't really teak or even teak veneer, but that is photographically reproduced teak grain on paper or plastic, overlaid on some other variety of wood, plywood, or "board." Nor can you say that the product, even when it is based on wood, is joined as much as installed, which means precut and screwed up in place. Depressing, isn't it? How fortunate for the craft of joinery that a fiberglass liner is too involved and expensive to make up for a one-off boat and that the only practical way to build her accommodations is with some type of joinerwork.

There is no part of a boat's joinerwork that cannot be built with solid, natural wood. Until 50 or 60 years ago, every bit of joinerwork in every boat, whatever its size or type, was so constructed, because there was nothing else. There was no waterproof glue, no plywood, and no thermoset laminates (like Micarta and Formica). Yet the techniques of joining solid wood reached such perfection that proper joinerwork still shows no sign of distortion after a century or longer, despite the drastic changes in moisture to which every piece of wood in a boat is subjected from season to season and year to year, with perhaps occasional flooding or years of dry storage thrown in.

The secret of such durable joinerwork is the arrangement of the wood comprising any large surface into some system of paneling or staving, so it can shrink and swell to its limits without disrupting the structure or destroying itself. But I only mention natural-wood joinerwork to highlight the all-but-forgotten fact that plywood is not a necessity. You can, if you want, build any part of your one-off's accommodations without it, and the result of so doing can create the most enjoyable joinerwork of all, provided only that you work within the bounds of long-established practice and common sense.

Meanwhile, plywood needs no advertising as a material for use in joinerwork. Hardly a boat is built today, no matter of what hull and deck materials, without some plywood in its interior, and in many boats plywood is used almost to the exclusion of natural wood. Although a person may deplore the plainness of an interior with too much plywood, he or she has to admit that there is no quicker type of joinerwork to build than that based on panels of plywood. Even the most stubborn purist must admit that it is useful for the bottoms of berths and drawers, for shelves, and for strength bulkheads (which paneling can cover).

You can attach joinerwork to the hull in the same ways that you attach bulkheads. You can tab it directly to a fiberglass skin or inner skin, fasten it to stringers or ribs of fiberglass laid up on them, or screw it to wooden cleats that are screwed to a sandwich or WLP construction. Remember that in tabbing joinerwork to fiberglass you are creating a watertight joint. After water has leaked into the boat, it becomes apparent that now there are some disadvantages. Although a watertight shelf, berth bottom, or counter top may keep whatever is beneath it dry from a deck leak, it may also retain a puddle or small pond that thoroughly saturates its own contents. You should therefore think about how to drain the water from a given area with the least danger of flooding another.

When it comes to planning and laying out the joinerwork of a boat, your conception or visualization of it is simplified and the building of it made easier by treating it in units between bulkheads. With few exceptions, all deckhouses, compartments, saloons, staterooms, galleys, heads, and their subdivisions into settees, berths, lockers, dinettes, dressers, counters, and shelves begin and end on bulkheads. These bulkheads or partial bulkheads, which are called half-bulkheads regardless of size, are the bases on which to lay out the shape of a unit. Because they are almost always in the plane of a true section of the boat, normal to the centerline and normal to the waterline, they are easy to draw into the plans, to pick up in the lofting, and to set up in the boat. That reminds me: You should always set a boat up level fore and aft and athwartships while you are doing your joinerwork. Once the limiting bulkheads or half-bulkheads are installed and the end sections of the unit are laid out on them, construction is but a matter of filling in between them. Again, this job is made easy, when the boat is leveled, by the fact that almost all of the flats or tops of joinerwork are dead level and most of its vertical surfaces plumb. Notable exceptions to this rule are those settee fronts raked inboard for foot room, backs raked outboard for lounging, and seats tilted slightly outboard (and curved) for comfort.

Since this book is not going into woodworking in detail, almost enough has been said on the subject of joinerwork. A few well-known rules, however, can always stand repetition:

1. No joinerwork corner should be sharp, lest somebody, sooner or later, dash himself or be dashed against it.

2. If there is not much about the interior to hang on to, you should consider installing handrails or posts. The wider and more open the cabin, the more important this is.

3. Plan the routing of wires, control or steering-system cables, or plumbing before you start building joinerwork, not after it is completed. Tab PVC tubes to the hull for conduits through which you can pull wires or tubes, or make some part of the joinerwork removable for servicing and replacing them.

4. Make sure that chainplates, deck hardware, through-hulls, or their fastenings and backing plates, will be accessible through joinerwork built over them without major surgery.

5. Keep joinerwork simple and relatively sturdy. Complicated, delicate, or lightly fastened joinerwork is soon damaged, and the same is true of its hardware.

HATCHES AND COAMINGS

I first describe the building of fiberglass hatches and coamings in molds in Chapter 2, pointing out that a hatch is a classic example of a part that should be built by this method. This is not necessarily true of coamings. Although the best fiberglass coaming is one built in a mold, especially when that mold is integral with a deck mold, it is not the easiest kind to build. After estimating the time it will take to construct a mold for one of these relatively small but complicated parts, you are likely to prefer laminating it over WLP or some other core installed around a raw opening in the deck.

Coamings form-built over a core require an all-mat laminate because of the many corners, although you can and should use some roving in the sides and deck flange of tall coamings, such as those that workboats and ocean-going craft often have. To ensure a good fit with its hatch, don't forget to allow for the thickness of the coaming's laminate when making up the core. You could wait to build the hatch mold until the coaming is built, but then you'd have to adjust the size of the mold to allow for the thickness of the hatch laminate. Either sequence, then, requires adjustment of the thickness of one laminate or the other for a good fit.

The most common hatch-to-coaming joints in fiberglass are variations of the matching rabbets long used in wooden hatches. In the fiberglass version, the coaming is rabbeted, but, usually, the whole, single-skin side of the hatch is brought down onto the outside ledge of that rabbet. This is convenient for the builder in fiberglass, because it would be much more trouble for him to fabricate a matching rabbet. It works all right because the relatively thin wall of fiberglass is tougher than wood two or three times its thickness; yet there is nothing to stop the builder from making it as thick as he thinks necessary.

Whether built of wood or fiberglass, the rabbeted hatch can be depended upon to shed falling water for its life without a tight fit or rubber gaskets. It has a smooth joint on the outside, which saves the hatch from snagging ropes, being torn open, or being flipped overboard. Neat fabric weather covers can be fitted to the hatch or even duct tape wrapped over the joint. In short, it is the perfect hatch for weathering all conditions, except for going under solid water or resisting water driven by high winds. For true watertight (and airtight) integrity, only a rubber gasket with a thin edge of hatch or coaming pressed into it with a number of dogs or a powerful screw will do. This principle, proven by years of use in traditional watertight doors, portlights, and hatches, is applicable to your fiberglass or wooden hatch in simpler but reasonably effective forms.

If you're wondering why I keep bringing wooden hatches and coamings into this section, it is because I know that some builders, despite building the hull and deck one-off in fiberglass, will nevertheless insist upon having the natural charm of wooden joinerwork on deck as well as below. Nor do I want to dissuade anyone from the rewarding experience of building hatches and coamings with perhaps dovetailed or half-lapped corners and a grooved and splined, ship-lapped, double-planked, or cold-molded top. Hatch building is the most pleasant sort of job to a woodworker.

Meanwhile, if you're not in the mood to build hatches, you can take the entirely different approach of buying and installing some of the ready-made aluminum-frame hatches a number of manufacturers offer. Based on the gasket principle mentioned previously, these hatches are really watertight when clamped down.

Their tops are clear, molded thermoplastic (like Plexiglass or Lexan) so that they are useful as skylights. With their narrow aluminum frames, they look like giant portlights mounted in the deck. The hatch and coaming come preassembled, complete with hardware to keep the hatch closed and open. Installation involves little more than fastening them down in bedding on a flat margin around the opening. That flat margin must really be in a flat place, for the aluminum coaming and hatch frame are quite flat and rigid. To provide this plane, you wedge up the curvature of the deck or build a low coaming with a flat top.

Still another type of deck hatch, well known to fishermen and workboat crews but rarely seen on yachts, is the "bunker plate." These circular metal hatches fit flush in a gasketed ring, which is usually let flush into the deck. They are fitted with dogs around their circumference to clamp them securely shut. A special T-handle wrench provided with them is used to apply the pressure on the dogs needed for tightness when underwater, to release the pressure, and to pry a stuck plate. These are great hatches for occasional access to space below busy deck areas. Years ago, bigger yachts had beautiful bronze bunker plates 30 inches or more in diameter in cockpit soles or in aft and forward decks over lazarettes and chain lockers. These included a second grating or openwork plate with which to replace the cover plate so that the area could be ventilated, yet safely walked over, in harbor and in fine weather. Today, this useful item is supplied mostly in aluminum or galvanized steel for commercial boats, although you can always have one cast in bronze if you're willing to pay the much higher price. Now and then, too, you can find a 50- to-75-year-old bronze bunker plate wherever used marine hardware is sold.

Companionway sliding hatches are not manufactured for boatbuilders as far as I know. But so many builders fail to build them quite right that it might be worthwhile for someone to market some sturdy models, guaranteed to slide smoothly for life. Until then, we can still expect to encounter occasional broken hatches, balkiness, jammed fingers, and bad language. Unlike the current remarkable automobile doors, trunk lids, and engine hoods, which operate perfectly after thousands of openings and closings, the development of the sliding hatch has actually regressed since this item was put into mass production. Many production builders are not putting out a sliding hatch you ought to copy on your one-off boat. It would be best if you went back to the traditional construction in wood. It slides quite dependably for life as long as it doesn't get broken, or as long as movement of the trunk structure itself doesn't throw the runs out of alignment. You can adapt the same basic design to a fiberglass hatch. Since the fiberglass usually needs no beams, the job of keeping it down on its runs is accomplished by hooking some part of it under the projecting inboard edge of the flat brass used for a bearing surface, rather than into a groove in the face of the run at the level of the underside of the beams, as is done in the wooden version.

Of course, if the fiberglass hatch is big and you wish to incorporate a beam or stiffener at each end, then you could build it and its runs with an arrangement just about identical to that of the wooden hatch. To take off those hatches with keepers in a groove, the aft keepers are removed, the aft end of the hatch is lifted over the forward coaming of the opening, and the hatch is slid forward until its forward keepers slide out the forward end of the groove. In some of the fiberglass hatches, however, no removable parts are used; instead, the brass bearing strips themselves are held captive in the hatch except for fore-and-aft motion. Taking off or reinstalling the hatch is then a matter of taking up or screwing down the bearing strips.

As you might expect with a new material, fiberglass precipitated a flurry of new designs for companionway slides as well as other types of hatches. One quite untraditional slide still showing up on a new production model now and then is the hat-shaped hatch, sliding on its brim or horizontal flange flat on the cabin-trunk top, captured and guided by wooden trim pieces along either side rabbeted to fit over the brim.

This slide is apparently designed for greater dryness. When closed it sits like a hat, or an upside-down box, over the coaming around the deck opening's sides and forward end, and it has no cutouts for runs such as the hatch on runs has. I cannot, however, vouch for its superior dryness, having never been under one in really wet going. I do know that some box deck hatches I built years ago, which were literally upside-down boxes fitted over high coamings, were no more able to keep out driving, solid water than an ordinary rabbeted hatch, without a gasket. I imagine that this hat-shaped companionway hatch might also need a gasket to be really watertight under such conditions. Anyway, I am far from convinced by the examples I have seen that this configuration is the final word in companionway slides. It has to be much wider than the opening it covers; therefore, it is heavier and more cumbersome to open than a traditional slide for the same size opening. It is also clumsier to have underfoot. On several I have seen, the rabbeted guides were broken up, obviously from being trampled.

When you think about it, the traditional sliding hatch on raised runs has a number of worthwhile features:

1. *a.* The runs raise the hatch joint above deck water.

   b. They are in effect parallel beams that stiffen the trunk top around the opening and forward for twice the length of the hatch, stiffening it more the higher they are.

   c. They serve as handrails for a person walking along the side deck and as toe rails on the trunk top.

   d. They provide additional headroom for a person going up and down the companionway or standing directly beneath the hatch. Many boats with limited headroom have an oversized slide on high runs, which creates one good standing area in the cabin without affecting the profile of the boat as adversely as a higher trunk.

2. *a.* The span of the sliding hatch is only as big as the opening and its total area not much greater; so it has maximum strength with minimum weight and can afford to have a flatter crown than a wider hatch, which makes stepping on it safer.

b. For the size opening it covers, it takes up less room on deck, which may be needed on some boats for lines and hardware.

To get better watertightness in a sliding hatch, a weather cover is the most popular arrangement. This is merely a three-sided box, not unlike the hat-shaped hatch described earlier, that is higher and wider than the sliding hatch and forms a watertight housing for it as it is pushed forward. Since the after end of the weather cover overlaps the forward end of the hatch when the latter is closed, the leaky notches in the hatch are shielded from driven water at all times.

Note that in addition to protecting the forward end of the sliding hatch, the weather cover provides a stationary base over the sliding hatch and runs to which a dodger can be solidly attached, and where the dodger can also rest, if folded down, without interfering with the opening and closing of the slide. Sometimes a weather cover also helps to keep the mainsheet or other rigging or gear from fouling the hatch. Fiberglass has done much to make the weather cover more practical and popular by reducing its bulk, weight, and cost, for the cover is an item suited by its nature to molding in fiberglass, but not nearly as well to fabrication in other materials.

COMPANIONWAY DOORS AND FISHERMAN SLIDES

By this time, you probably have chosen between doors or drop slides for closing the vertical part of the companionway. Even if you haven't, I would not argue that one is superior to the other for you and your boat. Over the years I have found that custom-boat owners, who are usually ambivalent about such matters, can be surprisingly didactic about which is best. For the purposes of this section, I simply enumerate the differences between doors and slides as I see them.

Companionway slides, also called fisherman slides and drop slides, are simpler, stronger, cheaper, and a better dam against solid water than most doors. A favorite argument of their adherents is that you can leave one or two slides in place to keep deck water from sloshing below and step over them to go in and out. This is undoubtedly true if the companionway opening extends to the level of deck or cockpit sole. However, slides hardly help in an opening with a threshold about 6 inches above a bridge deck that is inside a coaming in a cockpit with huge, ungasketed seat-locker covers that open into the entire hull.

The objections to slides are that they are a nuisance to put in and take out; they get mixed up, turned upside down or backward; they tend to jam even when made rattling loose; and they need identifying marks engraved in one corner if there is to be any hope of sorting them out in the dark. Then there is the problem of where to put them when they're out of their tracks. Left around on deck, they're in the way and are easily lost overboard. But unless a storage place is made for them, they take up precious space below decks, too. I have always found that a quarter berth, even if shunned for any other use, is worth having as a place handy to the companionway in which to stow (or throw) all the loose gear when it's time to clear the deck and get underway quickly.

Companionway doors have positive and negative features that are almost the reverse of those of slides. They are infinitely handier to use going below or on deck and are instantly ready to shut out weather as soon as you're through them. They pose no storage problem, as long as they are not in the way when hooked open. This, however, depends on the layout of the boat. They do cover a sizable area that in some boats is cherished for mounting instruments and in others for handling, or even hanging, lines that are led to the after end of the cabin trunk. You can sometimes solve problems of keeping open doors out of the way by using double doors, a vertically hinged door that folds upon itself, or "half hinges," which allow a door to be lifted off and stowed elsewhere for periods of fine weather.

Curiously, the use of companionway slides on sailboats has expanded to the point that they vastly outnumber doors on boats being produced today. I believe that this is due to several reasons: (1) they are so cheap and easy to build that production builders push them; (2) they are being copied along with a host of other features from racing boats (although it is certain that most boats rarely if ever race); and (3) many of today's owners have never sailed in a boat that didn't have slides and perhaps they associate doors only with powerboats. There's some humor, but not much sense, in two to five slides to take out and put back every time a sailor wishes to open and close the companionway on a boat that never carries sail deliberately to the verge of a knockdown, that rarely goes off soundings, and rarely sails in any but the best sailing weather of the year. But, lest anyone feel sorry for such sailors, the fine weather they boat in saves most of them from suffering unduly with slides: they simply take the slides out in the morning and don't put them in again until they want privacy or protection from rain, dew, or the chill of night.

DEADLIGHTS AND FIXED WINDOWS

Compared to opening portlights and windows, a deadlight or a fixed window is fixed, unopenable glass (or clear plastic) for letting in light and/or seeing through. Compared to each other, a deadlight and a fixed window are essentially the same thing. A deadlight, however, is small in area and rugged for its size, like its opening twin, the portlight. The idea is to let in light and to be able to look out without creating an area that is physically more vulnerable or less watertight than the surrounding construction.

It seems that deadlights are underutilized in most boats. Aside from their quite common use in trunk sides and hatches, we tend to forget their usefulness in brightening up all sorts of gloomy corners and in providing lookout peepholes, too. One man for whom we built a boat was very particular about the placement of a 6-

Fitting a Lexan deadlight. (Loy photo)

inch-diameter deadlight in the side of the hull over each V-berth. He said to me, "Sometimes I like to lie there and read by its light; and I can glance out through it once in a while to see that the boat is not dragging anchor or about to become the object of a collision. But I don't want an opening port; I'm too likely to forget to close it."

That's just one pair of deadlights, but a fairly universal pair of reasons. If you think about it, you'll realize that any boat over 25 feet, sail or power, but especially a cruising boat, would be improved by one or more additional deadlights, and still more so if it's to be a live-aboard boat. They're inexpensive for what they can do, completely safe if built with heavy enough glass or clear thermoplastic, and entirely trouble free for decade after decade if properly installed. They don't have to be circular. They can be rectangular, a long narrow slit, or any free shape, and any size, although at some size they begin to be called fixed windows. Nor do all deadlights have to be made with panes of sheet or plate stock. Some are prisms or other crystalline polyhedron shapes that refract light from above deck about the interior in a delightful way.

The method of installing deadlights and fixed windows depends upon the location and nature of the light and upon the shell or skin construction of the part. A deadlight in the hull's topsides needs to be recessed to minimize the chances of being bumped or snagged. For this reason, the deadlight, or its frame or retaining ring, if it has one, is usually bolted over the opening on the inside of the hull. However, in order not to trip the walker and to better bear his weight, a deadlight in the deck is invariably set flush with the surface in a recess made for it. To retain it, a thin metal frame is usually screwed down over the pane or prismatic shape, which may itself be recessed for the metal, according to whether or not the edges of the metal are needed to prevent slipping on the surface of the deadlight. Wet glass or plastic is indeed very slippery, but the size of the deadlight determines how far a foot might slip before it encounters more traction.

In contrast to deadlights in hull and deck, a wide variety of installations seem to work all right on cabin-trunk sides, a place where they are not usually as severely battered. Everybody except perhaps the Coast Guard expects them to grow larger in size and physically less rugged, also, until on many boats they are but fixed windows. The simplest installation on trunk sides is a piece of sheet thermoplastic bolted over the opening, usually on the outside. This is a practical arrangement, about as inexpensive as possible in labor. But materials like Plexiglas or Lexan are not cheap, and the results look a bit mechanical, what with all the bolts showing. A lot more refined, but more expensive, too, are deadlights or fixed windows that are panes fitted into a rabbeted opening and retained with a metal ring or puttied in, as they were for years on wooden boats. Also, there are the traditional, manufactured cast-bronze deadlights with glass set in them, which are sometimes called fixed portlights and are mounted the same way. As if these weren't enough, manufacturers now offer aluminum-framed fixed windows and windshields (as well as opening models of both), which they usually produce for recreational vehicles as well. In addition, they will make up virtually any shape or size from the smallest round lights on up. Innumerable examples of aluminum-framed windows can be seen in any marina or storage yard on various production sailboats or powerboats.

I ought to mention just one more type of fixed window installation: a pane that is fitted into a molded rubber frame that in turn is fitted onto the edge of the laminate around the opening. The rubber is supplied in strip form, grooved on one side to fit a given laminate thickness and on the other to fit a given glass or thermoplastic thickness. Very popular with some production builders in earlier years, the rubber channel or frame hasn't shown up lately on new boats as much as the aluminum frame, at least in New England.

Certainly, many more choices are available now than when the only deadlights were stout pieces of glass with or without a bronze frame and the only fixed windows were panes fitted into the wooden trunk sides. When considering what to do on your one-off, it is useful to weigh the advantages and disadvantages of the materials at your disposal.

Glass is relatively cheap, lasts a very long time, and does not scratch easily. It will not bend the least bit to fit a curved surface, however, and it is quite heavy. It also shatters dangerously if it is not the safety type.

The clear thermoplastics will bend to fit a developable curved surface (cylindrical or conical), but not a compound curve unless heat-formed to it. All of the thermoplastics are much less brittle than glass, and some kinds, like Lexan, can stand very hard impacts and considerable distortion.

One of the worst features of the thermoplastics is that they are softer than glass, soft enough that their excellent optical qualities and sparkling clear surfaces can become quite clouded and scratched after a number of years.

Another fault, one that can destroy the work of the unwary user of thermoplastics, is their high coefficient of thermal elongation.* Unless allowances are made for their growth and contraction as the ambient temperature changes, they will surely disrupt the join where fitted and fastened to more stable materials such as wood and fiberglass. Fastening holes in thermoplastics need to be oversize—the wider or longer the pane, the more so—lest crowding against the fastenings break pieces out of it. When you realize that in only a very narrow temperature range will a pane fit properly in a rabbet at the edge of an opening in fiberglass, then bolting the pane on the surface, covering the opening, which is very often done on fiberglass boats, makes a lot of sense. In that position, with a reasonably elastic bedding and enough play in the bolt holes, the pane is free to expand and contract with minimal restraint in response to temperature changes.

One more fault with thermoplastic windows often found on older boats are the myriad little "fiber-stress" cracks that appear on their surfaces, presumably due to too much bending. These certainly spoil both their optical qualities and their appearance, or I might say, both the looking through and the looks.

But for all its faults, clear thermoplastic has earned a place on boats where a more flexible, tougher, and lighter pane than glass is needed. When in good condition, it has excellent clarity, and it's readily available in many thicknesses. Some varieties are incredibly strong and tough. It also can be worked with the same tools used to work wood and soft metals.

Before leaving the subject of deadlights, I should remind you of the special opportunity that fiberglass itself offers to admit light to the interior of your one-off. You have only to leave off all paint, gelcoat, or other opaque materials, and light will shine through any solid fiberglass laminate. True, general-purpose resins like boat resins transmit a yellowish light, and their laminates are translucent, not transparent. However, it's light, a filtered, not unpleasant light, subdued in proportion to the thickness of the laminate, yet present in useful amounts through all normal skin thicknesses. Most commonly, a portion of the top of a fiberglass hatch is left ungelcoated so that it can act as a skylight, but other deck or trunk features or areas are left ungelcoated, too, with similar results. With a little imagination, you can have some lighting in many obscure corners, which might save hunting up a flashlight during daylight hours every time you wanted to look into them. Certainly, it's a good trick to remember. Meanwhile, if you wish to go to some extra trouble and expense, you can obtain clearer and nearly colorless resins

---

The coefficient of linear expansion of methyl methacrylate (Lucite and Plexiglas) is 5×10^{-5} in/in/°F. Fiberglass is 1.3×10^{-5}. Thus, Plexiglas will expand four times as much as fiberglass.

that are used to laminate fiberglass with optimum light-transmitting properties. You also might find handy somewhere on your boat a fiberglass sheet material manufactured in 4-by-8-foot sheets up to ⅛ inch thick for use as a cover or diffusion panel on large-area lighting systems. Originally, letting light pass through the fiberglass skin of a part did not come easily to builders. Right from the beginning, they had to make their laminates as completely opaque as possible with gelcoat on the outside and paint on the inside in order to head off complaints from the public that their work was "so thin you can see light through it." It seems that builders found it easier to block the light penetration than to put out the brush fires started by people who didn't understand that light easily penetrates any thickness of fiberglass likely to be found on a yacht, that they were looking at thin gelcoat, but not necessarily thin fiberglass.

OPENING PORTLIGHTS

I have no idea how the porthole of a ship came to be called the portlight, opening port, and—when rectangular—opening window on a yacht. These have been names for it in New England and in yacht hardware catalogs for many years. But to make the title of this section as explicit as possible, I use the most descriptive combination of them.

Whatever they're called, these clear panes in a hinged bronze frame, closing on a rubber gasket, made fast by tightening wing nuts, are still the ultimate seagoing windows. They detract little or nothing from the strength of the construction into which they are bolted, they open in fair weather, yet they are watertight in the worst of weather, and they will keep on working for at least a hundred years with only a new gasket every decade or two. The only reason bronze opening ports aren't used more than they are is that they are more expensive than some of the alternatives.

Two alternatives to bronze opening ports are aluminum and plastic facsimiles. The aluminum models, which have been on the market some 25 or 30 years, are in many cases identical to the bronze and are cast, no doubt, from the same patterns. They are lower in price than the bronze, and they work all right. But they cannot yet claim the endurance of bronze in a saltwater environment, despite the development of incredibly good seagoing aluminum alloys.

Just how durable the current crop of plastic opening ports is remains to be seen, as most of these ports have been in use for less than two decades. However, plastics with remarkable physical properties are available and are being improved constantly. Without a doubt, there will be more opening ports produced in this material, and they will be well worth watching.

The cost of all things being more or less relative in good times or bad, it is not surprising that designers and builders have been devising less-expensive alternatives since cast-bronze opening ports were developed. Two solutions to the problem that come to mind are Ralph Wiley's and L. Francis Herreshoff's. Both are based on the daring principle of pressing a loose pane of safety glass against the trunk side over the opening. You tilt it back to let in air and remove it to clear the opening or to replace it with a screen. Both designers got rid of the hinged metal frame, which is the greatest portion of the cost, although later Wiley's invention was manufactured with the gutter and wedge-shaped end brackets in a single bronze or aluminum casting. Some of these ports also use a turn button or two rather than wedges to hold the pane shut. Having installed all of the configurations mentioned here on various boats, I can say that I know that they all work. It is surprising how watertight and draft-free loose panes are when pressed against a truly flat surface around the opening, the reason being that a film of water completely seals the interface between two such smooth, flat planes. We built dozens of Meadow Lark ketches and other Herreshoff-designed boats on which his Marco Polo windows are still in service. You can be sure most of them would have been changed if they were unsatisfactory, for we were careful to make the openings not too big for standard cast-bronze opening ports. Wiley windows that we installed are still working out there, too, both the wood and metal versions.

Pleased as many owners are with these simple arrangements, others have rejected them out of hand, so I would not want to leave the impression that such windows are right for every owner, every boat, or every part of a boat. They do have their drawbacks, not the least of which is that the Wiley windows, especially, are hard to curtain. The wedge-shaped end projections on these, as well as the pane when it is tipped out in either style, present a hazard if located where you are likely to bump your head. Further, it is annoying to some people to live with so many loose parts likely to be in the way when taken out, yet lost when needed.

An entirely different way to avoid the expense of bronze opening ports, or of opening windows, is to assign their functions separately to deadlights or fixed windows for transmitting light and ventilators of some sort for transmitting air. Since we have considered the subject of deadlights and fixed windows and will soon take up ventilation, it should suffice to say here that more and more boats seem to be equipped this way. In larger boats furnished with air conditioning, opening ports and windows are generally unnecessary. If any boat, whether sail or power, needs funnels or Dorades because it is raced, driven hard, or taken across oceans, then it is possible to economize, as production builders have been quick to notice, by using more deadlights and fixed windows in conjunction with that ventilation.

OPENING WINDOWS

Except for windshields hinged at the top and large rectangular opening portlights, I recall very few hinged windows among the opening windows I have encountered on boats. There seems to be a consensus among boatbuilders that a large hinged sash, which might get loose and bang back and forth, is not appropriate aboard a boat; but that if there is to be such, it should be protected by a massive frame and preferably hinged at the top, which results in the least violent motion when it is unsecured. It also should be obvious that the pane of any opening window on a boat should be of nonsplintering material.

Pilothouse windshields that swing out and up—occasionally in and up—are well known on powerboats and motorsailers. With a brass flap covering the joints, a bead of rubber to close against for a seal, a strip of flexible waterproof material over the hinge (or a solid plastic hinge), some good leverage on the closing mechanism, and faithful maintenance, one of these windows can be kept reasonably weather tight. Although some water is bound to get in at times, the windshield is often located on the after end of a cabin-trunk top, where drips land and run off outboard without bothering the helmsman, who is 2 to 4 feet abaft the windshield.

My experience of living in New England has left me feeling somewhat ambivalent about these opening windshields, for in this particular climate the benefits hardly balance the potential problems. If you build some of them for your one-off with fiberglass and/or metal, you may make out all right. But I have found the wooden version to be in constant danger of rotting, especially when the forward face of the pilothouse rakes aft so that any sort of rabbet or groove in either the sash or the frame tends to retain wetness.

If you are in a climate where you can be satisfied with a fixed windshield at all times, except when obscured by rain or snow, you might like a neat arrangement in which the largest part of the windshield is fixed, except for a small section from just below eye level to the top. This section is hinged at the top, overlaps the lower section on the outside glass to glass by 1½ or 2 inches, and is swung up just enough to open a well-visored slot for uncluttered vision. Ordinarily, you might use windshield wipers on this windshield, and still, with the opening feature, have a back-up system that never fails, that exposes you much less to the weather than a full-opening model, and has fewer problems, too. Nevertheless, one customer who had a windshield like this put on his workboat has used it year-round for over 15 years with no wiper.

For opening windows along the sides of a pilothouse or deckhouse, horizontal-sliding windows are one popular mode. In their simplest form, the price could hardly be better, for they are but a piece of auto safety plate, or clear thermoplastic, sliding in a nylon-lined, channel-shaped track. The main problem with them in the past has been preventing the larger channel in the edge of the opening in a wooden deckhouse, in which the track and panes are fitted, from rotting out. It is impossible to keep the wooden channel cleaned out and properly bedded or painted without taking the windows apart. Dirt collecting around the track plugs the drain holes, holds moisture against the wood, and breeds decay. If you install sliding windows of this type, as other kinds of windows, in a fiberglass house side, you eliminate any possible problem with rot. I might add, however, that if the house is WLP construction, you should be very sure that there is a watertight fiberglass laminate between these windows and the wood everywhere.

The usual arrangement of horizontal-sliding windows consists of two panes. The after pane is fixed and mounted inboard of the forward pane, which overlaps it by 1 or 2 inches and slides over it when opened. The idea is that, as rain and spray come from forward most of the time, the forward edge of the forward sliding pane is protected from wind-driven water by the groove in the edge of the opening, while the overlap of its after edge shelters the forward edge of the aft pane. Obviously, this type of window needs a higher rail around the inside of the groove than outside so that water collecting there drains outboard if the scuppers are plugged. Further, any removable parts required in the assembly and disassembly of the window are best fitted on the outside, so that the entire interior surround of the window is seamless.

The track for sliding windows with plain glass panes, a metal channel lined with nylon "fuzz" on the sides and a strip of bearing material on the bottom, has been a standard marine-hardware item for years. The only other parts you have to purchase are the panes of auto safety glass, or some clear thermoplastic sheet, if that's what you're going to use. The auto glass shop will cut the glass to your pattern and polish its edges, grind shallow finger slots, bore holes for bolted-on handles, or supply you with cement for the stick-on kind. If you use clear thermoplastic, you can cut it from stock bought from a plastics supplier, one or two of whom should be listed in the Yellow Pages of the nearest sizable city's directory.

An alternative to building horizontal-sliding windows on the job is to order similar windows from a manufacturer of aluminum boat windows. As mentioned under fixed windows, almost any shape or size can be obtained from these companies.

Since long before my time, windows that drop down into the double-walled construction of deckhouses and pilothouses have been used on high-grade motor yachts. Some of these have bronze crank systems not unlike automobile window cranks; and the recess into which they lower is, in effect, a copper-lined tank that drains overboard. If you want a handsome opening window, that is certainly the way to hang it. Working with fiberglass in a fiberglass one-off, it should be both easier to do and even more durable, although I recently surveyed two different boats, one about 40 years old, the other over 50, on both of which such systems were operating very well. Who can complain about that sort of durability?

You might do well to copy one of these systems in a new one-off. You might also find it possible to copy an automobile window crank system, or even take one apart and have it hot-dip galvanized, although the height of auto windows is very low, relative to the window height in some deckhouses. Auto systems also bolt right to the bare glass, whereas the older boat systems raise and lower a sash—not that window cranks are a necessity. As is often done on workboats, you can simplify the drop-down window until it is nothing but a sash in grooves that you raise and lower by hand.

VENTILATION

There are three primary needs for ventilation, often overlapping, in any boat that has accommodations and an engine:
1. A fresh air supply for the occupants
2. A fresh air supply for air-burning equipment—the engine, cook stove, and any heaters
3. A change of air or removal of fumes, heat, and noxious odors from
    a. the engine space
    b. the fuel tank space
    c. the battery space
    d. the head
    e. the galley
    f. the bilges and other "dead-air" spaces

A ventilation system to sweep away any gasoline fumes that might be lingering in the engine or tank space, ready to blast the boat apart, is mandated by the Coast Guard. If your one-off will have an inboard gasoline engine, you should, as suggested in the section on fuel tanks, get a copy of *Rules and Regulations for Recreational Boats* (free, from any Coast Guard District office), which outlines in detail the rules for ventilation systems and other regulations that apply to gasoline-powered boats. The booklet contains regulations pertaining to LPG (liquefied petroleum gas) tanks and stoves, too, which you will need to know about in order to install these items without fear of future problems. Oh yes, it has rules about marine sanitation devices as well as a few others that might save you problems arising from possible Coast Guard inspections, from insurance surveys, or, someday when you want to sell the boat, from a buyer's survey. The intrusion of government into the private affairs of the yachtsman more and more each year is galling to me, as I'm sure it is to you. Still, we would be foolish to let these meddlesome attempts to save every heedless fool from himself blind us so with resentment that we deliberately flout common sense and proper safety precautions. I, for one, have been too familiar with incidents of boat explosions in which people were killed to do that.

In essence, heavier-than-air explosive fumes settle to the lowest point of a compartment, building up there like water collecting in a bowl. What best removes this bomb awaiting ignition is a set of ducts or tubes, some reaching from above decks to the lowest part of the bilge, in which a natural circulation of air down one duct and up the other occurs so that all of the air is being constantly replaced. In addition, an exhaust blower placed in one duct is used for a quick, forced replacement of the air around the engine before starting it, because the tiniest spark at a loose connection or leaking high-tension wire is enough to set off an explosive mixture of this nature.

The cheapest and simplest acceptable ducting for this ventilation is 4-inch plastic vacuum hose. However, while you are building your one-off, it might be better to build at least some portion of the ducting as a permanent fixture, depending on the location of the air scoops on deck and the layout of the space to be ventilated. Using fiberglass, metal, thin-walled PVC tubing, or some combination of these (and bearing in mind that it is only an air duct, not a coal chute), it should be relatively easy to install ducting that you will hardly ever have to concern yourself with again. Yet, balancing the low cost, ease of installation, and flexibility of vacuum hose against the convolutions that might be necessary to keep rigid ducting unobtrusive in crowded engine rooms, you might find a built-in system impracticable in your particular boat.

An easily utilized asset of wooden boats with engine and tank spaces under full-width cockpits is the enormous volume of ventilation made available by installing a ceiling on the inboard side of the ribs or frames and leaving an air strake, or gap, along the top under the side deck. You can create a row of ducts this way, leading to the space under the cockpit sole, that amounts to hundreds of square inches of ventilation. Few one-off fiberglass construction methods offer this useful feature; only WLP might have ribs or frames in place on which to install the ceiling. If you do intend to sheathe the sides of a full-width cockpit, you should certainly take the opportunity to use them for ventilation if that is practical.

One feature that many fiberglass sailboats have that helps with ventilation is a hollow cockpit coaming. Not only can air scoops be mounted against the sides of hollow coamings over a high hole, to avoid deck water, but the bottom of the coaming itself can be sealed over if need be, to form a horizontal fore-and-aft section of duct that connects the scoop to a point over the space to be vented.

In thinking about the location of a battery shelf or box, you should bear in mind that batteries give off highly explosive hydrogen gas while being charged. The amounts are relatively small, yet enough often collects to blow acid into your face if ignited by a spark, which happened to a friend of mine. What is needed is enough venting at the top of the battery space to let the lighter-than-air hydrogen float away. Also, you should guard against loose connections that can make a spark and cover or protect batteries against the possibility of short circuits created by metal objects contacting the terminals, the latter being more important electrically, due to the danger of fire and/or battery destruction. Still another requirement, albeit unconnected with ventilation, is the provision of an acid-proof battery box or shelf; but, since fiberglass is ideal for the job, this is hardly a serious problem to the builder of a one-off.

A similar project that you, as a fiberglass person, should be able to cope with is building a Coast Guard and insurer-mandated airtight LPG (gas-bottle) compartment with an overboard vent/drain. Any locker for LPG installed below the weather deck must be built this way. Alternatively, you can install the bottles in a box on deck. But I hasten to mention that you can also rid your boat of the danger of being split open like a pumpkin by LPG fumes settling into the bilge if you use CPG (compressed natural gas), which is lighter than air, provided it is available where you do your yachting.

Aside from the danger of explosions and fires, you should always bear in mind that galley stoves, cabin heaters, and engines, whether gas or diesel, are all oxygen depleters. A relatively small but constant supply of fresh air is needed for them generally, and larger than you might think for a diesel. Without ample air, engines will not operate efficiently; and stoves or heaters, which manufacture carbon dioxide at best and carbon monoxide at worst, will starve you for air and/or poison you.

One winter, several young workers from my shop who helped deliver an ocean racer to southern waters ran headlong into this problem. Someone got the idea to heat the unheated boat by running the alcohol cook stove and oven full blast with the cabin closed up as tight as possible. Said one of the youngsters, "We would get tired and chilled, go below to rest and warm up, then get a monstrous headache. Back on deck, we'd be rid of the headache after a while; but then we'd get chilled and exhausted again."

The boat had a number of Dorade ventilators. Had these been left open, the bitter cold notwithstanding, the crew might not have poisoned themselves with the products of the cook stove's combustion. (A Dorade, named for the 50-foot ocean racer on which such ventilators first appeared, is a deck box with an air funnel or scoop on one of two compartments and an air vent into the cabin out of the other. Air passing in and out of the boat through the box can go over the top of the dividing wall between the two compartments, but any water coming down the funnel is trapped in that compartment by the divider and runs out on deck through scuppers.) Obviously, you can't submerge Dorades, funnels and all, without water getting below; but they work well in going where the decks are constantly drenched with rain and spray, they are easy to build, and watertight caps are supplied for the standard deck plates and ventilator components, which are available from all sizable marine-hardware dealers.

In the 1960s, I developed a vertical water-trap ventilator and marketed it in fiberglass for a few years. At least one similar product has been on the market since that time, which I guess is flattering. For boats not intended to be driven regularly through heavy weather, ordinary scoops and funnels will do. They can be turned away from the wind and are usually replaceable with deck plates when need be.

A different proprietary item that is worthy of consideration for ventilation and a skylight effect is the dome-shaped, molded, clear-thermoplastic vent, of which the first on the market in my area was the Sudbury. These vents are deservedly very popular for installation on hatches and cabin trunks, wherever a dash of light and air would be welcome below. They are quite rain- and spray-proof, and the air flow can be easily controlled on most of them.

Another time-tested ventilating device is the mushroom vent. The mushroom-shaped lid's stem is threaded into a bracket or spider spanning the deck flange fitted to an opening. Spinning the mushroom raises it up like an umbrella over the opening or screws it down tight to the flange. Long made of bronze, some very old mushroom vents are still in service. But if you step on the edge of one when open, there is enough leverage to bend the stem, which you may have to replace.

It is important that every boat have some provision for elementary, semiautomatic ventilation, one other than partly opened hatches or windows, one that is rainproof, and one that allows a modest flow or change of air throughout the entire interior when everything else is closed up for long periods. In small boats with a relatively open interior layout, this might consist of one little funnel, scoop, or mushroom on the forward deck and another somewhere aft. The aft vent might be a plainer device that takes advantage of a less-exposed location, such as louvers in a companionway door or slide, a hole in a vertical cockpit surface with a cowl over it, or the aforementioned ventilation required for engine and tank spaces. The aim of this basic, permanent ventilation is to keep some air moving through the boat during its inactive periods so as to minimize the dampness of condensation, the buildup of excessive heat when sitting in the sun, and the growth of bacteria and fungi, like mildew. These conditions create an unhealthy interior and, where wood is involved, foster its destruction by rot. For releasing pent-up solar heat, it is very helpful if one vent is placed well up on any high cabin or deckhouse. As you install your one-off's joinerwork throughout the interior, you should keep in mind air holes or slots connecting enclosed spaces to the main, ventilated spaces. For a wholesome, sweet-smelling interior, ventilation must be thorough.

EXTERIOR TRIM

A fiberglass hull or deck is a shell that is absolutely watertight for all practical purposes. Barring accidents, it will remain so indefinitely. But every hole made through that shell is a potential leak; every smallest fastening that penetrates it might be knocked loose, might wiggle loose, expand, contract, stretch, or corrode until, one day, wetness follows it into the interior. How long can a fastening, a bolt or tapping screw, through fiberglass be expected to remain watertight? I think it is safe to say that I have never seen a fiberglass boat over 10 years old without some such fastenings that needed rebedding or replacement. And I have seen a few boats, including some I have built, already leaking through their fastenings during a rainstorm before their first launching. What experience tells us about exterior trim, then, is that someday its fastenings will leak. Knowing that, our common sense tells us never to fasten unnecessary trim to a fiberglass boat. What is necessary? As owner/builder of your one-off, it's up to you to decide. Toe rails and handrails are necessary certainly, if you were unable to build them as part of the deck, and guardrails, too, if the boat is to spend much time alongside piers. Are caps on bulwarks and coamings necessary? Well, yes, if the laminate's section is such that the fastenings do not go through into the interior. But if the construction is hollow, it puts you in a dilemma. Should you go for the trim and the aesthetic pleasure it gives you or for the freedom from potential problems you gain by leaving it off?

About the only time you can be absolutely sure that fastenings through a laminate won't leak is when their heads are covered over with at least two layers of

Racks for laminating curved parts of wood such as deck beams, tillers, and coamings.

mat. It is not possible, however, to cover the fastenings of trim this way. Thus, if you install trim over a sealed deck joint, you are reestablishing the conditions for leaking.

One thing you can do about trim fastenings is to cover their inboard ends. When you do this, you should include all of the fastenings and the seam, too, if the trim is covering a joint. After clipping or grinding off the projecting excess length of fastenings, you should lay up a continuous strip of glass over everything, sealing off all potential leaks. Besides being an inconvenient, onerous job, covering over fastenings on the inside theoretically is not as effective as on the outside, especially in a freezing climate. But I must admit that I have surveyed many 10- to 20-year-old boats in which the deck joint, its fastenings, and those of a toe rail or guardrail covering the joint are all buried under a hefty secondary laminate on the interior that has yet to show a trace of leaking.

In contrast, on a one-year-old 30-foot sailboat I recently surveyed, the deck joint and the toe rail covering it were both fastened at the same time with a row of pop rivets. The rivets were covered in the wooden rail with bungs and sealed, presumably, at the deck by the bedding in which the rail was set, but not by anything below decks, where almost all were now leaking.

"Wow," I thought, as silicone that someone had smeared along the toe rail-to-deck seam and stains running down the interior from the rivets mutely outlined the problem. "Probably someone got a raise in pay for cutting a day off the assembly of this boat. Now, to earn my fee, I'll have to recommend they pay back a day."

It is not only leakage through single skins into the boat that makes trim fastenings a worry. Water can migrate laterally into the core or perhaps between the core and skins of a sandwich construction, too. This leakage leads, in time, to destructive results. Trim fastenings also take some violent abuse and are often bent, broken off, or knocked loose. Thus, as with an old car, one of the first signs an old boat is failing is its loose or missing trim. Most of the time, undersized fastenings are used in trim. Were they bigger, many problems with the trim or its fastenings might not occur. Nor is there any excuse for skimping now that strong stainless-steel fastenings are plentiful and cheap.

There are innumerable kinds and configurations of trim that you might make up in wood or buy as a proprietary item in brass, galvanized or stainless steel, extruded vinyl, aluminum, rubber, or some combination of these. You can see them all in service wherever boats gather, and take your pick. But you'll be doing yourself a favor if you limit trim to that which is necessary.

DECK HARDWARE

You are in the same danger of creating leaks when you fasten deck hardware to your one-off boat as you are with exterior trim, except that leaks due to deck hardware are more common, more annoying, and indicative that the fitting may be working loose. We who blithely installed hardware on wooden boats for many years were spoiled. If we made the fastening holes a driving fit in the wood, bedded fitting and fastening well with white lead or a bedding compound, and wrapped a thread of cotton under the head of the fastening, there was hardly ever a problem. Even if water got by the bedding and the cotton, it would soon swell the wood around the fastening and shut itself off as neatly as you please. Most of the time, a well-driven fastening also compressed the wood enough to resist rotation and loosening up. A nut below deck was not likely to back off due to vibration either, once we tightened it enough to squeeze the wood.

Compared to wood, fiberglass is incompressible. Without a clearance hole, a fastening won't drive through it; nor will moisture swell it any tighter around a fastening. If you want to make the fastening watertight, you must bed its body, its head, and the base of the fitting very well to keep water from following along it, down the hole. A good bedding should do the job. But, forgive us our rabbit's foot, we old-fashioned boatbuilders might be wrapping a bit of cotton on each fastening, just because our experience tells us it is almost inevitable that some fastenings through fiberglass will leak.

The readiness of fiberglass to leak bothered me so much after a few encounters with it in fiberglass boats we built that I developed a washer to shut off leaks around bolts much as wood does. It consists of two parts: a thick leather washer and a bottle-cap-shaped stainless-steel washer into which the leather one fits. The hole in the leather is tight to the bolt, its outside circumference a tight fit in the metal, and its thickness greater than the depth of the cup. The theory is that water getting as far as the leather swells it tighter. There is no way, I reckoned, that water can leak past such a washer for very long, and, as far as I know, it never has.

These washers are probably too expensive, compared to bedding. Although surely all right for solid fiberglass, they don't stop the water from going down the hole and perhaps migrating sideways into a joint or the core of a sandwich construction. For this reason, they would worry me in a freezing climate if the boat was stored out of doors. The outcome as far as my shop was concerned was inconclusive. We often found them useful and always used up our supply of them fairly quickly; yet nobody was enthusiastic enough to beat a path to our door for them either.

Another approach to making bolts and tapping screws watertight in fiberglass is to thread the hole with a tap and screw the fastening into it in wet resin, preferably epoxy. When the fastening is a bolt or machine screw, this should be done in conjunction with, not in lieu of, using a nut and washer, unless the fiberglass happens to be extraordinarily thick, so there are a great many threads in it. The method seals against water penetration very well, but only in relatively thick laminates. Thin, flexible laminates bend too much and tend to break away around the fastening. Some builders, usually amateurs, rave about their success with this method, and I used it in setting nipples in fiberglass tanks and other wet, but static situations. However, as a busy boatbuilder, I found it too time consuming, what with tapping the hole and keeping resin at the ready to use on each fastening. Also, as implied above, I was never sure how long the seal would last around the fastenings of hardware subject to violent abuse, like a deck block, track, or traveler or the base of a lifeline stanchion.

One other system that boatbuilders have tried with some success is the use of a gasket under the base of the fitting. Such a gasket is usually cork or rubber, if supplied with the fitting. A number of sheet materials are sold for making the gasket on the job, also, some of which are solids and others semisolids. That gaskets can keep the water out from between two surfaces is too well known to need restatement. However, gaskets between parts do not stop water from following along fastenings that traverse the parts from the outside surface to the inside. Each fastening, therefore, must be made watertight with its own gasket, washer, smear of bedding, ring of cotton, or whatever under its head.

Of course, leaks along fastenings otherwise sealed by a gasket are not possible when the fastenings dead-end in the body of one of the parts, as they so often do where parts are bolted to engines and pumps. On fiberglass boats, however, the builder would have to thread the fastenings of hardware into metal buried in the laminate, cover the ends of the fastenings on the inside of the laminate with more fiberglass, or apply the fastenings from below decks up into the cast body of the fitting.

Obviously, the use of machine screws, tapping screws, bolts, or hanger bolts in these ways is much less convenient than plain fastening methods and bedding. I have found fastenings into buried metal backing plates useful, however, for struts, stern bearings, and other fittings where a backing plate is needed anyway, where it would be too difficult to reach nuts on the inside, or where it would be impossible to stop the leaking should the bolts be disrupted. Similar situations do occur on deck in out-of-the-way places in which it is difficult or impossible to nut up the bolts, so buried backing plates are a good stratagem to bear in mind, whether or not gaskets are used under the parts on deck. Meanwhile, if you use gaskets under fittings, you don't want to forget to ask yourself how to make the fastenings watertight.

There are innumerable good bedding compounds suitable for making your

A liberal smear of #5200 3M Scotch Seal, Sikaflex 241, or a similar bedding, sealant, and glue is a great thing to apply between parts and fiberglass. This part is the leeboard eyebolt bolster or pad. (Loy photo)

gasket in place, so to speak, under deck hardware and around its fastenings. To the older oil-based compounds that retain their "life" or gooeyness for a long time, modern chemistry has added the rubbery ones, the Thiokol, polyurethane, and silicone products, which retain a high degree of flexibility, and are, in some cases, powerful adhesives as well. 3M's Scotch Seal #5200 and Sikaflex 241 are two products that have both elasticity and adhesion. The number of these sealants or bedding compounds keeps growing. No one can know them all, and every builder has his favorite. In investigating those available to you, don't hesitate to make up some test samples. Trying a product yourself is far more instructive than reading the descriptions on packages or counter displays, or, I hate to say it, in a book like this. The best procedure is to utilize all of these sources and any other information you can glean.

Oddly enough, I have found that it is the best craftsmen, woodworkers, and boatbuilders who have to be watched in their use of bedding compounds. They're so fussy and careful and proud of their fine joints that they use it too sparingly, and their work often leaks. I don't care how wonderful a bedding compound is—it won't do much good if you're stingy with it.

Equally as important as watertightness in the installation of deck hardware is

Installing a boss, bolster, or pad for the leeboard eyebolt. (Loy photo)

the physical strength of the installation. The part, its fastenings, and the area of the deck to which it is fastened must be a proper match to the stresses to which it will be subjected. As has been mentioned many places in this book, it is often necessary, and it is always wise, to replace the core of a sandwich laminate, where any but the most trivial hardware is fastened, with a less-compressible material. Otherwise, the laminate will be crushed by bolts through it, the fitting will be loosened by strains on it, and the fastenings will leak. I should also remind you that, whenever possible, core replacements should be done as you build the deck, if for nothing but cosmetic reasons. The nature and use of the hardware in question relative to the nature of the deck to which it is fastened call for such a confusion of overlapping rules that I think a series of simple statements may work best.

   1. You should replace a patch of foam core with a material less compressible under any bolted-on hardware.

   2. Balsa core can take the bolting of light-duty hardware without collapsing; but as the pull gets heavier, you should use backing plates and/or replace the balsa.

3. You should always overbore, fill, and rebore balsa core for bolts through it and rout it out around any holes for fittings installed through it and then seal it off. Don't let anybody kid you: water leaking down into it does migrate laterally through it in time.

4. Cleats, bitts, or winches for ground tackle require very substantial reinforcement in or below the foredeck. This might be in the form of solid-wood core replacement, wooden backing blocks, metal backing plates, deckbeams, longitudinal stringers, or a combination of these features. When reinforcing this area of your boat, you should be thinking about the enormous strains on the foredeck that will be created by surging back on an anchor line in huge breakers, being taken in tow by a powerful vessel, and being dragged or kedging herself off when aground. In such circumstances, chunks of fiberglass deck have been broken out; and, in one well-known tragic accident, most of the forward deck was peeled away by a Coast Guard boat's towline.

5. The closer to the surface of the deck a line is belayed, the better. A deck structure, no matter the materials with which it is built, is far stronger along the plane of the deck than in bending, which is the type of force it has to resist when the line is fast to a tall object bolted to it. The old boatbuilders understood this; they took their bitt or bitts down to the stem or forekeel. A bitt with the heel fastened to the backbone transfers the forces applied to it above the deck into forces strictly in the plane of the deck.

6. When the pressure of a nut and washer is likely to be too great for the laminate through which a piece of deck hardware is bolted, backing plates will spread that pressure over a greater area. Blocks of plywood, hardwood, or metal plates are generally used for backing plates. Scrap pieces or cutouts of fiberglass laminate, too, are sometimes stiff enough to back up a light laminate for light hardware, although the material is too flexible for heavy loads unless very thick.

7. Metal backing plates bring the greatest stiffness to an area while adding the least thickness, which can be most important in the overhead of the boat's accommodations. If you want to streamline a metal backing plate and the fastenings through it to save scalps and at the same time to improve its appearance, you need only to make it thick enough to tap for the bolts, eliminate the nuts and washers, and grind the ends of the bolts off flush with it.

8. At my shop, we regularly employed backing plates of many shapes and sizes that were cast in bronze especially for use in the overhead. By having them cast, we avoided the labor of cutting them from sheet stock and of grinding their edges to a gentle radius. One pattern makes an indefinite number of identical parts that are ready to use. Some of these, not much bigger than half-dollars, albeit thicker, were used on the widely spaced bolts of handrails, each as an oversized washer/nut left exposed in the overhead; others were plates similar to or greater in area than the bases of eye plates, deck blocks, cleats, or other hardware.

9. Today, the need for backing plates is intensified by the use of small-diameter stainless-steel bolts with enormous tensile strength, which concentrates their

pressure on a tiny area of deck. Realizing this, some manufacturers supply punched-out stainless backing plates to match their deck hardware. When available, these are usually far cheaper to buy than they would be to make up.

10. Although everyone seems to know that hardware such as turn blocks, winches, backstay gear, and cleats puts cruel loads on decks, I am frequently shocked at how unaware some builders are of the force the base of a lifeline stanchion exerts when the weight of a heavy man is thrown against its top. If you multiply the weight of the person by the number of times greater the height of the stanchion is than the width of the base and add something for inertia if the person is in motion, you will see that hundreds of pounds of cause result in tons of effect. Yet of all the places where a backing plate is needed, this is the one where it is most frequently omitted.

I could go on indefinitely with these and other details. But often the real problem is saying too much, of trying to crowd too many bits and pieces of information into what is supposed to be an outline of principles, turning it into a litany of facts that are related but not always relevant. We can't keep this up forever. You have to get busy and build your one-off boat!

Glossary

Applesauce: A mixture of polyester resin and glass or asbestos fibers, resembling applesauce. Used as a strong glue, a bedding, and a filler of voids in fiberglass parts.

Catalyst: A chemical added to resin to cause it to harden into its solid state.

Coffee-can Joint: The joint formed where a deck laminate turns down into a vertical rabbet in the hull's topside to make an overlap that is flush at the exterior surface.

Cold-molding: Building a boat part by laminating layers of wood over or into a form in a cold-setting glue.

Compression: Pressure on a material tending to compress or squeeze it.

Core: A layer of another material, usually lighter in weight and/or less expensive, between two skins of fiberglass. It is used to make a "sandwich" laminate having better stiffness and insulating qualities for its weight and cost than a single-skin laminate.

Crown: The upward, convex curve of a surface; for example, deck crown.

CSM: Chopped-strand mat, chopped glass-fiber strands pressed into a mat that is held together with a resin-soluble binder.

CVC: A one-off system named for its developers, John Collamore, Jr., Allan H. Vaitses, and John Collamore III.

Fairing: Making a line or surface "fair"; that is, removing any unsightly bumps, hollows, or changes in direction.

Fer-a-lite: The trade name of a light aggregate mixed with resin, developed to replace cement and sand in ferrocement boatbuilding and used as a smoothing putty in wire-mesh laminates. Sold by Aladdin Products, Inc.

Flange: A border turned at an angle to the main body of a part.

Gelcoat: Resin compounded with pigments and inert fillers to make a cosmetically appealing surface coat that is resistant to weathering.

Hogged: A condition of older wooden boats wherein the ends sag and the middle becomes humped like a hog's back.

Horning: Squaring a part with the centerplane of a boat, form, or mold by measuring from a point along the centerplane to points (horns) on the same horizontal line on the part and equidistant from its vertical centerline. Equal measurements mean that the part is squared.

Lamination/Laminate: 1. Both words, as nouns, connote the product or material created by gluing layers together. 2. *Lamination* also connotes the act of laminating. 3. *Laminate*, as a verb, means to lay up the layers of material.

Layup *(noun)*: The product of laying up fiberglass. The laminate.

Lofting: Drawing the plans, lines, or parts of a boat full size in order to make and set up pieces around which or of which the boat is built.

Mandrel: An object or form on which to make something.

Mat: Short for chopped strand mat.

MEK: Methyl ethyl ketone peroxide, the most commonly used catalyst for general purpose polyester boat resins.

Mold: An object or structure with the shape of a part, in or upon which a fiberglass part is formed by causing fiberglass to harden while in contact with it.

Moulds: Forms, usually made of boards or plywood, having the full-size shape of a boat's cross sections, around or within which the boat, or a plug, mold, or form for the boat, can be built.

One-off: Built as a lone unit, not as one of a series.

Plug: 1. A mock-up of a boat part on which to build a fiberglass mold. 2. Any object, including a boat part, on which a fiberglass mold is built.

Pout: A joint, especially a deck joint, in which matching out-turned flanges on both parts are fastened together.

PVA: Polyvinyl alcohol, a water-soluble release coating sprayed on molds in addition to mold-release wax where release is at risk. Also sprayed over externally applied gelcoat to prevent air inhibition of its cure.

PVC: Polyvinyl chloride, the heat-formable plastic of which Airex foam is made. Also used to make cross-linked foams with polyurethane. Wide commercial use in water piping and other products.

Radius: 1. As a verb, to round a corner. 2. As a noun, a curved or rounded corner.

Roving: Continuous strands made up of glass fibers.

Shear: 1. As a verb, to cut apart or separate by sliding the parts on either side of a line in opposite directions. 2. As a noun, a shearing force or a situation in which that force exists. For example, bending can place the layers in shear, causing delamination.

Shoe-box joint: A joint in which one part fits down over another like the cover of a pasteboard shoe box.

Stringers: 1. Strips of wood fastened over moulds to give a hull or deck longitudinal shape. 2. Longitudinal stiffening members on the inside of a hull or deck.

Str-r-etch Mesh: The trade name of a specially made wire mesh sold by Aladdin Products, Inc., for one-off boatbuilding.

WLP: Wood left in place, a one-off boatbuilding procedure in which a part is formed of wood, fiberglass is laid up over it, and the wood is incorporated in the finished part.

Index

Above-deck features: provisions for in a mold, 28-29
Acetone: fumes of, 4
Airex foam, 63-64, 75, 77
"Applesauce," 26, 78

Ballast keels: bolted-on, 184-87; direct molds for, 181-82; external, 179; internal, 187-88; pouring a keel, 180-84; sand-cast keel, 182-84
Balsa core, 15, 205, 279-80
Bulkheads, 228-35; double-diagonal, 235; foam-core, 77, 234-35; fore-and-aft, 233-34; plywood for, 229-31; tabbing to hull, 231-33

Centerboard: building of, 198-203; case, 203-06; core material for, 201-02; hardware, 207-08; patent hanger for, 207-08; provision for, in hull mold, 60-61; tandem, 202-03; weight of, 198-99, 201
C-Flex: for decks, 85-86; fairness of, 80, 86; for hulls, 79-85; in inner skin versus outer, 83-84; shrinkage of, 81-82; strength of, directional, 84; wetting out, 81
Chainplates, 249-51
Chopper gun, 154
Cockpit: powerboat, 17; with PVC foam, 77-78; seat hatches, 31-33; seat lockers, 30; soles, full width, 254-55; tubs, provisions for in a mold, 29-30
Cold-molded, WLP, 122-24
Companionway: doors and slides, 262-63; provisions for in a mold, 26-27
Covering wooden boat with fiberglass, 108, 124-26
CVC: advantages of, 97; preparation of planks, 88-89

Daggerboard, 203
Deadlights. *See* Portlights and deadlights
Deck: from existing deck, 140; hardware, 276-81; hatches and skylights, provisions for in a mold, 27-28; house in a deck mold, 17; hull-deck joints, 19-22, 71; mold, building of,

16-44; mold design and materials, 18; mold, details in, 25-33; with PVC foam, 73-76; with Str-r-etch Mesh, 105
Diagonal-planked mold, 58-60
Diminution of planking widths, 109-10
Docking drain, 179
Doors, companionway, 262-63
"Draft" in a mold, 13

Engine position: in fiberglass boat, 243-44; in wooden boat, 238
Engine beds, 235-37

Fairing: putties, 167, 168; tools, 170
Fairness of finish, 166-70
Fastenings: fiberglass to wood, 111-13
Female-molded hull: from existing boat, 135-38
Fer-a-lite, 103, 105
Fiberglass materials: proportion of, in laminate, 147
Floors (floor timbers), 186-87
Foam sandwich, 234-35
Formica, 11, 19, 42, 73, 257

Gelcoat, 159-63, 174-75
Glass fibers: chopped strand and continuous, 147-51; skin rash from, 4

Hatch: and coamings, 258-62; laminating of, 14-16; mold for, 11-14
Hoops (with C-Flex), 80
Hot-melt glue, 12, 61, 113
Hull mold: details, 60-62; lining, 55

Intermediate bearings, 245-46

Joinerwork, 256-58

Keel: fiberglass versus wood, 176; putty, 179; solid filling in, 176-78, 241-42. *See also* Ballast keel
Klegecell foam, 64

Laminate schedule, 5, 151, 158; for a hatch, 14
Layup techniques, 151-65; over Str-r-etch Mesh, 99-102
Lead keel. *See* Ballast keel
Leeboards, 203
Linings, deck mold, 18-19
Lofting, 7; deck mold, 22-23; hull mold, 44

Male-molded hull: from existing boat, 128-34
Mat. *See* Glass fibers
Melamine-coated board, 11, 42, 44, 73, 89
Masonite, 11, 18, 19, 42, 73
Mast collar: formed in mold, 28
Mast step: on deck, 246-49; for through-deck masts, 251-52
Micarta, 11, 73, 257
Microballoons, 67, 167-68

Mold: deck, preparation for layup, 33-44; details of (portlights, bosses, etc.), 13-14, 25-33; existing boat as male mold or plug, 127-41; hatch, 11-14; hull, 44-62; material to use in, 18-19, 41; split molds, 49-54; use of, versus a form, 10-11
Molded hull, 44-62; of prefabricated sheets, 56-58
Moulds: for deck, stock to build, 23; for hulls, stock to build, 46; rocker moulds, 46-47; section moulds, picking up, 23; setting up, 23-25
Mylar, 70

Nonskid: hatch top, 12; pattern in a mold, 33-42

Oil pan, 178-79
One-off methods: choice of, 9
Outboard well: provision for, in hull mold, 61

Painting: versus gelcoat, 174-75
Plans, boat construction, 5
Plywood: bulkheads, 229-30; cabin sole, 253; in centerboard, 198; in centerboard case, 204; in cockpit sole, 197-98, 255; as core, 43, 70-71, 124, 280; for deck mold, 18; for moulds, 23; for rudder core, 189, 192
Portlights and deadlights: provision for in a mold, 26; types and installations, 263-68
Putty. *See under* Fairing; Smoothing; Keel
PVC (polyvinyl chloride) foam: core, 15, 205, 230, 234-35, 255; for deck, 73-76; glass ribs in, 77; for hull, 65-73; for other structures, 76-78; in rudder, 192; as scored sheets, 72-73; strength of, 64; types for boatbuilding, 63-64; in way of a ballast keel, 69

Radiusing mold corners, 163-64
Refrigerator: of PVC foam, 77
Releasing parts from molds, 139, 164-65
Resins: fumes of, 4; for hand layup, 145-47, 154-55, 156
Rocker moulds, 46-47
Roving. *See* Glass fibers
Rudder: building of, 188-93; materials for, 188-89; pintles and gudgeons, 195; rudder port, 61, 195-97; rudder stops, 197; shoal-draft, 193-95

Safety precautions, 4, 153
Sandwich construction, 15-16; stringers for, 89-97; weight of, 16
Shaft log, 237-42; positioning of hole for, 61, 243-44
Short-run mold, 51-54
Slides, fisherman, 262-63; provisions for in mold, 26-27
Split mold, 49-54
Smoothing, 170-74; putty, 171-72
Sole: cabin, 253; cockpit and deck, 254-55
Staples, 111-12
Steerers, 197-98
Str-r-etch Mesh: in decks, 105; fairness of, 102; form for, 99; as hull core material, 103-04

Stringers: for deck mold, 18; versus moulds to make a form for C-Flex, 80-81
Strip-planked WLP construction, 115-22
Strut, propeller shaft, 242-45
Stuffing box, 196, 237-38
Sumps, 178
Surfacers and primers, 172-74

Tabbing, 18, 20, 56, 73, 74, 78, 96, 113, 257; strength of, 231-33
Tank baffles, 211-12, 222, 225
Tanks: all-fiberglass, 209-14; Coast Guard regulations, 211-12, 216, 225; fiberglass over wood, 214-15; integral, 225-27; laminate schedule for, 214; metal-lined fiberglass, 215-25; metal, 208-09
Transom: in a female mold, 54-55
Trim, exterior, 274-76

Ventilation, 271-74

Wax: mold-release, 12-13; in resin, 56, 146-47; for rounding mold corners, 12
Windows: fixed, 263-67; opening, 268-70
Wooden coaming, 29
Wood left in place (WLP): as core material, 115-26; as liner for sandwich construction, 73, 113-15; as liner for single-skin construction, 108-13; variations of, 106
Wood: on interiors, 110-11, 257